The Great War
The British Campaign in France and Flanders, Vol. II

By Arthur Conan Doyle

TABLE OF CONTENTS
PREFACE
CHAPTER I. THE OPENING MONTHS OF 1915
Conflict of the 1st Brigade at Cuinchy, and of the 3rd Brigade at Givenchy—Heavy losses of the Guards—Michael O'Leary, V.C.—Relief of French Divisions by the Twenty-seventh and Twenty-eighth—British Pressure on the Fifth Corps—Force subdivided into two armies—Disaster to 16th Lancers—The dearth of munitions

CHAPTER II. NEUVE CHAPELLE AND HILL 60
The opening of the spring campaign—Surprise of Neuve Chapelle—The new artillery—Gallant advance and terrible losses—The Indians in Neuve Chapelle—A sterile victory —The night action of St. Eloi—Hill 60—The monstrous mine—The veteran 13th Brigade—A bloody battle—London Territorials on the Hill—A contest of endurance—The first signs of poison

CHAPTER III. THE SECOND BATTLE OF YPRES
Stage I. The Gas Attack, April 22-30
Situation at Ypres—The poison gas—The Canadian ordeal—The fight in the wood of St. Julien—The French recovery—Miracle days—The glorious Indians—The Northern Territorials—Hard fighting—The net result — Loss of Hill 60

CHAPTER IV. THE SECOND BATTLE OF YPRES
Stage II. The Bellewaarde Lines
The second phase—Attack on the Fourth Division— Great stand of the Princess Pats—Breaking of the line — Desperate attacks—The cavalry save the situation—The ordeal of the 11th Brigade—The German failure—Terrible strain on the British—The last effort of May 24—Result of the battle —Sequence of events

CHAPTER V. THE BATTLE OF RICHEBOURG FESTUBERT
May 9-24

The new attack—Ordeal of the 25th Brigade — Attack of the First Division—Fateful days—A difficult situation—Attack of the Second Division—Attack of the Seventh Division—British success—Good work of the Canadians — Advance of the Forty-seventh London Division—The lull before the storm

CHAPTER VI. THE TRENCHES OF HOOGE

The British line in June 1915—Canadians at Givenchy—Attack of 154th Brigade—8th Liverpool Irish Third Division at Hooge—11th Brigade near Ypres—Flame attack on the Fourteenth Light Division—Victory of the Sixth Division at Hooge

CHAPTER VII. THE BATTLE OF LOOS

The First Day—September 25
General order of battle—Check of the Second Division—Advance of the Ninth and Seventh Divisions—Advance of the First Division—Fine progress of the Fifteenth Division — Capture of Loos—Work of the Forty-seventh London Division

CHAPTER VIII. THE BATTLE OF LOOS

The Second Day—September 26
Death of General Capper—Retirement of the Fifteenth Division—Advance of the Twenty-fourth and Twenty-first Divisions—Heavy losses—Desperate struggle—General retirement on the right—Rally round Loos—Position in the evening

CHAPTER IX. THE BATTLE OF LOOS

From September 27 to the End of the Year
Loss of Fosse 8—Death of General Thesiger — Advance of the Guards—Attack of the Twenty-eighth Division — Arrival of the Twelfth Division—German counter-attacks—Attack by the Forty-sixth Division upon Hohenzollern Redoubt—Subsidiary attacks—General observations—Return of Lord French to England

Arthur Conan Doyle – A Short Biography

MAPS AND PLANS

British Front, 1915

Ypres District

Order of Battle, May 7th

Richebourg District

Loos District

Battle of Loos I

Battle of Loos II

The British Front in 1915

PREFACE

In the previous volume of this work, which dealt with the doings of the British Army in France and Flanders during the year 1914, I ventured to claim that a great deal of it was not only accurate but that it was very precisely correct in its detail. This claim has been made good, for although many military critics and many distinguished soldiers have read it there has been no instance up to date of any serious correction. Emboldened by this I am now putting forward an account of the doings of 1915, which will be equally detailed and, as I hope, equally accurate. In the late autumn a third volume will carry the story up to the end of 1916, covering the series of battles upon the Somme.

The three years of war may be roughly divided into the year of defence, the year of equilibrium, and the year of attack. This volume concerns itself with the second, which in its very nature must be less dramatic than the first or third. None the less it contains some of the most moving scenes of the great world tragedy, and especially the second Battle of Ypres and the great Battle of Loos, two desperate conflicts the details of which have not, so far as I know, been given up to now to the public.

Now, as before, I must plead guilty to many faults of omission, which often involve some injustice, since an author is naturally tempted to enlarge upon what he knows at the expense of that about which he is less well informed. These faults may be remedied with time, but in the meantime I can only claim indulgence for the obvious difficulty of my task. With the fullest possible information at his disposal, I do not envy the task of the chronicler who has to strike a just balance amid the claims of some fifty divisions.

Arthur Conan Doyle, Windlesham, Crowborough, April 1917.

I. THE OPENING MONTHS OF 1915

Conflict of the 1st Brigade at Cuinchy, and of the 3rd Brigade at Givenchy — Heavy losses of the Guards—Michael O'Leary, V.C. — Relief of French Divisions by the Twenty-seventh and Twenty-eighth — British Pressure on the Fifth Corps—Force subdivided into two armies —Disaster to 16th Lancers—The dearth of munitions

The weather after the new year was atrocious, heavy rain, frost, and gales of wind succeeding each other L with hardly a break. The ground was so sodden that all movements of troops became impossible, and the months trench work was more difficult than ever. The British, with their steadily increasing numbers, were now able to take over some of the trenches of the French and to extend their general line. This trench work came particularly hard upon the men who were new to the work and often fresh from the tropics. A great number of the soldiers contracted frost-bite and other ailments. The trenches were very wet, and the discomfort was extreme. There had been some thousands of casualties in the Fifth Corps from this cause before it can be said to have been in action. On the other hand, the medical service, which was extraordinarily efficient, did everything possible to preserve the health of the men. Wooden troughs were provided as a stance for them in the trenches, and vats heated to warm them when they emerged. Considering that typhoid fever was common among the civilian residents the health of the troops remained remarkably good, thanks to the general adoption of inoculation, a practice denounced by a handful of fanatics at home, but of supreme importance at the front, where the lesson of old wars, that disease was more deadly than the bullet, ceased to hold good.

On January 25 the Germans again became aggressive. If their spy system is as good as is claimed, they must by this time have known that all talk of bluff in connection with the new British armies was mere self-deception, and that if ever they were to attempt anything with a hope of success, it must be speedily before the line had thickened. As usual there was a heavy bombardment, and then a determined infantry advance this time to the immediate south of the Bethune Canal, where there was a salient held by the 1st Infantry Brigade with the French upon their right. The line was thinly held at the time by a half- battalion 1st Scots Guards and a half-battalion 1st Coldstream, a thousand men in all. One trench of the Scots Guards was blown up by a mine and the German infantry rushed it, killing, wounding, or taking every man of the 130 defenders. Three officers were hit, and Major Morrison-Bell, a member of parliament, was taken after being buried in the debris of the explosion. The remainder of the front line, after severe losses both in casualties and in prisoners, fell back from the salient and established themselves with the rest of their respective battalions on a straight line of defence, one flank on the canal, the other on the main Bethune-La Bassée high road. A small redoubt or keep had been established here, which became the centre of the defence.

Whilst the advance of the enemy was arrested at this line, preparations were made for a strong counter-attack. An attempt had been made by the enemy with their heavy guns to knock down the lock gates of the canal and to flood the ground in the rear of the position. This, however, was unsuccessful, and the counter-attack dashed to the front. The advancing troops consisted of the 1st Black Watch, part of the 1st Camerons, and the 2nd Rifles from the reserve. The London Scottish supported the movement. The enemy had flooded past the keep, which remained as a British island in a German lake. They were driven back with difficulty, the Black Watch advancing through mud up to their knees and losing very heavily from a cross fire. Two companies were practically destroyed. Finally, by an advance of the Rifles and 2nd Sussex after dark the Germans were ousted from all positions in advance of the keep, and this line between the canal and the road was held once more by the British. The night fell, and after dark the 1st Brigade, having suffered severely, was withdrawn, and the 2nd Brigade remained in occupation with the French upon their right. This was the action of Cuinchy falling upon the 1st Brigade, supported by part of the 2nd.

Whilst this long-drawn fight of January 25 had been going on to the south of the canal, there had been a vigorous German advance to the north of it, over the old ground which centres on Givenchy. The German attack, which came on in six lines, fell principally upon the 1st Gloucesters, who held the front trench. Captain Richmond, who commanded the advanced posts, had observed at dawn that the German wire had been disturbed and was on the alert. Large numbers advanced, but were brought to a standstill about forty yards from the position. These were nearly all shot down. Some of the stormers broke through upon the left of the Gloucesters, and for a time the battalion had the enemy upon their flank and even in their rear, but they showed great steadiness and fine fire discipline. A charge was made presently upon the flank by the 2nd Welsh aided by a handful of the Black Watch under Lieutenant Green, who were there as a working party, but found more congenial work awaiting them. Lieutenant Bush of the Gloucesters with his machine-guns did particularly fine work. This attack was organised by Captain Kees, aided by Major

MacNaughton, who was in the village as an artillery observer. The upshot was that the Germans on the flank were all killed, wounded, or taken. A remarkable individual exploit was performed by Lieutenant James and Corporal Thomas of the Welsh, who took a trench with 40 prisoners. A series of attacks to the north-east of the village were also repulsed, the South Wales Borderers doing some splendid work.

Thus the results of the day's fighting was that on the north the British gained a minor success, beating off all attacks, while to the south the Germans could claim an advantage, having gained some ground. The losses on both sides were considerable, those of the British being principally among Scots Guards, Coldstream and Black Watch to the south, and Welsh to the north. The action was barren of practical results.

There were some days of quiet, and then upon January 29 the Fourteenth German Corps buzzed out once more along the classic canal. This time they made for the keep, which has already been mentioned, and endeavoured to storm it with the aid of axes and scaling ladders. Solid Sussex was inside the keep, however, and ladders and stormers were hurled to the ground, while bombs were thrown on to the heads of the attackers. The Northamptons to the south were driven out for an instant, but came back with a rush and drove off their assailants. The skirmish cost the British few casualties, but the enemy lost heavily, leaving two hundred of his dead behind him. "Having arranged a code signal we got the first shell from the 40th R.F.A. twelve seconds after asking for it." So much for the co-operation between our guns and our infantry.

On February 1 the Guards who had suffered in the first fight at Cuinchy got back a little of what was owing to them. The action began by a small post of the 2nd Coldstream of the 4th Brigade being driven back. An endeavour was made to reinstate it in the early morning, but it was not successful. After daylight there was a proper artillery preparation, followed by an assault by a storming party of Coldstream and Irish Guards, led by Captain Leigh Bennett and Lieutenant Graham. The lost ground and a German trench beyond it were captured with 32 prisoners and 2 machine-guns. It was in this action that Michael O'Leary, the gallant Irish Guardsman, shot or bayoneted eight Germans and cleared a trench single-handed, one of the most remarkable individual feats of the War, for which a Victoria Cross was awarded. Again the fight fell upon the 4th Brigade, where Lord Cavan was gaining something of the reputation of his brother peer, Lord "Salamander" Cutts, in the days of Marlborough. On February 6 he again made a dashing attack with a party of the 3rd Coldstream and Irish, in which the Germans were driven out of the Brickfield position. The sappers under Major Fowkes rapidly made good the ground that the infantry had won, and it remained permanently with the British.

Another long lull followed this outburst of activity in the region of the La Bassée Canal, and the troops sank back once more into their muddy ditches, where, under the constant menace of the sniper, the bomb and the shell, they passed the weary weeks with a patience which was as remarkable as their valour. The British Army was still gradually relieving the French troops, who had previously relieved them. Thus in the north the newly-arrived Twenty-seventh and Twenty-eighth Divisions occupied several miles which had been held on the Ypres salient by General D'Urbal's men. Unfortunately, these two divisions, largely composed of men who had come straight from the tropics, ran into a peculiarly trying season of frost and rain, which for a time inflicted great hardship and loss upon them. To add to their trials, the trenches at the time they took them over were not only in a very bad state of repair, but had actually been mined by the Germans, and these mines were exploded shortly after the transfer, to the loss of the new occupants. The pressure of the enemy was incessant and severe in this part of the line, so that the losses of the Fifth Corps were for some weeks considerably greater than those of all the rest of the line put together. Two of the veteran brigades of the Second Corps, the 9th Fusilier Brigade (Douglas Smith) and the 13th (Wanless O'Gowan), were sent north to support their comrades, with the result that this sector was once again firmly held. Any temporary failure was in no way due to a weakness of the Fifth Army Corps, who were months to prove their mettle in many a future fight, but came from the fact, no doubt unavoidable but none the less unfortunate, that these troops, before they had gained any experience, were placed in the very worst trenches of the whole British line. "The trenches (so called) scarcely existed," said one who went through this trying experience, "and the ruts which were honoured with the name were liquid. We crouched in this morass of water and mud, living, dying, wounded and dead together for 48 hours at a stretch." Add to this that the weather was bitterly cold with incessant rain, and more miserable conditions could hardly be imagined. In places the trenches of the enemy were not more than twenty yards off, and the shower of bombs was incessant.

The British Army had now attained a size when it was no longer proper that a corps should be its highest unit. From this time onwards the corps were themselves distributed into different armies. At present, two of these armies were organised. The First, under General Sir Douglas Haig, comprised the First Corps, the Fourth Corps (Rawlinson), and the Indian Corps. The Second Army contained the Second Corps (Ferguson), the Third Corps (Pulteney), and the Fifth Corps (Plumer), all under Sir Horace Smith-Dorrien. The new formations as they came out were either fitted into these or formed part of a third army. Most of the brigades were strengthened by the addition of one, and often of two territorial battalions. Each army consisted roughly at this time of 120,000 men. The Second Army was in charge of the line to the north, and the First to the south.

On February 14 Snow's Twenty-seventh Division, which had been somewhat hustled by the Germans in the Ypres section, made a strong counter-attack under the cover of darkness, and won back four trenches near St. Eloi from which they had been driven by a German rush. This dashing advance was carried out by the 82nd Brigade (Longley's), and the particular battalions which were most closely engaged were the 2nd Cornwalls, the 1st Royal Irish, and 2nd Royal Irish Fusiliers. They were supported by the 80th Brigade (Fortescue's). The losses amounted to 300 killed and wounded. The Germans lost as many and a few prisoners were taken. The affair was of no great consequence in itself, but it marked a turn in the affairs of Plumer's Army Corps, whose experience up to now had been depressing. The enemy, however, was still aggressive and enterprising in this part of the line. Upon the 20th they ran a mine under a trench occupied by the 16th Lancers, and the explosion produced most serious effects. 5 officers killed, 3 wounded, and 60 men *hors de combat* were the fruits of this unfortunate incident, which pushed our trenches back for 40 yards on a front of 150 yards. The Germans had followed up the explosion by an infantry attack, which was met and held by the remains of the 16th, aided by a handful of French infantry and a squadron of the 11th Hussars. On this same day an accidental shot killed General Gough, chief staff officer of the First Corps, one of the most experienced and valuable leaders of the Army.

On the 21st, the Twenty-eighth Division near Ypres had a good deal of hard fighting, losing trenches and winning them, but coming out at the finish rather the loser on balance. The losses of the day were 250 killed and wounded, the greatest sufferers being months the Royal Lancasters. Somewhat south of Ypres, at Zwarteleen, the 1st West Kents were exposed to a shower of projectiles from the deadly *Minenwerfer*, which are more of the nature of aerial torpedoes than ordinary bombs. Their losses under this trying ordeal were 3 officers and 19 men killed, 1 officer and 18 men wounded. There was a lull after this in the trench fighting for some little time, which was broken upon February 28 by a very dashing little attack of the Princess Patricia's Canadian regiment, which as one of the units of the 80th Brigade had been the first Canadian Battalion to reach the front. Upon this occasion, led by Lieutenants Crabb and Papineau, they rushed a trench in their front, killed eleven of its occupants, drove off the remainder, and levelled it so that it should be untenable. Their losses in this exploit were very small. During this period of the trench warfare it may be said generally that the tendency was for the Germans to encroach upon British ground in the Ypres section and for the British to take theirs in the region of La Bassée.

With the opening of the warmer weather great preparations had been made by Great Britain for carrying on the land campaign, and these now began to bear fruit. Apart from the numerous Territorial regiments which had already been incorporated with regular brigades some fifty battalions in all there now appeared several divisions entirely composed of Territorials. The 46th North Midland and 48th South Midland Divisions were the first to form independent units, but they were soon followed by others. It had been insufficiently grasped that the supply of munitions was as important as that of men, and that the months expenditure of shell was something so enormous in modern warfare that the greedy guns, large and small, could keep a great army of workmen employed in satisfying their immoderate demands. The output of shells and cartridges in the month of March was, it is true, eighteen times greater than in September, and 3000 separate firms were directly or indirectly employed in war production; but operations were hampered by the needs of batteries which could consume in a day what the workshops could at that time hardly produce in a month. Among the other activities of Great Britain at this period was the great strengthening of her heavy artillery, in which for many months her well- prepared enemy had so vast an advantage. Huge engines lurked in the hearts of groves and behind hillocks at the back of the British lines, and the cheery news went round that even the heaviest bully that ever came out of Essen would find something of its own weight stripped and ready for the fray.

There was still considerable activity in the St. Eloi sector south-east of Ypres, where the German attacks were all, as it proved, the preliminaries of a strong advance. So persistent were they that Plumer's men were constantly striving for elbow room. On March 2 part of Fortescue's 80th Brigade, under Major Widdington of the 4th Rifles, endeavoured to push back the pressure in this region, and carried the nearest trench, but were driven out again by the German bombs. The losses were about 200, of which 47 fell upon the 3rd, and 110 upon the 4th Rifles. In these operations a very great strain came upon the Engineers, who were continually in front of the trenches at night, fixing the wire entanglements and doing other dangerous work under the very rifles of the Germans. It is pleasing to record that in this most hazardous task the Territorial sappers showed that they were worthy comrades of the Regulars. Major Gardner, Commander of the North Midland Field

Company, and many officers and men died in the performance of this dangerous duty.

II. NEUVE CHAPELLE AND HILL 60

The opening of the spring campaign—Surprise of Neuve Chapelle —The new artillery—Gallant advance and terrible losses — The Indians in Neuve Chapelle—A sterile victory—The night action of St. Eloi—Hill 60—The monstrous mine—The veteran 13th Brigade—A bloody battle—London Territorials on the Hill—A contest of endurance—The first signs of poison

WE now come to the close of the long period of petty and desultory warfare, which is only relieved from Neuve insignificance by the fact that the cumulative result during the winter was a loss to the Army of not less than twenty thousand men. With the breaking of the spring and the drying of the water-soaked meadows of Flanders, an era of larger and more ambitious operations had set in, involving, it is true, little change of position, but far stronger forces on the side of the British. The first hammer-blow of Sir John French was directed, upon March 10, against that village of Neuve Chapelle which had, as already described, changed hands several times, and eventually remained with the Germans during the hard fighting of Smith-Dorrien's Corps in the last week of October. The British trenches had been drawn a few hundred yards to the west of the village, and there had been no change during the last four months. Behind the village was the Aubers Ridge, and behind that again the whole great plain of Lille and Turcoing. This was the spot upon which the British General had determined to try the effects of his new artillery.

His secret was remarkably well kept. Few British and and no Germans knew where the blow was to fall. The boasted spy system was completely at fault. British The success of

Sir John in keeping his secret was surprisingly largely dependent upon the fact that above the British lines an air space had been cleared into which no German airman could enter save at his own very great peril. No great movement of troops was needed since Haig's army lay opposite to the point to be attacked, and it was to two of his corps that the main assault was assigned. On the other hand, there was a considerable concentration of guns, which were arranged, over three hundred in number, in such a position that their fire could converge from various directions upon the area of the German defences.

It was planned that Smith-Dorrien, along the whole line held by the Second Army to the north, should demonstrate with sufficient energy to hold the Germans from reinforcing their comrades. To the south of the point of attack, the First Army Corps in the Givenchy neighbourhood had also received instructions to make a strong demonstration. Thus the Germans of Neuve Chapelle, who were believed to number only a few battalions, were isolated on either side. It was advisable also to hinder their reinforcements coming from the reserves in the northern towns behind the fighting lines. With this object, instructions were given to the British airmen at any personal risk to attack all the railway points along which the trains could come. This was duly done, and the junctions of Menin, Courtrai, Don, and Douai attacked, Captain Carmichael and other airmen bravely descending within a hundred feet of their mark.

The troops chosen for the assault were Rawlinson's Fourth Army Corps upon the left and the Indian Corps upon the right, upon a front of half a mile, which as the operation developed broadened to three thousand yards. The object was not the mere occupation of the village, but an advance to the farthest point attainable. The Second Division of Cavalry was held in reserve, to be used in case the German line should be penetrated. All during the hours of the night the troops in single file were brought up to the advanced trenches, which in many cases were less than a hundred yards from the enemy. Before daylight they were crammed with men waiting most eagerly for the signal to advance. Short ladders had been distributed, so that the stormers could swarm swiftly out of the deep trenches.

The obstacle in front of the Army was a most serious one. The barbed wire entanglements were on an immense scale, the trenches were bristling with machine-guns, and the village in the rear contained several large outlying houses with walls and orchards, each of which had been converted into a fortress. On the other hand, the defenders had received no warning, and therefore no reinforcement, so that the attackers were far the more numerous. It is said that a German officer's attention was called to the stir in the opposing trenches, and that he was actually at the telephone reporting his misgivings to headquarters when the storm broke loose.

It was at half-past seven that the first gun boomed from the rear of the British position. Within a few minutes three hundred were hard at work, the gunners striving desperately to pour in the greatest possible number of shells in the shortest period of time. It had been supposed that some of the very heavy guns could get in forty rounds in the time, but they actually fired nearly a hundred, and at the end of it the huge garrison gunners were lying panting like spent hounds round their pieces. From the 18-pounder of the field- gun to the huge 1400-pound projectile from the new monsters in the rear, a shower of every sort and size of missile poured down upon the Germans, many of whom were absolutely bereft of their senses by the sudden and horrible experience. Trenches, machine-guns, and human bodies flew high into the air, while the stakes which supported the barbed wire were uprooted, and the wire itself torn into ribbons and twisted into a thousand fantastic coils with many a gap between. In front of part of the Indian line there was a clean sweep of the impediments. So also to the right of the British line. Only at the left of the line, to the extreme north of the German position, was the fatal wire still quite unbroken and the trenches unapproachable. Meanwhile, so completely was the resistance flattened out by the overpowering weight of fire that the British infantry, with their own shells flowing in a steady stream within a few feet of their heads, were able to line their parapets and stare across at the wonderful smoking and roaring swirl of destruction that faced them. Here and there men sprang upon the parapets waving their rifles and shouting in the hot eagerness of their hearts. "Our bomb-throwers," says one correspondent, "started cake-walking." It was but half an hour that they waited, and yet to many it seemed the longest half-hour of their lives. It was an extraordinary revelation of the absolute accuracy of scientific gunfire that the British batteries should dare to shell the German trenches which were only a hundred yards away from their own, and this at a range of five or six thousand yards.

At five minutes past eight the guns ceased as suddenly as they had begun, the shrill whistles of the officers sounded all along the line, and the ardent infantry poured over the long lip of the trenches. The assault upon the left was undertaken by Pinney's 23rd Infantry Brigade of the Eighth Division. The 25th Brigade of the same division (Lowry-Cole's) was on the right, and on the right of them again were the Indians. The 25th Brigade was headed by the 2nd Lincolns (left) and the 2nd Berkshires (right), who were ordered to clear the trenches, and then to form a supporting line while their comrades of the 1st Irish Rifles (left) and the 2nd Rifle Brigade (right) passed through their ranks and carried the village beyond. The 1st Londons and 13th

London (Kensingtons) were pressing up in support. Colonel McAndrew, of the Lincolns, was mortally hit at the outset, but watched the assault with constant questions as to its progress until he died. It was nothing but good news that he heard, for the work of the brigade went splendidly from the start. It overwhelmed the trenches in an instant, seizing the bewildered survivors, who crouched, yellow with lyddite and shaken by the horror of their situation, in the corners of the earthworks. As the Berkshires rushed down the German trench they met with no resistance at all, save from two gallant German officers, who fought a machine- gun until both were bayoneted.

It was very different, however, with the 23rd Brigade upon the left. Their experience was a terrible one. As they rushed forward, they came upon a broad sheet of partly-broken wire entanglement between themselves and the trenches which had escaped the artillery fire. The obstacle could not be passed, and yet the furious men would not retire, but tore and raged at the edge of the barrier even as their ancestors raged against the scythe-blades of the breach of Badajoz. The 2nd Scottish Rifles and the 2nd Middlesex were the first two regiments, and their losses were ghastly. Of the Scottish Rifles, Colonel Bliss was killed, every officer but one was either killed or wounded, and half the men were on the ground. The battalion found some openings, however, especially B Company (Captain Ferrers), upon their right flank, and in spite of their murderous losses made their way into the German trenches, the bombardiers, under Lieutenant Bibby, doing fine work in clearing them, though half their number were killed. The Middlesex men, after charging through a driving sleet of machine-gun bullets, were completely held up by an unbroken obstacle, and after three gallant and costly attacks, when the old "Diehards" lived up to their historic name, the remains of the regiment were compelled to move to the right and make their way through the gap cleared by the Scottish Rifles. "Rally, boys, and at it again!" they yelled at every repulse. The 2nd Devons and 2nd West Yorkshires were in close support of the first line, but their losses were comparatively small. The bombers of the Devons, under Lieutenant Wright, got round the obstacle and cleared two hundred yards of trench. On account of the impregnable German position upon the left, the right of the brigade was soon three hundred yards in advance and suffered severely from the enfilade fire of rifles and machine-guns, the two flanks being connected up by a line of men facing half left, and making the best of the very imperfect cover.

It should be mentioned that the getting forward of the 23rd Brigade was largely due to the personal intervention of General Pinney, who, about 8:30, hearing of their difficult position, came forward himself across the open and inspected the obstacle. He then called off his men for a breather while he telephoned to the gunners to reopen fire. This cool and practical manoeuvre had the effect of partly smashing the wires. At the same time much depended upon the advance of the 25th Brigade. Having, as stated, occupied the position which faced them, they were able to outflank the section of the German line which was still intact. Their left flank having been turned, the defenders fell back or surrendered, and the remains of the 23rd Brigade were able to get forward into an alignment with their comrades, the Devons and West Yorkshires passing through the thinned ranks in front of them. The whole body then advanced for about a thousand yards.

At this period Major Carter Campbell, who had been wounded in the head, and Second Lieutenant Somervail, from the Special Reserve, were the only officers left with the Scottish Rifles; while the Middlesex were hardly in better case. Of the former battalion only 150 men could be collected after the action. The 24th Brigade was following closely behind the other two, and the 1st Worcesters, 2nd East Lancashires, 1st Sherwood Foresters, and 2nd Northampton were each in turn warmly engaged as they made good the ground that had been won. The East Lancashires materially helped to turn the Germans out of the trenches on the left.

Whilst the British brigades had been making this gallant advance upon the left the Indians had dashed forward with equal fire and zeal upon the right. It was their first real chance of attack upon a large scale, and they rose grandly to the occasion. The Garhwali Brigade attacked upon the left of the Indian line, with the Dehra Duns (Jacob) upon their right, and the Bareillys (Southey) in support, all being of the Meerut Division. The Garhwalis, consisting of men from the mountains of Northern India, advanced with reckless courage, the 39th Regiment upon the left, the 3rd Gurkhas in the centre, the 2nd Leicesters upon the right, while the 8th Gurkhas, together with the 3rd London Territorials and the second battalion of the Garhwalis, were in support. Part of the front was still covered with wire, and the Garhwalis were held up for a time, but the Leicesters, on their right, smashed a way through all obstacles. Their Indian comrades endured the loss of 20 officers and 350 men, but nonetheless they persevered, finally swerving to the right and finding a gap which brought them through. The Gurkhas, however, had passed them, the agile little men slipping under, over, or through the tangled wire in a wonderful fashion. The 3rd Londons closely followed the Leicesters, and were heavily engaged for some hours in forcing a stronghold on the right flank, held by 70 Germans with machine-guns. They lost 2 officers, Captain Pulman and Lieutenant Mathieson, and 50 men of A Company, but stuck to their task, and eventually, with the help of a gun overcame the resistance, taking 50 prisoners. The battalion lost 200 men and did very fine work.

Gradually the Territorials were winning their place and in the Army. "They can't call us Saturday night soldiers now," said a dying lad of the 3rd Londons; and he spoke for the whole force who have endured perverse criticism for so long.

The moment that the infantry advance upon the trenches had begun, the British guns were turned upon the village itself. Supported by their fire, as already described, the victorious Indians from the south and the 25th Brigade from the west rushed into the streets and took possession of the ruins which flanked them, advancing with an ardour which brought them occasionally into the zone of fire from their own guns. By twelve o'clock the whole position, trenches, village, and detached houses, had been carried, while the artillery had lengthened its range and rained shrapnel upon the ground over which reinforcements must advance. The Rifles of the 25th Brigade and the 3rd Gurkhas of the Indians were the first troops in Neuve Chapelle.

It is not to be imagined that the powerful guns of the enemy had acquiesced tamely in these rapid developments. On the contrary, they had kept up a fire which was only second to that of the British in volume, but inferior in effect, since the latter had registered upon such fixed marks as the trenches and the village, while the others had but the ever-changing line of an open order attack. How dense was the fall of the German shells may be reckoned from the fact that the telephone lines by which the observers in the firing line controlled the gunners some miles behind them were continually severed, although they had been laid down in duplicate, and often in triplicate. There were heavy losses among the stormers, but they were cheerfully endured as part of the price of victory. The jovial exultation of the wounded as they were carried or led to the dressing stations was one of the recollections which stood out clearest amid the confused impressions which a modern battle leaves upon the half-stunned mind of the spectator.

At twelve o'clock the position had been carried, and yet it was not possible to renew the advance before three. These few hours were consumed in rearranging the units, which had been greatly mixed up during the advance, in getting back into position the left wing of the 25th Brigade, which had been deflected by the necessity of relieving the 23rd Brigade, and in bringing up reserves to take the place of regiments which had endured very heavy losses. Meanwhile the enemy seemed to have been completely stunned by the blow which had so suddenly fallen upon him. The fire from his lines had died down, and British brigades on the right, forming up for the renewed advance, were able to do so unmolested in the open, amid the horrible chaos of pits, mounds, wire tangles, splintered woodwork, and shattered bodies which marked where the steel cyclone had passed. The left was still under very heavy fire.

At half-past three the word was given, and again The the eager khaki fringe pushed swiftly to the front, On the extreme left of the line of attack Watts's 21st Brigade pushed onwards with fierce impetuosity. This attack was an extension to the left of the original attack. The 21st was the only brigade of the Seventh Division to be employed that day. There is a hamlet to the north- east of Neuve Chapelle called Moulin-du-Piètre, and this was the immediate objective of the attack. Several hundreds of yards were gained before the advance was held up by a severe fire from the houses, and by the discovery of a fresh, undamaged line of German trenches opposite to the right of the 21st

Brigade. Here the infantry was held, and did no more than keep their ground until evening. Their comrades of the Eighth Division upon their right had also advanced, the 24th Brigade (Carter's) taking the place of the decimated 23rd in the front line; but they also came to a standstill under the fire of German machine-guns, which were directed from the bridge crossing the stream of the little Des Layes River in front of them.

The Bois du Biez is an important wood on the south-east of Neuve Chapelle, and the Indians, after their successful assault, directed their renewed advance upon this objective. The Garhwali Brigade, which had helped to carry the village, was now held back, and the Dehra Dun Brigade of 1st and 4th Seaforths, Jats, and Gurkhas, supported by the Jullundur Brigade from the Lahore Division, moved forward to carry the wood. They gained a considerable stretch of ground by a magnificent charge over the open, but were held up along the line of the river as their European comrades had been to the north. More than once the gallant Indians cleared the wood, but could not permanently hold it. The German post at the bridge was able to enfilade the line, and our artillery was unable to drive it out. Three regiments of the 1st Brigade were brought up to Richebourg in support of the attack, but darkness came on before the preparations were complete. The troops slept upon the ground which they had won, ready and eager for the renewal of the battle in the morning. The losses had been heavy during the day, falling with undue severity upon a few particular battalions; but the soldiers were of good heart, for continual strings of German prisoners, numbering nine hundred in all, had been led through their lines, and they had but to look around them to assure themselves of the loss which they had inflicted upon the enemy. In that long winter struggle a few yards to west or east had been a matter for which a man might gladly lay down his life, so that now, when more than a thousand yards had been gained by a single forward spring, there was no desire to flinch from the grievous cost.

It has already been stated that the British had made demonstrations to right and to left in order to hold the enemy in their trenches. In the case of Smith-Dorrien's Second Army, a bombardment along the line was sufficient for the purpose. To the south, however, at Givenchy, the First Corps made an attack upon the trenches two hundred yards in front of them, which had no success, as the wire had been uncut. This attack was carried out by Fanshawe's 6th Infantry Brigade, and if it failed the failure was not due to want of intrepid leading by the officers and desperate courage of the men. The 1st King's (Liverpool) suffered very heavily in front of the impassable wire. "Our boys took their bayonets and hacked away. It was impossible to break through." Colonel Carter was wounded, but continued to lead his men. Feveran and Suatt, who led the assault, were respectively killed and wounded. The officers were nearly all hit, down to the young Subaltern Webb, who kept shouting "Come on, the King's!" until he could shout no more. A hundred were killed and 119 wounded in the ranks. Both the 2nd South Staffords and the 1st King's Royal Rifles joined in this brave, but ineffectual, attack, and lost very heavily. The total loss of the brigade was between six and seven hundred, but at least it had prevented this section of the line from reinforcing Neuve Chapelle. All along the line the night was spent in making good the ground that had been won.

The morning of the 11th broke with thick mist, a condition which continued during the whole of the day. Both the use of the aircraft and the direction of the artillery were negatived by the state of the weather—a grievous piece of ill-fortune, as it put a stop to any serious advance during the day, since it would have been a desperate business to march infantry against a difficult front without any artillery preparation. In this way the Germans gained a precious respite during which they might reinforce their line and prepare for a further attack. They essayed a counter-attack from the Bois du Biez in the morning, but it was easily repulsed by the Indians. Their shell-fire, however, was very murderous. The British infantry still faced Moulin-du-Piètre in the north and the Bois du Biez in the south, but could make no progress without support, while they lost heavily from the German artillery. The Indians were still at the south of the line, the 24th Brigade in the middle and the 21st in the north. Farther north still, at a point just south of Armentières, a useful little advance was made, for late at night, or early in the morning of the 12th, the 17th Infantry Brigade (Harper's) had made a swift dash at the village of l'Epinette, calculating, no doubt, that some of its defenders had been drafted south to strengthen the stricken line. The place was carried by storm at the small cost of five officers and thirty men, and the line carried forward at this point to a depth of three hundred yards over a front of half a mile. A counter-attack upon the 13th was driven off with loss.

So far as the main operation was concerned, the weather upon the 12th was hardly more favourable than upon the 11th. The veil of mist still intervened between the heavy artillery and its target. Three aeroplanes were lost in the determined efforts of the airmen to get close observation of the position. It also interfered with the accuracy of the German fire, which was poured upon the area held by the British troops, but inflicted small damage upon them. The day began by an attack in which the Germans got possession of a trench held by the 1st Sherwood Foresters. As the mist rose the flank company of the 2nd West Yorks perceived these unwelcome neighbours and, under the lead of Captain Harrington, turned them out again. Both the Indians on the right and the Seventh Division on the left lost a number of men during the morning in endeavouring, with poor success, to drive the German garrisons out of the various farmhouses, which were impregnable to anything but artillery. The gallant 20th Brigade, which had done such great work at Ypres in October, came into action this day and stormed up to the strongholds of the Moulin-du-Piètre. One of them, with three hundred Germans inside, was carried by the 2nd Borders, the defenders being made prisoners. All the battalions of the brigade the 2nd Scots Guards, the 1st Grenadiers, the 2nd Gordons, and their Territorial comrades, the 6th Gordons lost heavily in this most desperate of all forms of fighting. Colonel McLean of the latter regiment died at the head of his men. "Go about your duty," was his last speech to those who tended him. The Grenadiers fought like heroes, and one of them, Corporal Fuller, performed the extraordinary feat of heading off fifty Germans by fleetness of foot, and single-handed compelling the surrender of all of them. At the other end of the line, the 25th Brigade, led by the Rifle Brigade, also made desperate efforts to get on, but were brought to a standstill by the trenches and machine-guns in the houses. The losses of the British upon this day were heavy, but they were a small matter compared to those of the Germans, who made several counter-attacks in close formation from dawn onwards in the vain hope of recovering the ground that had been lost. It is doubtful if in the whole war greater slaughter has been inflicted in a shorter time and in so confined a space as in the case of some of these advances, where whole dense bodies of infantry were caught in the converging fire of machine-guns and rifles. In front of the 1st Worcesters, of the 24th Brigade, alone more than a thousand dead were counted. From the ridge of Aubers, half a mile to the eastward, down to the front of the Indian and British line, the whole sloping countryside was mottled grey with the bodies of the fallen. All that the British had suffered in front of the barbed wire upon the 10th was repaid with heavy interest during the counter-attacks of the 12th. Gradually they faded away and were renewed no more. For the first time in the war the Germans finally abandoned a position that they had lost, and made no further attempt to retake it. The Battle of Neuve Chapelle was at an end, and the British, though their accomplishment fell far short of their hopes, had none the less made a permanent advance of a thousand yards along a front of three thousand, and obtained a valuable position for their operations in the future. The sappers were busy all evening in wiring and sand-bagging the ground gained, while the medical organisation, which was strained to the uttermost, did its work with a bravery and a technical efficiency which could not be surpassed.

Upon the last day of the fighting some 700 more Result of prisoners had been taken, bringing the total number to 30 officers and 1650 men. The original defenders had been men of the Seventh German Corps, raised from Karlsruhe in Westphalia; but the reinforcements which suffered so heavily were either Saxons or Bavarians. The losses of the Germans were estimated, and possibly overestimated, at 18,000 men. The British losses were very heavy, consisting of 562 officers and 12,239 men. Some 1800 of these were returned as "Missing," but these were the men who fell in the advanced attack upon ground which was not retained. Only the wounded fell into the enemy's hands. The Fourth Corps lost 7500 men, and the Indians about 4000.

Of the six brigades of the Fourth Corps, all suffered about equally, except the 22nd, which was not so hard hit as the others. The remaining brigades lost over 25 per cent of their numbers, but nothing of their efficiency and zeal, as they were very soon to show in the later engagements. When one remembers that Julius Caesar describes an action as a severe one upon the ground that every tenth man was wounded, it may be conjectured that he would have welcomed a legion of Scottish Rifles or Sherwood Foresters.

Certainly no British soldier was likely to live long enough to have his teeth worn down by the ration bread, as was the case with the Tenth Legion. The two units named may have suffered most, but the 2nd Lincolns, 2nd Berkshires, 2nd Borders, 2nd Scots Fusiliers, 1st Irish Rifles, 2nd Rifle Brigade, the two battalions of Gordons, and the 1st Worcesters were all badly cut up. Of the five commanding officers of the 20th Brigade, Uniacke of the 2nd Gordons, McLean of the 5th Gordons, and Fisher Rowe of the Grenadiers were killed, while Paynter of the 2nd Scots Guards was wounded. The only survivor, the Colonel of the Borders, was shot a few days later. It was said at the time of the African War that the British colonels had led their men up to and through the gates of Death. The words were still true. Of the brave Indian Corps, the 1st Seaforths, 2nd Leicesters, 39th Garhwalis, with the 3rd and 4th Gurkhas, were the chief sufferers. The 1st Londons, 3rd Londons, and 13th (Kensingtons) had also shown that they could stand punishment with the best.

So ended the Battle of Neuve Chapelle, a fierce and murderous encounter in which every weapon of modern warfare the giant howitzer, the bomb, and the machine-gun was used to the full, and where the reward of the victor was a slice of ground no larger than a moderate farm. And yet the moral prevails over the material, and the fact that a Prussian line, built up with four months of labour, could be rushed in a couple of hours, and that by no exertion could a German set foot upon it again, was a hopeful first lesson in the spring campaign.

On March 12 an attack was made upon the enemy's trenches south-west of the village of Wytschaete—the region where, on November 1, the Bavarians had forced back the lines of our cavalry. The advance was delayed by the mist, and eventually was ordered for four in the afternoon. It was carried out by the 1st Wilts and the 3rd Worcesters, of the 7th Brigade (Ballard), advancing for two hundred yards up a considerable slope. The defence was too strong, however, and the attack was abandoned with a loss of 28 officers and 343 men. It may be said, however, to have served the general purpose of diverting troops from the important action in the south. It is to be hoped that this was so, as the attack itself, though fruitless, was carried out with unflinching bravery and devotion.

On March 14, two days after the Battle of Neuve Action of Chapelle, the Germans endeavoured to bring about a counter-stroke in the north which should avenge their defeat, arguing, no doubt, that the considerable strength which Haig's First Army had exhibited in the south meant some subtraction from Smith- Dorrien at the other end of the line. This new action broke out at the hamlet of St. Eloi, some miles to the south-east of Ypres, a spot where many preliminary bickerings and a good deal of trench activity had heralded this more serious effort. This particular section of the line was held by the 82nd Brigade (Longley's) of the Twenty-seventh Division, the whole quarter being under the supervision of General Plumer. There was a small mound in a brickfield to the south-east of the village with trenches upon either side of it which were held by the men of the 2nd Cornish Light Infantry. It is a mere clay dump about seventy feet long and twenty feet high. After a brief but furious bombardment, a mine which had been run under this mound was exploded at five in the evening, and both and mound and trenches were carried by a rush of German stormers. These trenches in turn enfiladed other ones, and a considerable stretch was lost, including two support trenches west of the mound and close to it, two breastworks and trenches to the north-east of it, and also the southern end of St. Eloi village.

So intense had been the preliminary fire that every wire connecting with the rear had been severed, and it was only the actual explosion upon the mound an explosion which buried many of the defenders, including two machine-guns with their detachments which made the situation clear to the artillery in support. The 19th and 20th Brigades concentrated their thirty-six 18-pounders upon the mound and its vicinity. The German infantry were already in possession, having overwhelmed the few survivors of the 2nd Cornwalls and driven back a company of the 2nd Irish Fusiliers, who were either behind the mound or in the adjacent trenches to the east of the village. The stormers had rushed forward, preceded by a swarm of men carrying bombs and without rifles. Behind them came a detachment of sappers with planks, fascines, and sand-bags, together with machine-gun detachments, who dug themselves instantly into the shattered mound. The whole German organisation and execution of the attack were admirable. Lieutenants Fry and Aston of the Cornwall Light Infantry put up a brave fight with their handful of shaken men. As the survivors of the British front line fell back, two companies of the 1st Cambridge Territorials took up a rallying position. The situation was exceedingly obscure from the rear, for, as already stated, all wires had been cut, but daring personal reconnaissance by individual officers, notably Captain Follett and and Lieutenant Elton, cleared it up to some extent. By nine o'clock preparations had been made for a counter-attack, the 1st Leinsters and 1st Royal Irish, of the 82nd Brigade, being brought up, while Fortescue's 80th Brigade was warned to support the movement.

It was pitch-dark, and the advance, which could only be organised and started at two in the morning, had to pass over very difficult ground. The line was formed by two companies of the Royal Irish, the Leinster Regiment, and the 4th Rifles in general support. The latter regiment was guided to their position by Captain Harrison, of the Cornwalls, who was unfortunately shot, so that the movement, so far as they were concerned, became disorganised. Colonel Prowse, of the Leinsters, commanded the attack. The Irishmen rushed forward, but the Germans fought manfully, and there was a desperate struggle in the darkness, illuminated only by the quick red flash of the guns and the flares thrown up from the trenches. By the light of these the machine-guns installed upon the mound held up the advance of the Royal Irish, who tried bravely to carry the position, but were forced in the end, after losing Colonel Forbes, to be content with the nearest house, and with gaining a firm grip upon the village. The Leinsters made good progress and carried first a breastwork and then a trench in front of them, but could get no farther. About 4:30 the 80th Brigade joined in the attack. The advance was carried out by the 4th Rifle Brigade upon the right and the Princess Patricia's (Canadians) upon the left, with the Shropshires and the 3rd Rifles in support.

It was all-important to get in the attack before day-light, and the result was that the dispositions were necessarily somewhat hurried and incomplete. The Canadians attacked upon the left, but their attack was lacking in weight, being confined to three platoons, and they could make no headway against the fire from the mound. They lost 3 officers and 24 men in the venture. Thesiger's 4th Rifle Brigade directed its attack, not upon the mound, but on a trench at the side of it. This was carried with a rush by Captain Mostyn Pryce's company. Several obstacles were also taken in succession by the Riflemen, but though repeated attempts were made to get possession of the mound, all of them were repulsed. One company, under Captain Selby-Smith, made so determined an attack upon one barricade that all save four were killed or wounded, in spite of which the barricade was actually carried. A second one lay behind, which was taken by Lieutenant Sackville's company, only to disclose a third one behind. Two companies of the Shropshires were brought up to give weight to the further attack, but already day was breaking and there was no chance of success when once it was light, as all the front trenches were dominated by the mound. This vigorous night action ended, therefore, by leaving the mound itself and the front trench in the hands of the Germans, who had been pushed back from all the other trenches and the portion of the village which they had been able to occupy in the first rush of their attack. The losses of the British amounted to 40 officers and 680 men killed, wounded, and missing, about 100 coming under the last category, who represent the men destroyed by the explosion.

The German losses were certainly not less, but it must be admitted that the mound, as representing the trophy of victory, remained in their hands. In the morning of the 15th the Germans endeavoured to E turn the Leinsters out of the trench which they had recaptured, but their attack was blown back, and they left 34 dead in front of the position.

It is pleasing in this most barbarous of all wars to be able to record that all German troops did not debase themselves to the degraded standards of Prussia. Upon this occasion the Bavarian general in charge consented at once to a mutual gathering in of the wounded and a burying of the dead things which have been a matter of course in all civilised warfare until the disciples of Kultur embarked upon their campaign. It is also to be remarked that in this section of the field a further amenity can be noted, for twice messages were dropped within the British lines containing news as to missing aviators who had been brought down by the German guns. It was hoped for a time that the struggle, however stern, was at last about to conform to the usual practices of humanity a hope which was destined to be wrecked for ever upon that crowning abomination, the poisoning of Langemarck.

A month of comparative quiet succeeded the battle of Neuve Chapelle, the Germans settling down into their new position and making no attempt to regain their old ones. Both sides were exhausted, though in the case of the Allies the exhaustion was rather in munitions than in men. The regiments were kept well supplied from the depots, and the brutality of the German methods of warfare ensured a steady supply of spirited recruits. That which was meant to cow had in reality the effect of stimulating. It is well that this was so, for so insatiable are the demands of modern warfare that already after eight months the whole of the regiments of the original expeditionary force would have absolutely disappeared but for the frequent replenishments, which were admirably supplied by the central authorities. They had been far more than annihilated, for many of the veteran corps had lost from one and a half times to twice their numbers. The 1st Hants at this date had lost 2700 out of an original force of 1200 men, and its case was by no means an exceptional one. Even in times of quiet there was a continual toll exacted by snipers, bombers, and shells along the front which ran into thousands of casualties per week. The off-days of Flanders were more murderous than the engagements of South Africa. Now and then a man of note was taken from the Army in this chronic and useless warfare. The death of General Gough, of the staff of the First Army, has already been recorded. Colonel Farquhar, of the Princess Patricia Canadians, lost his life in a similar fashion. The stray shell or the lurking sniper exacted a continual toll, General Maude of the 14th Brigade, Major Leslie Oldham, one of the heroes of Chitral, and other valuable officers being killed or wounded in this manner.

Battle of On April 17 there began a contest which was destined to rage with great fury, though at intermittent intervals, for several weeks. This was the fight for Hill 60. Hill 60 was a low ridge about fifty feet high and two hundred and fifty yards from end to end, which faced the Allied trenches in the Zillebeke region to the south-east of Ypres. This portion of the line had been recently taken over by Smith Dorrien's Army from the French, and one of the first tasks which the British had set themselves was to regain the hill, which was of considerable strategic importance, because by their possession of it the Germans were able to establish an observation post and direct the fire of their guns towards any portion of the British line which seemed to be vulnerable. With the hill in British hands it would be possible to move troops from point to point without their being overseen and subjected to fire. Therefore the British had directed their mines towards the hill, and ran six underneath it, each of them ending in a chamber which contained a ton of gunpowder. This work, begun by Lieutenant Burnyeat and a hundred miners of the Monmouth battalions, was very difficult owing to the wet soil. It was charged by Major Norton Griffiths and the 171st Mining Company Royal Engineers. At seven in the evening of Saturday, April 17, the whole was exploded with terrific effect. Before the smoke had cleared away the British infantry had dashed from their trench and the hill was occupied. A handful of dazed Germans were taken prisoners and 150 were buried under the debris.

The storming party was drawn from two battalions storming of the veteran 13th Brigade, and the Brigadier

Wanless O'Gowan was in general control of the operations under General Morland, of the Fifth Division. The two battalions immediately concerned were the 1st Royal West Kents and the 2nd Scottish Borderers. Major Joslin, of the Kents, led the assault, and C Company of that regiment, under Captain Moulton Barrett, was actually the first to reach the crest while it was still reeking and heaving from the immense IL explosion. Sappers of the 2nd Home Counties Company raced up with the infantry, bearing sandbags and entrenching tools to make good the ground, while a ponderous backing of artillery searched on every side to break up the inevitable counter- attack. There was desperate digging upon the hill to raise some cover, and especially to cut back communication trenches to the rear. Without an over- crowding which would have been dangerous under artillery fire, there was only room for one company upon the very crest. The rest were in supporting trenches immediately behind. By half-past one in the morning of the 18th the troops were dug in, but the Germans, after a lull which followed the shock, were already thickening for the attack. Their trenches came up to the base of the hill, and many of their snipers and bomb-throwers hid themselves amid the darkness in the numerous deep holes with which the whole hill was pocked. Showers of bombs fell upon the British line, which held on as best it might.

At 3:30 A.M. the Scots Borderers pushed forward to take over the advanced fire trench from the Kents, who had suffered severely. This exchange was an expensive one, as several officers, including Major Joslin, the leader of the assault, Colonel Sladen, and Captains Bering and Burnett, were killed or wounded, and in the confusion the Germans were able to get more of their bombers thrown forward, making the front trench hardly tenable. The British losses up to this time had almost entirely arisen from these bombs, and two attempts at regular counter-attacks had been nipped in the bud by the artillery fire, aided by motor machine-guns. As the sky was beginning to whiten in the east, however, there was a more formidable advance, supported by heavy and incessant bombing, so that at half-past five the 2nd West Ridings were sent forward, supported by the 1st Bedfords from the 15th Brigade. A desperate fight ensued. In the cold of the morning, with bomb and bayonet men stood up to each other at close quarters, neither side flinching from the slaughter. By seven o'clock the Germans had got a grip of part of the hill crest, while the weary Yorkshiremen, supported by their fellow-countrymen of the 2nd Yorkshire Light Infantry, were hanging on to the broken ground and the edge of the mine craters. From then onwards the day was spent by the Germans in strengthening their hold, and by the British in preparing for a renewed assault. This second assault, more formidable than the first, since it was undertaken against an expectant enemy, was fixed for six o'clock in the evening.

At the signal five companies of infantry, three from the West Ridings and two from the Yorkshire Light Infantry, rushed to the front. The losses of the storming party were heavy, but nothing could stop them. Of C Company of the West Ridings only Captain Barton and eleven men were left out of a hundred, but none the less they carried the point at which their charge was aimed. D Company lost all its officers, but the men carried on. After a fierce struggle the Germans were ejected once again, and the whole crest held by the British. The losses had been very heavy, the various craters formed by the mines and the heavy shells being desperately fought for by either party. It was about seven o'clock on the evening of the 18th that the Yorkshiremen of both regiments drew together in the dusk and made an organised charge across the whole length of the hill, sweeping it clear from end to end, while the 59th and

Company Royal Engineers helped in making good the ground. It was a desperate tussle, in which men charged each other like bulls, drove their bayonets through each other, and hurled bombs at a range of a few yards into each other's faces. Seldom in the war has there been more furious fighting, and in the whole Army it would have been difficult to find better men for such work than the units engaged.

From early morning of that day till late at night the Brigadier- General o' Go wan was in the closest touch with the fighting line, feeding it, binding it, supporting it, thickening it, until he brought it through to victory. His Staff-Captain Egerton was killed at his side, and he had several narrow escapes. The losses were heavy and the men exhausted, but the German defence was for the time completely broken, and the British took advantage of the lull to push fresh men into the advanced trenches and withdraw the tired soldiers. This was done about midnight on the 18th, and the fight from then onwards was under the direction of General Northey, who had under him the 1st East Surrey, the 1st Bedfords, and the 9th London (Queen Victoria) Rifles. Already in this murderous action the British casualties had been 50 officers and 1500 men, who lay, with as many of the Germans, within a space no larger than a moderate meadow.

During the whole of the daylight hours of April 19 a furious bombardment was directed upon the hill, on and behind which the defenders were crouching. Officers of experience described this concentration of fire as the worst that they had ever experienced. Colonel Griffith of the Bedfords held grimly to his front trench, but the losses continued to be heavy. During that afternoon a new phenomenon was observed for the first time an indication of what was to come. Officers seated in a dug-out immediately behind the fighting line experienced a strong feeling of suffocation, and were driven from their shelter, the candles in which were extinguished by the noxious air. Shells bursting on the hill set the troops coughing and gasping. It was the first German experiment in the use of poison an expedient which is the most cowardly in the history of warfare, reducing their army from being honourable soldiers to the level of assassins, even as the sailors of their submarines had been made the agents for the cold- blooded murder of helpless civilians. Attacked by this new agent, the troops still held their ground.

Tuesday, April 20, was another day of furious Desperate shell-fire. A single shell upon that morning blew in a parapet and buried Lieutenant Watson with twenty men of the Surreys. The Queen Victorias under Colonel Shipley upheld the rising reputation of the Territorial troops by their admirable steadiness. Major Lees, Lieutenant Summerhays, and many others died an heroic death; but there was no flinching from that trench which was so often a grave. As already explained, there was only one trench and room for a very limited number of men on the actual crest, while the rest were kept just behind the curve, so as to avoid a second Spion Kop. At one time upon this eventful day a handful of London Territorials under a boy officer, Woolley of the Victorias, were the only troops upon the top, but it was in safe keeping none the less. This officer received the Victoria Cross. Hour after hour the deadly bombardment went on. About 7:30 in the evening the bombers of the enemy got into some folds in the ground within twenty yards and began a most harassing attack. All night, under the sudden glare of star shells, there were a succession of assaults which tried the half-stupefied troops to the utmost. Soon after midnight in the early morning of Wednesday, April 21, the report came in to the Brigadier that the 1st Surreys in the trenches to the left had lost all their officers except one subaltern. As a matter of fact, every man in one detachment had been killed or wounded by the grenades. It was rumoured that the company was falling back, but on a message reaching them based upon this supposition, the answer was, "We have not budged a yard, and have no intention of doing so." At 2:30 in the morning the position seemed very precarious, so fierce was the assault and so worn the defence. Of A Company of the Surreys only 55 privates were left out of 180, while of the five officers none were now standing, Major Paterson and Captain Wynyard being killed, while Lieutenant Koupell, who got the Cross, and two others were wounded. It was really a subalterns' battle, and splendidly the boys played up.

All the long night trench-mortars and mine-throwers played upon them, while monstrous explosions flung shattered khaki figures amid a red glare into the drifting clouds of smoke, but still the hill was British. With daylight the 1st Devons were brought up into the fight, and an hour later the hill was clear of the enemy once more, save for a handful of snipers concealed in the craters of the north-west corner. In vain the Germans tried to win back a foothold. Nothing could shift that tenacious infantry. Field-guns were brought up by the attackers and fired at short range at the parapets hastily thrown up, but the Devons lay flat and held tight. It had been a grand fight. Heavy as were the strokes of the Thor hammer of Germany, they had sometimes bent but never shattered the iron line of Britain. Already the death-roll had been doubled, and 100 officers with 3000 of our men were stretched upon that little space, littered with bodies and red with blood from end to end. But now the action was at last drawing to its close. Five days it had raged with hardly a break. British guns were now run up and drove the German ones to cover. Bombers who still lurked in the craters were routed out with the bayonet. In the afternoon of the 21st the fire died gradually away and the assaults came to an end. Hill 60 remained with the British. The weary survivors were relieved, and limped back singing ragtime music to their rest-camps in the rear, while the 2nd Cameron Highlanders, under Colonel Campbell, took over the gruesome trenches.

It was a fine feat of arms for which the various brigadiers, with General Morland of the Fifth Division, should have the credit. It was not a question of the little mound important as that might be, it could not justify so excessive a loss of life, whether German or British. Hill 60 was a secondary matter. What was really being fought for was the ascendancy of the British or the Prussian soldier that subtle thing which would tinge every battle which might be fought thereafter. Who would cry "Enough!" first? Who would stick it to the bitter end? Which had the staying-power when tried out to a finish? The answer to that question was of more definite military importance than an observation post, and it was worth our three thousand slain or maimed to have the award of the God of battles to strengthen us hereafter.

This description may well be ended by the general order in which Sir John French acknowledged the services of the troops engaged in this arduous affair: "I congratulate you and the troops of the Second Army on your brilliant capture and retention of the important position at Hill 60. Great credit is due to Lieutenant- General Sir Charles Ferguson, commanding Second Corps; Major- General Morland, commanding Fifth Division; Brigadier-General Wanless O'Gowan, commanding 13th Brigade; and Brigadier-General Northey, commanding 15th Brigade, for their energy and skill in carrying out the operations. I wish particularly to express my warmest admiration for the splendid dash and spirit displayed by the battalions of the 13th, 14th, and 15th Brigades which took part under their respective commanding officers. This has been shown in the first seizure of the position, by the fire attack of the Royal West Kents and the King's Own Scottish Borderers, and in the heroic tenacity with which the hill has been held by the other battalions of these brigades against the most violent counter-attacks and terrific artillery bombardment. I also must commend the skilful work of the Mining Company R.E., of the 59th Field Company R.E., and 2nd Home Counties Field Company R.E., and of the Artillery. I fully recognise the skill and foresight of Major-General Bulfin, commanding Twenty- eighth Division, and his C.R.E., Colonel Jerome, who are responsible for the original conception and plan of the undertaking."

It will be noticed that in his generous commendation Sir John French quotes the different separate units of Engineers as a token of his appreciation of the heavy work which fell upon them before as well as and during the battle. Many anecdotes were current in the Army as to the extraordinary daring and energy of the subterranean workers, who were never so happy as when, deep in the bowels of the earth, they were planning some counter-mine with the tapping of the German picks growing louder on their ears. One authentic deed by Captain Johnston's 172nd Mining Company may well be placed upon record. The sapping upon this occasion was directed against the Peckham Farm held by the Germans. Finding that the enemy were countermining, a camouflet was laid down which destroyed their tunnel. After an interval a corporal descended into the shaft, but was poisoned by the fumes. An officer followed him and seized him by the ankles, but became unconscious. A private came next and grabbed the officer, but lost his own senses. Seven men in succession were in turn rescuers and rescued, until the whole chain was at last brought to the surface. Lieutenants Severne and Williams, with Corporal Gray and Sappers Hattersley,

Hayes, Lannon, and Smith, were the heroes of this incident. It is pleasant to add that though the corporal died, the six others were all resuscitated.

It is with a feeling of loathing that the chronicler turns from such knightly deeds as these to narrate the next episode of the war, in which the gallant profession of arms was degraded to the level of the assassin, and the Germans, foiled in fair fighting, stole away a few miles of ground by the arts of the murderer. So long as military history is written, the poisoning of Langemarck will be recorded as a loathsome incident by which warfare was degraded to a depth unknown Neuve among savages, and a great army, which had long been and honoured as the finest fighting force in the world, became in a single day an object of horror and contempt, flying to the bottles of a chemist to make the clearance which all the cannons of Krupp were unable to effect. The crime was no sudden outbreak of spite, nor was it the work of some unscrupulous subordinate. It could only have been effected by long preparation, in which the making of great retorts and wholesale experiments upon animals had their place. Our generals, and even our papers, heard some rumours of such doings, but dismissed them as being an incredible slur upon German honour. It proved now that it was only too true, and that it represented the deliberate, cold-blooded plan of the military leaders. Their lies, which are as much part of their military equipment as their batteries, represented that the British had themselves used such devices in the fighting on Hill 60. Such an assertion may be left to the judgment of the world.

III. THE SECOND BATTLE OF YPRES
Stage I. The Gas Attack, April 22-30

Situation at Ypres—The poison gas—The Canadian ordeal —The fight in the wood of St. Julien—The French recovery —Miracle days—The glorious Indians—The Northern Territorials—Hard fighting—The net result—Loss of Hill 60

It may be remembered that the northern line of the Ypres position, extending from Steenstraate to Langemarck, with Pilken somewhat to the south of the centre, had been established and held by the British during the fighting of October 21, 22, and 23. Later, when the pressure upon the British to the east and south became excessive, the French took over this section. The general disposition of the Allies at the 22nd of April was as follows.

The Belgians still held the flooded Yser Canal up to the neighbourhood of Bixschoote. There the line was carried on by the French Eighth Army, now commanded by General Putz in the place of General d'Urbal. His troops seem to have been all either Colonial or Territorial, two classes which had frequently shown the utmost gallantry, but were less likely to meet an unexpected danger with steadiness than the regular infantry of the line. These formations held the trenches from Bixschoote on the canal to the Ypres-Poelcapelle road, two thousand yards east of Langemarck, on the right. At this point they joined on to Plumer's Fifth Corps, the Canadian Division, Twenty-eighth and Twenty-seventh British Divisions, forming a line which passed a mile north of Zonnebeke, curling round south outside the Polygon Wood to the point where the Fifth Division of the Second Corps kept their iron grip upon Hill 60. The average distance from Ypres to all these various lines would be about five miles. Smith-Dorrien, as commander of the Second Army, was general warden of the district.

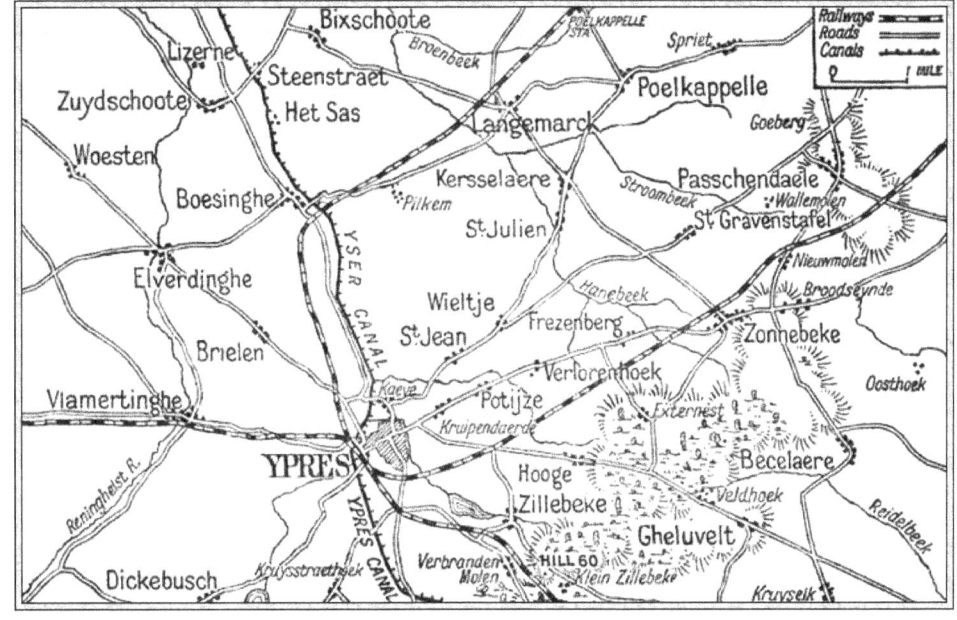

Ypres District

Up to the third week of April the enemy opposite the French had consisted of the Twenty-sixth Corps, with the Fifteenth Corps on the right, all under the Duke of Würtemberg, whose headquarters were at Thielt. There were signs, however, of secret concentration which had not entirely escaped the observation of the Allied aviators, and on April 20 and 21 the German guns showered shells on Ypres. About 5 P.M. upon Thursday, April 22, a furious artillery bombardment from Bixschoote to Langemarck began along the French lines, including the left of the Canadians, and it was reported that the Forty- fifth French Division was being heavily attacked. At the same time a phenomenon was observed which would seem to be more in place in the pages of a romance than in the record of an historian. From the base of the German trenches over a considerable length there appeared jets of whitish vapour, which gathered and swirled until they settled into a definite low cloudbank, greenish-brown below and yellow above, where it reflected the rays of the sinking sun. This ominous bank of vapour, impelled by a northern breeze, drifted swiftly across the space which separated the two lines.

The French troops, staring over the top of their parapet at this curious screen which ensured them a temporary relief from fire, were observed suddenly to throw up their hands, to clutch at their throats, and to fall to the ground in the agonies of asphyxiation. Many lay where they had fallen, while their comrades, absolutely helpless against this diabolical agency, rushed madly out of the mephitic mist and made for the rear, over-running the lines of trenches behind them. Many of them never halted until they had reached Ypres, while others rushed westwards and put the canal between themselves and the enemy. The Germans, meanwhile, advanced, and took possession of the successive lines of trenches, tenanted only by the dead garrisons, whose blackened faces, contorted figures, and lips fringed with the blood and foam from their bursting lungs, showed the agonies in which they had died. Some thousands of stupefied prisoners, eight batteries of French field-guns, and four British 4-7's, which had been placed in a wood behind the French position, were the trophies won by this disgraceful victory. The British heavy guns belonged to the Second London Division, and were not deserted by their gunners until the enemy's infantry were close upon them, when the strikers were removed from the breech-blocks and the pieces abandoned. It should be added that both the young officers present, Lieuts. Sandeman and Hamilton Field, died beside their guns after the tradition of their corps.

By seven o'clock the French had left the Langemarck district, had passed over the higher ground about Pilken, and had crossed the canal towards Brielen. Under the shattering blow which they had received, a blow particularly demoralising to African troops, with their fears of magic and the unknown, it was impossible to rally them effectually until the next day. It is be remembered in explanation of this disorganisation that it was the first experience of these poison tactics, and that the troops engaged received the gas in a very much more severe form than our own men on the right of Langemarck. For a time there was a gap five miles broad in the front of the position of the Allies, and there were many hours during which there was no substantial force between the Germans and Ypres. They wasted their time, however, in consolidating their ground, and the chance of a great coup passed for ever. They had sold their souls as soldiers, but the Devil's price was a poor one. Had they had a corps of cavalry ready, and pushed them through the gap, it would have been the most dangerous moment of the war.

A portion of the German force, which had passed through the gap left by the retirement of the French, moved eastwards in an endeavour to roll up the Canadian line, the flank of which they had turned. Had they succeeded in doing this the situation would have become most critical, as they would have been to the rear of the whole of the Fifth Army Corps. General Alderson, commanding the Canadians, took instant measures to hold his line. On the exposed flank were the 13th (Royal Highlanders) and 15th (48th Highlanders), both of the 3rd Brigade. To the right of these were the 8th Canadians and 5th Canadians in the order named. The attack developed along two-thirds of a front of five thousand yards, but was most severe upon the left, where it had become a flank as well as a frontal assault; but in spite of the sudden and severe nature of the action, the line held splendidly firm. Any doubt as to the quality of our Canadian troops if any such doubt had existed was set at rest for ever, for they met the danger with a joyous and disciplined alacrity. General Turner, who commanded the 3rd Brigade upon the left, extended his men to such an extent that, while covering his original front, he could still throw back a line several thousand yards long to the south-west and so prevent the Germans breaking through. By bending and thinning his line in this fashion he obviously formed a vulnerable salient which was furiously attacked by the Germans by shell and rifle fire, with occasional blasts of their hellish gas, which lost something of its effectiveness through the direction of the wind. The Canadian guns, swinging round from north to west, were pouring shrapnel into the advancing masses at a range of two hundred yards with fuses set at zero, while the infantry without trenches fired so rapidly and steadily that the attack recoiled from the severity of the punishment. The British 118th and 365th Batteries did good work in holding back this German advance.

Two reserve battalions had been brought up in hot haste from Ypres to strengthen the left of the line. These were the 16th (Canadian Scottish) and the 10th Canadians. Their advance was directed against the wood to the west of St. Julien, in which lay our four guns which, as already described, had fallen into the hands of the Germans. Advancing about midnight by the light of the moon, these two brave regiments, under Colonels Leckie and Boyle, rushed at the wood which the Germans had already entrenched and carried it at the point of the bayonet after a furious hand-to-hand struggle. Following at the heels of the flying Germans, they drove them ever deeper into the recesses of the wood, where there loomed up under the trees the huge bulk of the captured guns. For a time they were once again in British hands, but there was no possible means of removing them, so that the Canadians had to be content with satisfying themselves that they were unserviceable. For some time the Canadians held the whole of the wood, but Colonel Leckie, who was in command, found that there were Germans on each side of him and no supports. It was clear, since he was already a thousand yards behind the German line, that he would be cut off in the morning. With quick decision he withdrew unmolested through the wood, and occupied the German trenches at the south end of it. Colonel Boyle lost his life in this very gallant advance, which may truly be said to have saved the situation, since it engaged the German attention and gave time for reinforcements to arrive. The immediate pressing necessity was to give the French time to re-form, and to make some sort of line between the Canadian left and the French right. As early as half-past two in the morning, while the two Canadian regiments were struggling in the wood of St. Julien, the First Cavalry Division were showing once again the value of a mobile reserve. De Lisle's horsemen were despatched at full speed to get across the Canal, so as to act as a support and an immediate reserve for the French. The 2nd East Yorks from the Twenty-eighth Division was also sent on the same errand.

April 23. With the dawn it became of most pressing importance to do something to lessen, if not to fill, the huge gap which yawned between the left of the Canadians and the canal, like a great open door five miles wide leading into Ypres. Troops were already streaming north at the call of Smith-Dorrien from all parts of the British lines, but the need was quick and pressing. The Canadian 1st Brigade, which had been in reserve, was thrown into the broad avenue down which the German army was pouring. The four battalions of General Mercer's Brigade the 1st (Ontario), 4th, 2nd, and 3rd (Toronto) advanced south of Pilken. Nearer still to St. Julien was the wood, still fringed by their comrades of the 10th and the 16th, while to the east of St. Julien the remaining six battalions of Canadians were facing north-eastwards to hold up the German advance from that quarter, with their flank turned north-west to prevent the force from being taken in the rear. Of these six battalions the most northern was the 13th Royal Canadian Highlanders, and it was on the unsupported left flank of this regiment that the pressure was most severe, as the Germans were in the French trenches alongside them, and raked them with their machine-guns without causing them to leave their position, which was the pivot of the whole line.

Gradually, out of the chaos and confusion, of the crisis, facts of the situation began to emerge, and in the early morning of April 23 French saw clearly how great an emergency he had to meet and what forces he had with which to meet it. The prospect at first sight was appalling if it were handled by men who allowed themselves to be appalled. It was known now that the Germans had not only broken a five-mile gap in the line and penetrated two miles into it, but that they had taken Steenstraate, had forced the canal, had taken Lizerne upon the farther side, and had descended the eastern side as far south as Boesinghe. At that time it became known, to the great relief of the British higher command, that the left of the Canadian 1st Brigade, which had been thrown out, was in touch with six French battalions much exhausted by their terrible experience on the east bank of the canal, about a mile south-east of Boesinghe. From that moment the situation began to mend, for it had become clear where the reinforcements which were now coming to hand should be applied. A line had been drawn across the gap, and it only remained to stiffen and to hold it, while taking steps to modify and support the salient in the St. Julien direction, where a dangerous angle had been created by the new hasty rearrangement of the Canadian line.

It has been said that a line had been drawn across the gap, but dots rather than a line would have described the situation more exactly. Patrols had reached the French, but there was no solid obstacle to a German advance. This was partially remedied through the sacrifices of a body of men, who have up to now received the less credit in the matter because, being a mere chance collection of military atoms, they had no representative character. No finer proof of soldierly virtue could be given than the behaviour of these isolated British regiments which were now pushed up out of their rest camps near Ypres, many of them wearied from recent fighting, and none of them heartened by the presence of the comrades and superior officers who had formed their old brigades. The battalions were the 2nd Buffs, half of the 3rd Middlesex, the 1st York and Lancasters, the 5th Royal Lancasters, the 4th Rifle Brigade, the 2nd Cornwalls, the 9th Royal Scots, and half the 2nd Shropshires. These odd battalions were placed under the command of Colonel Geddes of the Buffs, and may be described as Geddes' Detachment. These scattered units, hardly conscious of each other's presence, were ordered upon April 23 not only to advance and fill the gap, but actually to attack the German Army, so as to give the impression of strength, and bring the assailants to a halt while reinforcements were being hurried to the Ypres front. These battalions, regardless of fire and gas, marched straight across country at the Germans, got right up to their line, and though unable to break it, held them fast in their positions. The 1st Royal Irish, under Colonel Gloster, had done the same farther to the eastward. For three days these battalions played their part in the front line, deliberately sacrificing themselves for the sake of the army. Colonel Geddes himself, with many senior officers, was killed, and the losses of some of these stubborn units were so heavy that it is reported that an observer approached a long row of prostrate men, whom he took to be the 1st York and

Lancaster, only to find that it was the helpless swathe of their dead and wounded filling a position from which the survivors had been moved. The other battalions were in no better case, but their audacity in attacking at a time when even a defence might seem a desperate business, had its effect, and held up the bewildered van of the enemy. It might well be quoted as a classical example of military bluff. Nearly all these battalions were in reserve to the 27th or 28th Divisions, who were themselves holding a long line in face of the enemy, and who, by turning their reserves to the West, were like a bank which transfers money to a neighbour at a time when it may have to face a run upon its own resources. But the times were recognised as being desperate, and any risk must be run to keep the Germans out of Ypres and to hold the pass until further help should come from the south. It was of course well understood that, swiftly as our reinforcements could come, the movement of the German troops, all swirling towards this sudden gap in the dam, would necessarily be even swifter, since they could anticipate such a situation and we could not. The remains of these battalions had by the evening of the 23rd dug themselves in on a line which roughly joined up the French and the Canadians.

In the afternoon of the 23rd those of the French troops who had escaped the gas attack advanced gallantly to recover some of their ground, and their movement was shared by the Canadian troops on the British left wing and by Geddes' detachment. The advance was towards Pilken, the French being on the left of the Ypres-Pilken road, and the British on the right. Few troops would have come back to the battle as quickly as our allies, but these survivors of the Forty-fifth Division were still rather a collection of brave men than an organised force. The strain of this difficult advance upon a victorious enemy fell largely upon the 1st and 4th Battalions of Mercer's 1st Canadian Brigade. Burchall, of the latter regiment, with a light cane in his hand, led his men on in a debonair fashion, which was a reversion to more chivalrous days. He fell, but lived long enough to see his infantry in occupation of the front German line of trenches. No further progress could be made, but at least the advance had for the moment been stayed, and a few hours gained at a time when every hour was an hour of destiny.

A line had now been formed upon the left, and the Canadian Germans had been held off. But in the salient to gal1 the right in the St. Julien section the situation was becoming ever more serious. The gallant 13th Canadians (Royal Highlanders) were learning something of what their French comrades had endured the day before, for in the early dawn the horrible gases were drifting down upon their lines, while through the yellow mist of death there came the steady thresh of the German shells. The ordeal seemed mechanical and inhuman such an ordeal as flesh and blood can hardly be expected to bear. Yet with admirable constancy the 13th and their neighbours, the 15th, held on to their positions, though the trenches were filled with choking and gasping men. The German advance was blown back by rifle-fire, even if the fingers which pulled the triggers were already stiffening in death. No soldiers in the world could have done more finely than these volunteers, who combined the dashing American spirit with the cool endurance of the North. Little did Bernhardi think when he penned his famous paragraph about our Colonial Militia and their uselessness upon a European battlefield that a division of those very troops were destined at a supreme moment to hold up one of the most vital German movements in the Western campaign.

The French upon the left were not yet in a position to render much help, so General Alderson, who was in command of this movement, threw back his left wing and held a line facing westwards with the 4th Rifle Brigade and a few Zouaves, so as to guard against a German advance between him and the canal. When the night of the 23rd fell it ended a day of hard desultory fighting, but the Allies could congratulate themselves that the general line held in the morning had been maintained, and even improved.

Reinforcements were urgently needed by the advanced line, so during the early hours of the morning of April 24 two battalions of the York and Durham Territorial Brigade the 4th East Yorkshires and another were sent from the west to Ypres to reinforce the weary 13th Brigade, much reduced by its exertions at Hill 60, which was in immediate support near Brielen. There was no fighting at this point during the night, but just about daybreak some of the 2nd Canadian Brigade upon the right of the British line, who were still holding their original trenches, were driven out of them by gas, and compelled to re-form a short distance behind them.

Though the British advance upon the left had gained touch with the Canadian 3rd Brigade, the latter still formed a salient which was so exposed that the edge of it, especially the 13th and 15th battalions, were assailed by infantry from the flank, and even from the rear. To them it seemed, during the long morning of April 24, as if they were entirely isolated, and that nothing remained but to sell their lives dearly. They were circumstances under which less spirited troops might well have surrendered. So close was the fighting that bayonets were crossed more than once, Major Norsworthy, of the 13th, among others, being stabbed in a fierce encounter. Very grim was the spirit of the Canadians. "Fine men, wonderful fellows, absolutely calm, and I have never seen such courage," wrote a Victoria Rifle Territorial, who had himself come fresh from the heroic carnage of Hill 60. It may be added that, good as the Canadian infantry was, their artillery was worthy to stand behind it. It is on record that one Canadian heavy battery, that of Colonel McGee, was so pre-eminently efficient that it was in demand at any threatened portion of the line.

It was clear on the morning of April 24 that the advanced angle, where the French and Canadians had been torn apart, could no longer be held in face of the tremendous shell-fire which was directed upon it and the continuous pressure of the infantry attacks. The 3rd Canadian Brigade fell slowly back upon the village of St. Julien. This they endeavoured to hold, but a concentrated fire rained upon it from several sides and the retreat continued. A detachment of the 13th and 14th Canadians were cut off before they could get clear, and surrounded in the village. Here they held out as long as their cartridges allowed, but were finally all killed, wounded, and taken. The prisoners are said to have amounted to 700 men. The remainder of the heroic and decimated 3rd Brigade rallied to the south of St. Julien, but their retirement had exposed the flank of the 2nd Canadian Brigade (Curry's), even as their own flank had been exposed by the retirement of the French Forty-fifth Division. This 2nd Brigade flung back its left flank in order to meet the situation, and successfully held its ground.

In doing this they were greatly aided by supports The arrival which came from the rear. This welcome reinforcement consisted of three battalions of the 84th Brigade, under Colonel Wallace. These three battalions were ordered to advance about four o'clock in the afternoon, their instructions being to make straight for Fortuin. Their assault was a desperate one, since there was inadequate artillery support, and they had to cross two miles of open ground under a dreadful fire. They went forward in the open British formation the 1st Suffolks in the van, then the 12th London Rangers, and behind them the 1st Monmouths.

Numerous gassed Canadians covered the ground over which they advanced. The losses were very heavy, several hundred in the Suffolks alone, but they reached a point within a few hundred yards of the enemy, where they joined hands with the few Canadians who were left alive in those trenches. They hailed their advent with cheers. The whole line lay down at this point, being unable to get farther, and they were joined at a later date by the 9th Durhams, who came up on the right. This body, which may be called Wallace's detachment, remained in this position during the night, and were exposed to severe attack next day, as will be seen later. So perilous was their position at the time the 9th Durhams came up that preparations had been made for destroying all confidential records in view of the imminent danger of being overwhelmed.

In this and subsequent fighting the reader is likely to complain that he finds it difficult to follow the movements or order of the troops, but the same trouble was experienced by the generals at the time. So broken was the fighting that a regimental officer had units of nine battalions under him at one moment. The general situations both now and for the next three days may be taken to be this: that certain well-defined clumps of British troops Twenty-eighth Division, 10th Brigade, Canadians, and so forth are holding back the Germans, and that odd battalions or even companies are continually pushed in, in order to fill the varying gaps between these ragged forces and to save their flanks, so far as possible, from being turned. These odd battalions coalesced into irregular brigades which are named here Geddes', Tuson's, or Wallace's detachment, after their senior officer.

Every hour of this day was an hour of danger, fresh ground had been abandoned and heavy losses incurred. None the less it may be said that on the evening of Saturday, April 24, the worst was over. From the British point of view it was a war of narrow escapes, and this surely was among the narrowest. The mystics who saw bands of bowmen and of knights between the lines during the retreat from Mons did but give definite shape to the undeniable fact that again and again the day had been saved when it would appear that the energy, the numbers, or the engines of the enemy must assure a defeat. On this occasion the whole front had, from an unforeseen cause, fallen suddenly out of the defence. Strong forces of the Germans had only five miles to go in order to cut the great nerve ganglion of Ypres out of the British system. They were provided with new and deadly devices of war. They were confronted by no one save a single division of what they looked upon as raw Colonial Militia, with such odds and ends of reinforcements as could be suddenly called upon. And yet of the five miles they could only accomplish two, and now after days of struggle the shattered tower of the old Cloth Hall in front of them was as inaccessible as ever. It needs no visions of overwrought men to see the doom of God in such episodes as that. The innocent blood of Belgium for ever clogged the hand of Germany.

Reinforcements were now assembling to the immediate south of St. Julien. By evening the Northumberland Brigade and the Durham Light Infantry Brigade both of the Fiftieth Territorial Division had reached Potijze. More experienced, but not more eager, was Hull's 10th Regular Brigade, which had come swiftly from the Armentières region. All these troops, together with Geddes' detachment and two battalions of the York and Durham Territorials, were placed under the hand of General Alderson for the purpose of a strong counter-attack upon St. Julien. This attack was planned to take place on the morning of Sunday, April 25. When night fell upon the 24th the front British line was formed as follows:

The Twenty-seventh and Twenty-eighth Divisions held their original trenches facing eastwards. In touch with their left was the 2nd Canadian Brigade, with one battalion of the 1st Canadian Brigade. Then came Wallace's detachment with two battalions of the York and Durham Territorials joining with the remains of the 3rd Canadian Brigade. Thence Geddes' detachment and the 13th Brigade prolonged the line, as already described, towards the canal. Behind this screen the reinforcements gathered for the attack.

April 25. The advance was made at 6:30 in the morning of April 25, General Hull being in immediate control of the attack. It was made in the first instance by the 10th Brigade and the 1st Royal Irish from the 82nd Brigade. The remains of the indomitable 3rd Canadian Brigade kept pace with it upon the right. Little progress was made, however, and it became clear that there was not weight enough behind the advance to crush a way through the obstacles in front. Two flank battalions retired, and the 2nd Seaforths were exposed to a terrible cross-fire. "We shouted to our officers (what was left of them) to give the order to charge, knowing in our minds that it was hopeless, as the smoke was so thick from their gas shells that we could see nothing on either side of us." Some cavalry was seen, the first for many days, but was driven off by the machine-gun of the Highlanders. Finally a brigade of Northumberland Territorials came up to sustain the hard-pressed line, passing over some two miles of open country under heavy fire on their advance. It was then nearly mid-day. From that point onwards the attackers accepted the situation and dug themselves in at the farthest point which they could reach near the hamlet of Fortuin, about a mile south of St. Julien.

It will be remembered that Wallace's detachment had upon the day before already reached this point. They were in a position of considerable danger, forming a salient in front of the general line. Together with the 9th Durhams upon their right, they sustained several German assaults, which they drove back while thrusting wet rifle rags into their mouths to keep out the drifting gas. From their right trenches they had the curious experience of seeing clearly the detraining of the German reserves at Langemarck Station, and even of observing a speech made by a German general before his troops hurried from the train into the battle. This advanced line was held by these troops, not only during the 25th, but for 1 three more days, until they were finally relieved after suffering very heavy losses, but having rendered most vital service.

Whilst the British were vainly endeavouring to advance to the north, a new German attack developed suddenly from the north-east in the region of Broodseinde, some five miles from St. Julien. This attack was on a front of eight hundred yards. The trenches attacked were those of the 84th and 85th Brigades of the Twenty-eighth Division, and no doubt the Germans held the theory that these would be found to be denuded or at least fatally weakened, their occupants having been drafted off to stiffen the Western line. Like so many other German theories, this particular one proved to be a fallacy. In spite of a constant shower of poison shells, which suffocated many of the soldiers, the enemy were vigorously repulsed, the 2nd East Surrey Regiment getting at one time to hand-to-hand fighting. The few who were able to reach the trenches remained in them as prisoners. Great slaughter was caused by a machine-gun of the 3rd Royal Fusiliers under Lieutenant Mallandain. Still, the movement caused a further strain upon the resources of the British General, as it was necessary to send up three battalions to remain in reserve in this quarter in case of a renewal of the attack. On the other hand, the 1 1th Brigade (Hasler), less the 1st East Lancashires, came up from the south to join the 10th, and Indian troops were known to be upon the way. The flank of the 85th Brigade was in danger all day, and it was covered by the great devotion of the 8th Durham Light Infantry to the north of it. This battalion lost heavily both in killed, wounded, and prisoners, but it fought with remarkable C valour in a very critical portion of the field. Early in the morning of the 26th the 1st Hants, on the right of the newly-arrived 11th Brigade, joined up with the 3rd Royal Fusiliers on the left of the 85th Brigade, and so made the line complete. Shortly after the arrival of the Hampshires the enemy charged through the dim dawn with a shout of "Ve vos the Royal Fusiliers." Wily Hampshire was awake, however, and the trick was a failure.

Up to the evening of Sunday, April 25, the 2nd Canadian Brigade had succeeded in holding its original line, which was along a slight eminence called the Gravenstrafel Ridge. All the regiments had fought splendidly, but the greatest pressure had been borne by Colonel Lipsett's 8th Battalion (90th Winnipeg Rifles), who had been gassed, enfiladed, and bombarded to the last pitch of human endurance. About five o'clock their trenches were obliterated by the fury of the German bombardment, and the weary soldiers, who had been fighting for the best part of four days, fell back towards Wieltje. That evening a large part of the Canadian Division, which had endured losses of nearly 50 per cent and established a lasting reputation for steadfast valour, were moved into reserve, while the Lahore Indian Division (Keary) came into the fighting line. It is a remarkable illustration, if one were needed, of the unity of the British Empire that, as the weary men from Montreal or Manitoba moved from the field, their place was filled by eager soldiers from the Punjab and the slopes of the Himalayas.

That evening a fresh French Division, the One Hundred and Fifty-second, under General de Ligne, came up from the south, and two others were announced as being on their way, so that a powerful French offensive was assured for next day upon the further side of the Canal. De Lisle's First Division of Cavalry continued to support the French opposite Lizerne, while Kavanagh's Second Division was dismounted and pushed into the French territorial trenches in front of Boesinghe. The enemy had come within shelling distance of Poperinghe, and caused considerable annoyance there, as the town was crowded with wounded.

Splendid work was done during these days by the motor ambulances, which on this one evening brought 600 wounded men from under the very muzzles of the German rifles in front of St. Julien. Several of them were destroyed by direct hits, but no losses damped their splendid ardour.

The Lahore Division having now arrived, it was directed to advance on the left of the British and on the right of the French, along the general line of the Ypres-Langemarck road. Encouraged by this reinforcement, and by the thickening line of the French, General Smith-Dorrien, who had spent several nightmare days, meeting one dire emergency after another with never-failing coolness and resource, ordered a general counter-attack for the early afternoon of April 26. There was no sign yet of any lull in the German activity which would encourage the hope that they had shot their bolt. On the contrary, during the whole morning there had been confused and inconclusive fighting along the whole front, and especially along the Gravenstrafel Ridge, where the British 10th and 11th Brigades were now opposing the advance. The 11th Brigade and 85th Brigade suffered heavily from shell-fire. About two o'clock the counter-attack was set in motion, all forces co-operating, the general idea being to drive the enemy back from the line between Boesinghe on the left and Zonnebeke on the right. Of the French attack on the east of the Canal one can only say that it kept pace generally with the British, but on the west of the Canal it was pushed very strongly in the direction of the village of Lizerne, where the Germans had established an important bridge-head.

The Indians advanced to the right of the French, with the Jullundur Brigade upon the right and the Ferozepore Brigade upon the left, the Sirhind Brigade in reserve. This Indian advance was an extraordinarily fine one over fifteen hundred yards of open under a very heavy shell-fire. They had nearly reached the front line of German trenches, and were making good progress, when before them there rose once more the ominous green-yellow mist of the poisoners. A steady north-east wind was blowing, and in a moment the Indians were encircled by the deadly fumes. It was impossible to get forward. Many of the men died where they stood. The mephitic cloud passed slowly over, but the stupefied men were in no immediate condition to resume their advance. The whole line was brought to a halt, but the survivors dug themselves in, and were eventually supported and relieved by the Sirhind Brigade, who, with the help of the 3rd Sappers and Miners and the 34th Pioneers, consolidated the front line. General Smith-Dorrien tersely summed up the characteristics of this advance of the Lahore Division when he said that it was done "with insufficient artillery preparation, up an open slope in the face of overwhelming shell, rifle, and machine-gun fire and clouds of poison gas, but it prevented the German advance and ensured the safety of Ypres." In this war of great military deeds there have been few more heroic than this, but it was done at a terrible cost. Of the 129th Baluchis, only a hundred could be collected that night, and many regiments were in little better case. The 1st Manchesters and 1st Connaughts had fought magnificently, but it cannot be said that there was any difference of gallantry between Briton and Indian.

Farther to the eastwards another fine advance had been made by the Northumberland Brigade of Territorials (Eiddell) of the Fiftieth Division, who had just arrived from England. Some military historian has remarked that British soldiers never fight better than in their first battle, and this particular performance, carried out by men with the home dust still upon their boots, could not have been improved upon. In this as in other attacks it was well understood that the object of the operations was rather to bluff the Germans into suspending their dangerous advance than to actually gain and permanently hold any of the lost ground. The brigade advanced in artillery formation which soon broke into open order. The fire, both from the German guns, which had matters April 26. all their own way, and from their riflemen, was incessant and murderous. The 6th Northumberland Fusiliers were on the left with the 7th upon the right, the other two battalions being nominally in second line but actually swarming up into the gaps. In spite of desperately heavy losses the gallant Geordies won their way across open fields, with an occasional rest behind a bank or hedge, until they were on the actual outbuildings of St. Julien. They held on to the edge of the village for some time, but they had lost their Brigadier, the gallant Eiddell, and a high proportion of their officers and men. Any support would have secured their gains, but the 151st Durham Light Infantry Brigade behind them had their own hard task to perform. The battalions which had reached the village were compelled to fall back. Shortly after six in the evening the survivors had dropped back to their own trenches. Their military career had begun with a repulse, but it was one which was more glorious than many a facile success.

On their right the Twenty-eighth Division had been severely attacked, and the pressure was so great that two and a half battalions had to be sent to their help, thus weakening the

British advance to that extent. Had these battalions been available to help the Northumbrians, it is possible that their success could have been made good. The strain upon our overmatched artillery may be indicated by the fact that on that one afternoon the 366th Battery of the Twenty-eighth Division fired one thousand seven hundred and forty rounds. The troops in this section of the battlefield had been flung into the fight in such stress that it had been very difficult to keep a line without gaps, and great danger arose from this cause on several occasions. Thus a gap formed upon the left of the Hampshire Regiment, the flank of the 11th Brigade, through which the Germans poured. Another gap formed on the right of the Hampshires between them and the 3rd Royal Fusiliers of the 85th Brigade. One company of the 8th Middlesex was practically annihilated in filling this gap, but by the help of the 8th Durham Light Infantry and other Durham and Yorkshire Territorials the line was restored. The 2nd Shropshire Light Infantry also co- operated in this fierce piece of fighting, their Colonel Bridgford directing the operation.

The Indians upon the left had suffered from the gas attack, but the French near the Canal had been very badly poisoned. By 3:30 they had steadied themselves, however, and came forward once again, while the Indians kept pace with them. The whole net advance of the day upon this wing did not exceed three hundred yards, but it was effected in the face of the poison fumes, which might well have excused a retreat. In the night the front line was consolidated and the Sirhind reserve brigade brought up to occupy it. It was a day of heavy losses and uncertain gains, but the one vital fact remained that, with their artillery, their devil's gas, and their north-east wind, the Germans were not a yard nearer to that gaunt, tottering tower which marked the goal of their desire.

The night of the 26th was spent by the British in reorganising their line, taking out the troops who were worn to the bone, and substituting such reserves as could be found. The French had been unable to get forward on the east of the Canal, but on the west, where they were farther from the gas, they had made progress, taking trenches between Boesinghe and Lizerne, and partially occupying the latter village. April 27. In the early afternoon of the 27th our indomitable Allies renewed their advance upon our left. They were held up by artillery fire, and finally, about 7 P.M., were driven back by gas fumes. The Sirhind and Ferozepore Indian Brigades kept pace with the French upon the right, but made little progress, for the fire was terrific. The losses of the Sirhind Brigade were very heavy, but they held their own manfully. The 1st and 4th Gurkhas had only two officers left unwounded in each battalion. The 4th King's also made a very fine advance. Four battalions from Ypres. corps reserve the 2nd Cornwalls, 2nd West Ridings, 5th King's Own, and 1st York and Lancaster were sent up at 3 P.M., under Colonel Tuson, to support the Indians. The whole of this composite brigade was only one thousand three hundred rifles, three out of the four battalions having been with Geddes' decimated force. The advance could not get forward, but when in the late evening the French recoiled before the deadly gas, the left of the Sirhind Brigade would have been in the air but for the deployment of part of Tuson's detachment to cover their flank. At 9 P.M. the Morocco Brigade of the French Division came forward once more and the line was re-formed, Tuson's detachment falling back into support. Once again it was a day of hard fighting, considerable losses, and inconclusive results, but yet another day had gone and Ypres was still intact. On the right of the British the 10th and 11th Brigades had more than held their own, and the line of the Gravenstrafel Ridge was in their hands. Across the Canal also the French had come on, and the Germans were being slowly but surely pushed across to the farther side. By the evening of the 28th a continuation of this movement had entirely cleared the western side, and on the eastern had brought the French line up to the neighbourhood of Steenstraate.

At this point the first phase of the second battle Results. of Ypres may be said to have come to an end, although for the next few days there was desultory fighting here and there along the French and British fronts. The net result of the five days' close combat had been that the Germans had advanced some two miles nearer to Ypres. They had also captured the four large guns of the London battery, eight batteries of French field-guns, a number of machine-guns, several thousand French, and about a thousand British prisoners. The losses of the Allies had been very heavy, for the troops had fought with the utmost devotion in the most difficult circumstances. Our casualties up to the end of the month in this region came to nearly 20,000 men, and at least 12,000 French would have to be added to represent the total Allied loss. The single unit which suffered most was the British 10th Brigade (Hull), consisting of the 1st Warwicks, 2nd Seaforths, 1st Irish Fusiliers, 2nd Dublin Fusiliers, and 7th Argyll and Sutherlands. These battalions lost among them no fewer than 63 officers and 2300 men, a very high proportion of their total numbers. Nearly as high were the losses of the three Canadian brigades, the first losing 64 officers and 1862 men; the second 71 officers and 1770 men; while the third lost 62 officers and 1771 men. The Northumbrian Division was also very hard hit, losing 102 officers and 2423 men, just half of the casualties coming from the Northumberland Infantry Brigade. The Lahore Division had about the same losses as the Northern Territorials, while the Twenty-seventh and Twenty-eighth Divisions each lost about 2000. General Hasler, of the 11th Brigade, General Riddell, of the Northumberlands, Colonel Geddes, of the Buffs, Colonels Burchall, McHaig, and Boyle, of the 4th, 7th, and 10th Canadians, Colonel Martin, of the 1st King's Own Lancasters, Colonel Hicks, of the 1st Hants, with many senior regimental officers, were among the dead. No British or Canadian guns were lost save the four heavy pieces, which were exposed through the exceptional circumstance of the gas attack. The saving of all the Canadian guns was an especially fine achievement, as two-thirds of the horses were killed, and it was necessary to use the same teams again and again to get away pieces which were in close contact with the enemy.

The airmen, too, did great work during this engagement, bombarding Steenstraate, Langemarck, Poelcapelle, and Paschendaale. In so short an account of so huge an operation it is difficult to descend to the individual, but no finer deed could be chronicled in the whole war than that of Lieutenant Rhodes-Moorhouse, who, having been mortally wounded in the execution of his duty, none the less steered his machine home, delivered her at the hangar, and made his report before losing consciousness for ever.

As to the German losses, they were very considerable. The Twenty-sixth Corps returned a casualty list of 10,572, and the Twenty-seventh of 6101. These are great figures when one considers that it was almost entirely to their rifles that the British had to trust. There were many other units engaged, and the total could not have been less than 25,000 killed, wounded, or taken.

In this hard-fought battle the British, if one includes the whole area of contest, had seven divisions engaged the Fourth, Fifth, Twenty-seventh, Twenty- eighth, Fiftieth, Canadian, and Lahore. Nearly half of these were immobile, however, being fixed to the long line of eastern trenches. Forty thousand men would be a fair estimate of those available from first to last to stop the German advance. It would be absurd to deny that the advantage rested with the Germans, but still more absurd to talk of the honours of war in such a connection. By a foul trick they gained a trumpery advantage at the cost of an eternal slur upon their military reputation. It was recognised from this time onwards that there was absolutely nothing at which these people would stick, and that the idea of military and naval honour or the immemorial customs of warfare had no meaning for them whatever. The result was to infuse an extraordinary bitterness into our soldiers, who had seen their comrades borne past them in the agonies of asphyxiation. The fighting became sterner and more relentless, whilst the same feeling was reflected in Great Britain, hardening the resolution with which the people faced those numerous problems of recruiting, food supply, and munitions which had to be solved. Truly honesty is the better policy in war as in peace, for no means could have been contrived by the wit of man to bring out the full, slow, ponderous strength of the British Empire so effectively as the long series of German outrages, each adding a fresh stimulus before the effect of the last was outworn. Belgium, Louvain, Rheims, Zeppelin raids, Scarborough, poison-gas, the *Lusitania*, Edith Cavell, Captain Fryatt these were the stages which led us on to victory. Had Germany never violated the Belgian frontier, and had she fought an honest, manly fight from first to last, the prospect would have been an appalling one for the Allies. There may have been more criminal wars in history, and there may have been more foolish policies, but the historian may search the past in vain for any such combination of crime and folly as the methods of "frightfulness " by which the Germans endeavoured to carry out the schemes of aggression which they had planned so long.

The gain of ground by the Germans from north to south in this engagement necessitated a drawing-in of the line from east to west over a front of nearly eight miles in order to avoid a dangerous projecting salient at Zonnebeke. It was hard in cold blood to give up ground which had been successfully held for so many months, and which was soaked with the blood of our bravest and best. On the other hand, if it were not done now, while the Germans were still stunned by the heavy losses which they had sustained and wearied out by their exertions, it might be exposed to an attack by fresh troops, and lead to an indefensible strategic position.

Upon Sunday, May 2, they made a fresh attack May 2. on the north of Ypres along the front held by the French to the immediate south of Pilken and along the British left to the east of St. Julien, where the newly-arrived 12th Brigade (Anley) and the remains of the 10th and 11th were stationed. The 12th Brigade, which came up on May 1, consisted at that time of the 1st King's Own Lancasters, 2nd Lancashire Fusiliers, 2nd Essex, 5th South Lancashires (T.F.), 2nd Monmouths (T.F.), and 2nd Royal Irish. The attack was in the first instance carried out by means of a huge cloud of gas, which was ejected under high pressure from the compressed cylinders in their trenches, and rapidly traversed the narrow space between the lines. As the troops fell back to avoid asphyxiation they were thickly sprayed by shrapnel from the German guns. The German infantry followed on the fringe of their poison cloud, but they brought themselves into the zone of the British guns, and suffered considerable losses. Many of the troops in the trenches drew to one side to avoid the gas, or even, in some cases, notably that of the 7th Argyll and Sutherland Highlanders, waited for the gas to come, and then charged swiftly through it to reach the stormers upon the other side, falling upon them with all the concentrated fury that such murderous tactics could excite. The result was that neither on the French nor on the British front did the enemy gain any ground. Two battalions of the 12th Brigade the 2nd Lancashire Fusiliers and the 2nd Essex suffered heavily, many of the men being poisoned. The Lancashire Fusiliers lost 300 men from this cause, among them the heroic machine-gunner, Private Lynn, who stood without a respirator in the thick of the fumes, and beat off a German attack almost single-handed, at the cost of a death of torture to himself.

It was found that even when the acute poisoning had been avoided, a great lassitude was produced for some time by the inhalation of the gas. In the case of Hull's 10th Brigade, which had been practically living in the fumes for a fortnight, but had a specially bad dose on May 2, it was found that out of 2500 survivors, only 500 were really fit for duty. The sufferings of the troops were increased by the use of gas shells, which were of thin metal with highly-compressed gas inside. All these fiendish devices were speedily neutralised by means of respirators, but a full supply had not yet come to hand, nor had the most efficient type been discovered, so that many of the Allies were still poisoned.

Upon May 3 the enemy renewed his attack upon the 11th Brigade, now commanded by Brigadier General Prowse, and the 1st Rifle Brigade, which was the right flank regiment, was badly mauled, their Ypres. trenches being almost cleared of defenders. The Mays. 1st Somersets also suffered heavily. Part of the 1st York and Lancasters and the 5th King's Own Lancasters were rushed up to the rescue from the supports of the Twenty-eighth Division. The gallant Colonel of the latter battalion, Lord Richard Cavendish, was wounded while waving on his men with his cane and shouting, "Come along, King's Own." At the same time the German infantry tried to push in between the 11th Brigade on our left and the 85th on the right, at the salient between the Fourth and Twenty- eighth Divisions, the extreme north-east corner of the British lines. The fight was a very desperate one, being strongly supported by field-guns at short ranges. Three more British battalions the 2nd Buffs, 3rd Fusiliers, and 2nd East Yorks were thrown into the fight, and the advance was stopped. That night the general retirement took place, effected in many cases from positions within a few yards of the enemy, and carried out without the loss of a man or a gun. The retirement was upon the right of the British line, and mainly affected the Twenty-seventh, and to a less degree the Twenty-eighth, Divisions. The Fourth Division upon the left or north did not retire, but was the hinge upon which the others swung. During the whole of these and subsequent operations the Fourth Division was splendidly supported by the French artillery, which continually played upon the attacking Germans.

Before closing this chapter, dealing with the gas attacks to the north of Ypres, and beginning the next one, which details the furious German assault upon the contracted lines of the Fifth Army Corps, it would be well to interpolate some account of the new development at Hill 60. This position was a typical one for the German use of gas, just as the Dardanelles lines would have been for the Allies, had they condescended to such an atrocity upon a foe who did not themselves use such a weapon. Where there is room for flexibility of manoeuvre, and a temporary loss of ground is immaterial, the gas is at a discount; but where there is a fixed and limited position it is without respirators practically impossible to hold it against such an agency. Up to now the fighting at Hill 60 had furnished on both sides a fine epic of manliness, in which man breasted man in honest virile combat. Alas, that such a brave story should have so cowardly an ending! Upon the evening of May 1 the poisoners got to work, and the familiar greenish gas came stealing out from the German trenches, eddied and swirled round the base of the hill, and finally submerged the summit, where the brave men of the Dorsets in the trenches were strangled by the chlorine as they lay motionless and silent, examples of a discipline as stern as that of the Roman sentry at Herculaneum. So dense were the fumes that the Germans could not take possession, and it was a reinforcement of Devons and Bedfords of the 15th Brigade who were the first to reach the trenches, where they found the bodies of their murdered comrades, either fixed already in death or writhing in the agonies of choking. It is said that the instructions of the relieving force were to carry up munitions and to carry down the Dorsets. One officer and 50 men had been killed at once, while 4 officers and 150 men were badly injured, many of them being permanently incapacitated. The 59th Company of the Royal Engineers were also overwhelmed by the fumes, three officers and many men being poisoned.

The gas attack upon Hill 60 on May 1 may have been a mere experiment upon the part of the Germans to see how far they could submerge it, for it was not followed up by an infantry advance. A more sustained and more successful attack was made by the same foul means upon May 5. Early in the morning the familiar cloud appeared once more, and within a few minutes the British position was covered by it. Not only the hill itself, but a long trench to the north of it was rendered untenable, and so was another trench two thousand yards north of Westhoek.

The 2nd West Ridings were holding the front trench at the time, and suffered horribly from the poison. Mr. Valentine Williams, in his admirable account of the episode, says: "There appeared staggering towards the dug-out of the commanding officer of the Duke's in the rear two figures, an officer and an orderly. The officer was as pale as death, and when he spoke his voice came hoarsely from his throat.

Beside him his orderly, with unbuttoned coat, his rifle clasped in his hand, swayed as he stood. The officer said slowly, in his gasping voice, 'They have gassed the Duke's. I believe I was the last man to leave the hill. The men are all up there dead. They were splendid. I thought I ought to come and report.' That officer was Captain Robins... They took him and his faithful orderly to hospital, but the gallant officer died that night." His two subalterns, Lieut. Miller and another, both remained in the front trench until they died.

Such was the upshot of the fighting at Hill 60. What with the shells and what with the mines, very little of the original eminence was left. The British still held the trenches upon the side while the Germans held the summit, if such a name could be applied. The British losses, nearly all from poison, had been considerable in the affair, and amounted to the greater part of a thousand men, the Dorsets, Devons, Bedfords, and West Ridings being the regiments which suffered most heavily. When the historian of the future sums up the deeds of the war it is probable that he will find nothing more remarkable than the patient endurance with which the troops faced a death of torture from the murderous gas in the days when no protection had yet been afforded them.

One incident of this period may be quoted as showing the peculiar happenings of modern warfare. The village of Poperinghe was at this time the chief depot for stores and resting-place for wounded, being ten miles to the rear of the line. Great surprise and confusion were caused, therefore, by a sudden fall of immense shells, which came out of space with no indication whatever as to their origin. They caused more fright than damage, but were excessively unnerving. From their measured fall it was clear that they all came from one single gun of gigantic power behind the far distant

German line. To the admirable aeroplanes was given the task of solving the mystery, and regardless of gun-fire or hostile craft they quartered the whole country round until at last, by a combination of luck and skill, they concluded that a Belgian barn, five miles behind the enemy line and fifteen from Poperinghe, was the lair of the monster. A large British gun came stealthily up and lay concealed till dawn when it opened upon the barn. The third or fourth shell went home, a magazine exploded, the barn went up, and there was peace henceforth in Poperinghe.

IV. THE SECOND BATTLE OF YPRES

Stage II. The Bellewaarde Lines

The second phase—Attack on the Fourth Division—Great stand of the Princess Pats—Breaking of the line—Desperate attacks —The cavalry save the situation—The ordeal of the 11th Brigade —The German failure—Terrible strain on the British—The last effort of May 24—Result of the battle—Sequence of events

It was upon the evening of May 4 that the difficult operations were finished by which the lines of the British Army on the north-east of Ypres were brought closer to the city. The trenches which faced north, including those which looked towards Pilken and St. Julien, were hardly affected at all by this rearrangement. The section which was chiefly modified was the long curved line which was held from Zonnebeke southwards by the Twenty-seventh and Twenty-eighth Divisions. Instead of averaging five miles from Ypres, these troops were now not more than three from that centre, and the curve of their line was from Wieltje and Frezenberg to past the Bellewaarde wood and lake, and so through Hooge and on to Hill 60.

The second phase of this great battle, which began with the poisoning of Langemarck, is dated from the time that the British line was readjusted. The Germans were naturally much encouraged by so general a withdrawal, and it seemed to them that, with a further effort, they would be able to burst their way through and take possession at last of this town which faced them, still inviolate, after nearly eight months of incessant attack. Their guns, aided by their aeroplanes, after wasting a day in bombarding the empty trenches, hastened to register upon the new line of defences.

During the 5th, 6th, and 7th the enemy were perfecting their new arrangements, but no peace or rest was given to that northern portion of the line which was still in its old trenches. The bombardment was turned on to this or that battalion in turn. On the evening of the 5th it was the 5th South Lancashires, on the right of the 12th Brigade, who were torn to pieces by jets of steel from the terrible hose. The battalion was relieved by the 2nd Monmouths, who beat off an attack next morning. All day upon the 7th the Germans were massing for an attack, but were held back by the steady fire of the French and British batteries. On the 8th, however, the new preparations were complete, and a terrible storm, destined to last for six unbroken days days never to be forgotten by those who endured them broke along the whole east, north-east, and north of the British line.

It has been shown in the last chapter that during the long and bitter fight which had raged from the 22nd to the 28th of April the two British divisions which together formed the Fifth Army Corps had not only been closely engaged in their own trenches, but had lent battalions freely to the Canadians, so that they had at one time only a single battalion in their own reserve. During the period of the readjustment of the line nearly all these troops returned, but they The second came back grievously weakened and wearied by the desperate struggle in which they had been involved. None the less, they got to work at once in forming and strengthening the new dyke which was to keep the German flood out of Ypres. Day and night they toiled at their lines, helped by working parties from the Fifth Division, the 50th Northumbrian Division, and two field companies of sappers from the Fourth Division. All was ready when the German attack broke upon the line. The left of this attack was borne by the Fourth Division, the centre, in the Frezenberg sector, was held by the Twenty- eighth Division, and the right by the Twenty-seventh Division, who joined up with the Fifth Division in the south. This was at first almost entirely an artillery attack, and was of a most destructive character. Such an attack probably represents the fixed type of the future, where the guns will make an area of country impossible for human life, and the function of the infantry will simply be to move forward afterwards and to occupy. Along the whole line of the three divisions for hour after hour an inexhaustible rain of huge projectiles fell with relentless precision into the trenches, smashing them to pieces and burying the occupants in the graves which they had prepared for themselves. It was with joy that the wearied troops saw the occasional head of an infantry assault and blew it to pieces with their rifles. For the greater part it was not a contest between men and men, but rather one between men and metal, in which our battalions were faced by a deserted and motionless landscape, from which came the ceaseless downpour of shells and occasional drifting clouds of chlorine. At one point, near Frezenberg, the trenches had been sited some 70 yards down the forward slope of a hill, with disastrous results, as the 3rd Monmouths Ypres. and part of the 2nd Royal Lancasters who held this section were almost destroyed. When the 3rd Monmouths were eventually recalled the Battalion H.Q. and some orderlies and signallers were all who appeared in answer to the summons.

About seven o'clock the German infantry attack developed against that part of the line—the northern or left wing—which was held by the Fourth Division. The advance was pushed with great resolution and driven back with heavy losses, after getting within a hundred yards of the trenches. "Company after company came swinging forward steadily in one long, never-ending line," says an observer of the 11th Brigade, describing the attack as it appeared from the front of the 1st East Lancashires and of the 5th London Rifle Brigade. "Here and there their attack slackened, but the check was only temporary. On they came again, and the sight was one that almost mesmerised us. They were near enough for us to hear the short, sharp cries of the officers, and the rain of bullets became more deadly than ever. It was simple murder." The barbed wire in front of the defences was choked and heaped with dead and wounded men. This desperate German attack had more success farther to the south.

At this part of the line the Germans had pushed through a gap and had seized the village of Wieltje, thus getting behind the right rear of the 12th Brigade. It was essential to regain the village, for it was a vital point in the line. The 1st Royal Irish, which had been attached to this brigade, together with two companies of the 5th South Lancashire, were ordered to advance, while two reserve battalions of the 1st Irish Fusiliers and the 7th Argyll and Sutherlands, all under General Anley, supported the attack. It is no light matter with an inferior artillery to attack a village held by German troops, but the assault was brilliantly successful and the village was regained, while the dangerous gap was closed in the British line. That night there was some desperate righting round Wieltje, which occasionally got down to bayonet work. The 1st Hants and 1st East Lancashire from the 11th Brigade had come up and helped in the fierce defence, which ended where it began, with the British line still intact.

So much for the fighting on May 8 in front of the Fourth Division. Farther down the line to the south the situation was more serious. A terrific bombardment had demolished the trenches of the Fifth Corps, and a very heavy infantry advance had followed, which broke the line in several places.

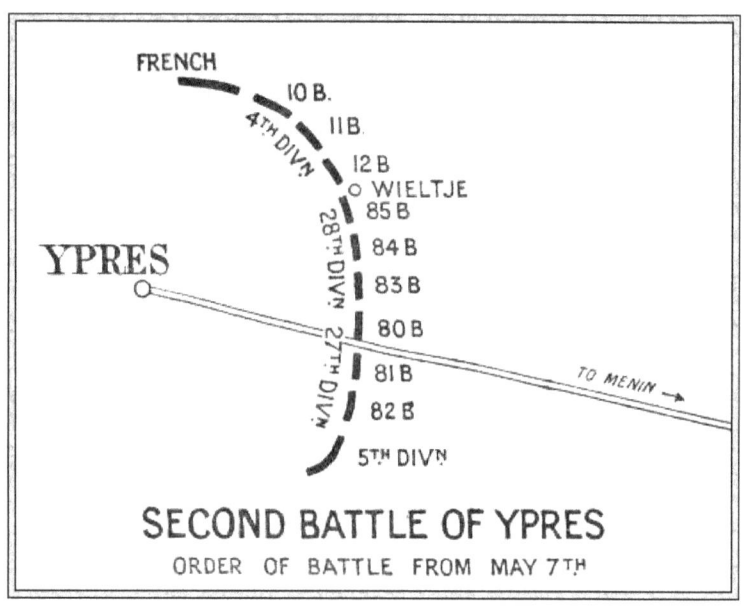

Order Of Battle from May 7th

The weight of this attack fell upon the Twenty-eighth Division in front of Frezenberg, and very particularly upon the 83rd Brigade, which formed the unit on the right flank. The German rush was stemmed for a time by the staunch North of England battalions which made up this brigade the

1st Yorkshire Light Infantry on the extreme right, and their neighbours of the 5th Royal Lancasters, the 2nd Royal Lancasters, and the 2nd East Yorkshires. Great drifts of gas came over, and the gasping soldiers, with their hands to their throats and the tears running down their cheeks, were at the same time cut to pieces by every kind of shell beating upon them in an endless stream. Yet they made head against this accumulation of horrors. The East Yorkshires were particularly badly cut up, and the Monmouths, who were in support, endured a terrible and glorious baptism of fire while advancing in splendid fashion to their support. But the losses from the shell-fire had been very heavy, and the line was too weak to hold. Of 2500 men in the Frezenberg trenches only 600 men were left standing. The brigade had to fall back. The left flank of the 80th Brigade of the Twenty-seventh Division upon the right was consequently exposed and in the air. A glance at the accompanying diagram will show the situation created by the retirement of any unit.

The flank trench was held by the Princess Patricia Great Canadians, and their grand defence of it showed once more the splendid stuff which the Dominion had sent us. Major Gault and all the other senior officers were killed or wounded, and the command devolved upon Lieutenant Niven, who rose greatly to the occasion. Besides the heavy shelling and the gas, the trenches were raked by machine-guns in neighbouring buildings. So accurate was the German artillery that the machine-guns of the Canadians were buried again and again, but were dug up and spat out their defiance once more. Corporal Dover worked one of these guns till both his leg and his arm had been shot away. When the trenches were absolutely obliterated the Canadians manned the communication trench and continued the desperate resistance. The 4th Rifle Brigade sent up a reinforcement and the fight went on. Later a party of the 2nd Shropshires pushed their way also into the fire-swept trenches, bringing with them a welcome supply of cartridges. It was at this hour that the 83rd Brigade upon the right of the Twenty-eighth Division had to fall back, increasing the difficulty of holding the position. The enemy charged once more and got possession of the trench at a point where all the defenders had been killed. There was a rush, however, by the survivors in the other sections, and the Germans were driven out again. From then until late at night the shell-fire continued, but there was no further infantry advance. Late that night, when relieved by the Rifles, the Canadian regiment, which had numbered nearly 700 in the morning, could only muster 150 men. Having read the service over their comrades, many of whom had already been buried by the German shells, they were led back by Lieutenants Niven, Clark, Vandenburg, and Papineau after a day of great stress and loss, but of permanent glory. "No regiment could have fought with greater determination or endurance," said an experienced British general. "Many would have failed where they succeeded."

It has already been described how the 83rd Brigade had been riven back by the extreme weight of the German advance. Their fellow brigade upon the left, the 84th (Bowes), had a similar experience. They also held their line under heavy losses, and were finally, shortly after mid-day, compelled to retire. The flank regiment on the right, the 1st Suffolk, were cut off and destroyed even as their second battalion had been at Le Cateau.

At this time the 1st Suffolk was so reduced by the losses sustained when it had formed part of Wallace's detachment, as described in the last chapter, that there were fewer than 300 men with the Colours.

When the Germans broke through the left flank of the 83rd Brigade they got partly to the rear of the Suffolk trenches. The survivors of the Suffolks were crowded down the trench and mixed up with the 2nd Cheshires, who were their immediate neighbours. The parapets were wrecked, the trenches full of debris, the air polluted with gas, and the Germans pushing forward on the flank, holding before them the prisoners that they had just taken from the 83rd Brigade. It is little wonder that in these circumstances this most gallant battalion was overwhelmed. Colonel Wallace and 130 men were taken. The 2nd Northumberland Fusiliers and the 1st Monmouths sustained also very heavy losses, as did the 12th London Rangers. The shattered remains of the brigade were compelled to fall back in conformity with the 83rd upon the right, sustaining fresh losses as they were swept with artillery fire on emerging from the trenches. This was about 11:30 in the morning. The 1st Monmouths upon the left of the line seem, however, to have kept up their resistance till a considerably later hour, and to have behaved with extraordinary gallantry. Outflanked and attacked in the rear after the Germans had taken the trenches on the right, they still, under their gallant Colonel Robinson, persevered in what was really a hopeless resistance. The Germans trained a machine-gun upon them from a house which overlooked their trench, but nothing could shift the gallant miners who formed the greater part of the regiment. Colonel Robinson was shot dead while passing his men down the trench one by one in the hope of forming a new front. Half the officers and men were already on the ground. The German stormers were on the top of them with cries of "Surrender! Surrender!" "Surrender be damned!" shouted Captain Edwards, and died still firing his revolver into the grey of them. It was a fine feat of arms, but only 120 men out of 750 reassembled that night.

After this severe blow battalions held back in reserve were formed up for a counter-attack, which was launched about half-past three. The attack advanced from the point where the Fourth and Twenty-eighth Divisions adjoined, and two battalions of the Fourth Division the 1st Warwicks and the 2nd Dublin Fusiliers together with the 2nd East Surreys, 1st York and Lancasters, and 3rd Middlesex, of the 85th Brigade, took part in it, pushing forwards towards the hamlet of Frezenberg, which they succeeded in occupying. On their left the 12th London Regiment (the Rangers) won their way back to the line which their brigade, the 84th, had held in the morning, but they lost very heavily in their gallant attack. Two other reserve battalions, the 1st East Lancashires, of the 11th Brigade, and the 7th Argyll and Sutherland Highlanders, of the 10th, fought their way up as already mentioned on the extreme left in the neighbourhood of Wieltje, and spliced the line at the weak point of the junction of divisions. All these attacks were made against incessant drifts of poison-gas, as well as heavy rifle and shell fire. It was a day of desperate and incessant fighting, where all General Plumer's skill and resolution were needed to restore and to hold his line. The Germans claimed to have taken 500 prisoners, mostly of the 84th Brigade.

The net result of the fighting upon May 8 was that the area held in the north-east of Ypres was further diminished. Early upon the 9th the Germans, encouraged by their partial success, continued their attack, still relying upon their massive artillery, which far exceeded anything which the British could put against it. The attack on this morning came down the Menin road, and the trenches on either side of it were heavily bombarded. At ten o'clock there was an infantry advance upon the line of the 81st Brigade (Croker), which was driven back by the 2nd Cameron Highlanders and the 2nd Gloucesters. The shell-fire was continued upon the same line until 4 P.M., when the trench was obliterated, and a second advance of the German infantry got possession of it. A counter-attack of the Gloucesters was held up with considerable loss, the advance of the regiment through the wood being greatly impeded by the number of trees cut down by shells and forming abattis in every direction, like the windfalls of a Canadian forest. This trench was the only capture made by the Germans during the day, and it did not materially weaken the position. The Gloucesters lost Colonel Tulloh, five other officers, and 150 men.

These attacks along the line of the Menin road and to the north of Lake Bellewaarde were all directed upon the Twenty-seventh Division, but the Twenty- eighth Division immediately to the north, which had been defending the sector which runs through Frezenberg and Wieltje, had also been most violently shelled, but had held its line, as had the Fourth Division to the north. All these divisions had considerable losses. The general result was a further slight contraction of the British line. It could not be broken, and it could not be driven in upon Ypres, but the desperate and (apart from the gas outrages) valorous onslaughts of Germans, aided by their overpowering artillery, gained continually an angle here and a corner there, with the result that the British position was being gradually whittled away.

On the 10th the Germans again attacked upon the line of the Menin road, blasting a passage with their artillery, but meeting with a most determined resistance. The weight of their advance fell chiefly upon the 80th Brigade to the north of the road, the 4th Rifle Brigade and the 4th Rifles bearing the brunt of it and suffering very severely, though the 2nd Camerons and 9th Royal Scots, of the 81st Brigade, were also hard hit. So savage had been the bombardment, and so thick the gas, that the German infantry thought that they could safely advance, but the battalions named, together with the 3rd Battalion of Rifles, drove them back with heavy loss. It was always a moment of joy for the British infantry when for a brief space they were faced by men rather than machines. The pitiless bombardment continued; the garrison of the trenches was mostly killed or buried, and the survivors fell back on to the support trenches west of the wood. This defence of the Riflemen was as desperate a business as that of the Canadians upon the 8th. Several of the platoons remained in the shattered trenches until the Germans had almost surrounded them, and finally shot and stabbed a path for themselves till they could rejoin their comrades. It was on this day that the 9th Argyll and Sutherland Highlanders suffered heavy losses, including their splendid Colonel, James Clark.

On May 11 the attack was still very vigorous. The Twenty-seventh Division was strongly pressed in the morning. The 80th Brigade was to the north and somewhat to the west of the 81st, which caused the latter to form a salient. With their usual quickness in taking advantage of such things, the Germans instantly directed their fire upon this point. After several hours of heavy shelling, an infantry attack about 11 A.M. got into the trenches, but was driven out again by the rush of the 9th Royal Scots. The bombardment was then renewed, and the attack was more successful at 4 P.M. an almost exact repetition of the events upon the day before, save that the stress fell upon the 81st instead of the 80th Brigade. During the night the Leinsters of the 82nd Brigade drove the Germans out again, but found that the trench was untenable on account of the shell-fire. It was abandoned, therefore, and the line was drawn back into the better cover afforded by a wood. Afterwards the trench was partly reoccupied by a company of the 2nd Gloucestershires under Captain Fane.

By this date many of the defending troops had been fighting with hardly a break from April 22. It was an ordeal which had lasted by day and by night, and had only been interrupted by the labour of completing the new lines. The losses had been very heavy, and reinforcements were most urgently needed. Some idea of the stress may be gathered from the fact that at the time the six battalions of the 83rd Brigade had been formed into one composite battalion under Colonel Worsley Gough. At the same time it was impossible to take any troops from the northern sector, which was already hardly strong enough to hold a violent German attack. In the south the Army had, as will be shown, become involved in the very serious and expensive operations which began at Kichebourg on May 9. In these difficult circumstances it was to the never-failing cavalry that General Plumer had to turn. It is sinful extravagance to expend these highly trained horsemen, who cannot be afterwards improvised, on work that is not their own, but there have been many times in this war when it was absolutely necessary that the last man, be he who he might, should be put forward. So it was now, and the First and Third Cavalry Divisions, under General de Lisle, were put into the firing line to the north of Lake Bellewaarde, taking the place of the Twenty-eighth Division, which at that time had hardly a senior regimental officer left standing. The First Cavalry Division took the line from Wieltje to Verlorenhoek, while the Third carried it on to Hooge, where it touched the Twenty-seventh Division. Their presence in the front firing line was a sign of British weakness, but, on the other hand, it was certain that the Germans had lost enormously, that they were becoming exhausted, and that they were likely to wear out the rifling of their cannon before they broke the line of the defence. A few more days would save the situation, and it was hoped that the inclusion of the cavalry would win them.

May 12. They took over the lines just in time to meet the brunt of what may have been the most severe attack of all. The shelling upon May 12 can only be described as terrific. The Germans appeared to have an inexhaustible supply of munitions, and from morning to night they blew to pieces the trenches in front and the shelters behind which might screen the supports.

It was a day of tempestuous weather, and the howling wind, the driving rain, and the pitiless fire made a Dantesque nightmare of the combat. The attack on the right fell upon the Third Cavalry Division. This force had been reorganised since the days in October when it had done so splendidly with the Seventh Infantry Division in the fighting before Ypres. It consisted now of the 6th Brigade (1st Royals, 3rd Dragoon Guards, North Somerset Yeomanry), the 7th Brigade (1st and 2nd Life Guards and Leicestershire Yeomanry), and the 8th Brigade (Blues, 10th Hussars, and Essex Yeomanry). This Division was exposed all morning to a perfectly hellish fire, which was especially murderous to the north of the Ypres-Roulers road. At this point the 1st Royals, 3rd Dragoon Guards, and Somerset Yeomanry were stationed, and were blown, with their trenches, into the air by a bombardment which continued for fourteen hours. A single sentence may be extracted from the report of the Commander-in-Chief , which the Somersets should have printed in gold round the walls of their headquarters. "The North Somerset Yeomanry on the right of the brigade," says the General, "although also suffering severely, hung on to their trenches throughout the day and actually advanced and attacked the enemy with the bayonet." The Royals came up in support, and the brigade held its own. On one occasion the enemy actually got round the left of the 3rd Dragoon Guards, who were the flank regiment, upon which Captain Neville, who was killed later upon the same day, gave the order, "Even numbers deal with the enemy in the rear, odd numbers carry on!" which was calmly obeyed with complete success. On the right the flank of the Twenty-seventh Division had been exposed, but the 2nd Irish Fusiliers were echeloned back so as to cover it. So with desperate devices a sagging line was still drawn between Ypres and the ever-pressing invaders. The strain was heavy, not only upon the cavalry, but upon the Twenty- seventh Division to the south of them. There was a time when the pressure upon the 4th Rifle Brigade, a battalion which had endured enormous losses, was so great that help was urgently needed. The Princess Patricia's had been taken out of the line, as only 100 men remained effective, and the 4th Rifles were in hardly a better position, but the two maimed battalions were formed into one composite body, which pushed up with a good heart into the fighting line and took the place of the 3rd Rifles, who in turn relieved the exhausted Rifle Brigade.

On the left of the cavalry line, where the First Cavalry Division joined on to the Fourth Infantry Division, near Wieltje, the artillery storm had burst also with appalling violence. The 18th Hussars lost 150 men out of their already scanty ranks. The Essex Regiment on their left helped them to fill the gap until the 4th Dragoon Guards came up in support. This fine regiment and their comrades of the 9th Lancers were heavily punished, but bore it with grim stoicism. To their right Briggs' 1st Brigade held splendidly, though all of them, and especially the Bays, were terribly knocked about. In the afternoon the 5th Dragoon Guards were momentarily driven in by the blasts of shell, but the 11th Hussars held the line firm.

The situation as the day wore on became somewhat more reassuring. The British line had been badly dented in the middle, where the cavalry had been driven back or annihilated, but it held firm at each end. South of the Menin road the Twenty-seventh The Division, much exhausted, were still holding on, officers and men praying in their weary souls that the enemy might be more weary still. These buttressed the right of the line, while three miles to the north the Fourth Division, equally worn and ragged, was holding the left. The 10th Brigade had sustained such losses in the gas battle that it was held, as far as possible, in reserve, but the 11th and 12th were hard pressed during the long, bitter day, in which they were choked by gas, lashed with artillery fire, and attacked time after time by columns of infantry. The 11th Brigade in that dark hour showed to a supreme degree the historic qualities of British infantry, their courage hardening as the times grew worse. The 1st East Lancashires had their trenches destroyed, lost Major Rutter and many of their officers, but still, under their gallant Colonel Lawrence, held on to their shattered lines. Every point gained by the stubborn Germans was wrenched from them again by men more stubborn still. They carried a farmhouse near Wieltje, but were turned out again by the indomitable East Lancashires after desperate fighting at close quarters. It is said to have been the fourth time that this battalion mended a broken line. Severe attacks were made upon the trenches of the 1st Hampshires and the 5th London Rifle Brigade, but in each case the defenders held their line, the latter Territorial battalion being left with fewer than 200 men. It was in this action that Sergeant Belcher, of the London Rifle Brigade, with eight of his Territorials and two Hussars, held a vital position against the full force of a German infantry attack, losing half their little band, but saving the whole line from being enfiladed.

The 12th Brigade had been drawn back into reserve, but it was not a day for rest, and the 2nd Essex was hurried forward to the relief of the extreme left of the cavalry, where their line abutted upon the Fourth Division. The battalion made a very tine counter-attack under a hail of shells, recovering some trenches and clearing the Germans out of a farmhouse, which they subsequently held against all assailants. This attack was ordered on the instant by Colonel Jones, of the Essex, and was carried out so swiftly that the enemy had no time to consolidate his new position.

Whilst each buttress held firm, a gallant attempt was made in the afternoon to straighten out the line hi the centre where the Third Cavalry Division had been pushed back. The 8th Brigade of Cavalry, under Bulkeley- Johnson, pushed forward on foot and won their way to the original line of trenches, chasing the Germans out of them and making many prisoners, but they found it impossible to hold them without supports under the heavy shell-fire. They fell back, therefore, and formed an irregular line behind the trenches, partly in broken ground and partly in the craters of explosions. This they held for the rest of the day.

Thus ended a truly desperate conflict. The had failed in this, which proved to be their final and supreme effort to break the line. On the other hand, the advance to the north of the Bellewaarde Lake necessitated a further spreading and weakening of the other forces, so that it may truly be said that the prospects never looked worse than at the very moment when the Germans had spent their strength and could do no more. From May 13 the fighting died down, and for some time the harassed and exhausted defenders were allowed to re-form and to recuperate. The 80th Brigade, which had suffered very heavily, was drawn out upon the 17th, the Second Cavalry Division, under Kavanagh, taking its place. Next day the 81st Brigade, and on May 22 the 82nd, were also drawn back to the west of Ypres, their place being taken by fresh troops. The various units of the Twenty-eighth Division were also rested for a time. For the gunners and sappers there was no rest, however, but incessant labour against overmastering force.

The second phase of this new Battle of Ypres may be said to have lasted from May 4 to May 13. It consisted of a violent German attack, pushed chiefly by poison and by artillery, against the Twenty-seventh and Twenty-eighth Divisions of the Fifth British Corps and the Fourth Division to the north of them. Its aim was, as ever, the capture of Ypres. In this aim it failed, nor did it from first to last occupy any village or post which gave it any return for its exertions. It inflicted upon the British a loss of from 12,000 to 15,000 men, but endured itself at the very least an equal slaughter without any compensating advantage. The whole operation can only be described, therefore, as being a costly failure. Throughout these operations the British infantry were provided with respirators soaked in alkalis, while many wore specially- constructed helmets to save them from being poisoned.

To such grotesque expedients had Germany brought the warfare of the twentieth century.

There is no doubt that the three British regular divisions and the cavalry were worn to a shadow at the end of these operations. Since the enemy ceased to attack, it is to be presumed that they were in no better case. The British infantry had been fighting almost day and night for three weeks, under the most desperate conditions. Their superiority to the infantry of the Germans was incontestable, but there was no comparison at all between the number of heavy guns available, which were at least six to one in favour of the enemy. Shells were poured down with a profusion, and also with an accuracy, never before seen in warfare, and though the British infantry continually regained trenches which had been occupied by the German infantry, it was only to be shelled out of them again by a fire against which they could make no adequate answer. An aerial observer has described that plain simply flaming and smoking from end to end with the incessant heat of the shells, and has expressed his wonder that human life should have been possible under such a fire. And yet the road to Ypres was ever barred.

All the infantry losses, heavy as they were, are eclipsed by those of the Third Cavalry Division, which bore the full blast of the final whirlwind, and was practically destroyed in holding it back from Ypres. This splendid division, to whom, from first to last, the country owes as much as to any body of troops in the field, was only engaged in the fighting for one clear day, and yet lost nearly as heavily in proportion as either of the infantry divisions which had been in the firing line for a week. Their casualties were 91 officers and 1050 men. This will give some idea of the concentrated force of the storm which broke upon them on May 12. It was a most murderous affair, and they were only driven from their trenches when the trenches themselves had been blasted to pieces. It is doubtful whether any regiments have endured more in so short a time. These three brigades were formed of *corps d'élites*, and they showed that day that the blue blood of the land was not yet losing its iron. The casualty lists in this and the succeeding action of the 24th read like a society function. Colonel Ferguson, of the Blues, Colonel the Hon. Evans-Freke, Lord Chesham, Captain the Hon. J. Grenfell, Lord Leveson-Gower, Sir Robert Sutton, Lord Compton, Major the Hon. C. B. Mitford, the Hon. C. E. A. Phillips, Viscount Wendover so runs the sombre and yet glorious list. The sternest of Radicals may well admit that the aristocrats of Britain have counted their lives cheap when the enemy was at the gate. Colonel Smith-Bingham, of the 3rd Dragoon Guards, Colonel Steele, of the 1st Royals, Colonel Freke, of the Leicestershire Yeomanry, and many other senior officers were among the dead or wounded. The Leicester Yeomanry suffered very severely, but their comrades of Essex and of

Somerset, the Blues and the 1st Royals, were also hard hit. The losses of the First Cavalry Division were not so desperately heavy as those of the Third, but were none the less very serious, amounting to 54 officers and 650 men.

It is possible that the German attack desisted because the infantry were exhausted, but more probable that the great head of shells accumulated had been brought down to a minimum level, and that the gas cylinders were empty. For ten days, while the British strengthened their battered line, there was a lull in the fighting.

There was no change, however, in the German plan of campaign, and the fight which broke out again upon May 24 may be taken as the continuation of the battle which had died down upon the 13th. Fresh reservoirs of poison had been accumulated, and early in the morning in the first light of dawn the infernal stuff was drifting down wind in a solid bank some three miles in length and forty feet in depth, bleaching the grass, blighting the trees, and leaving a broad scar of destruction behind it. A roaring torrent of shells came pouring into the trenches at the instant that the men, hastily aroused from sleep, were desperately fumbling in the darkness to find their respirators and shield their lungs from the strangling poison. The front of this attack was from a farm called "Shell-trap," between the Poelcapelle and Langemarck roads on the north, to Bellewaarde Lake on the south. The surprise of the poison in that weird hour was very effective, and it was immediately followed by a terrific and accurate bombardment, which brought showers of asphyxiating shells into the trenches. The main force of the chlorine seems to have struck the extreme right of the Fourth Division and the whole front of the Twenty-eighth Division, but the Twenty-seventh and the cavalry were also involved in a lesser degree.

Anley's 12th Brigade was on the left of the British line, with Hull's 10th Brigade upon its right, the 11th being in reserve. On the 12th and 10th fell the full impact of the attack. The 12th, though badly mauled, stood like a rock and blew back the Germans as they tried to follow up the gas. "They doubled out of their trenches to follow it up half an hour after the emission," wrote an officer of the Essex. "They were simply shot back into them by a blaze of fire. They bolted back like rabbits." All day the left and centre of the 12th Brigade held firm. The Royal Irish upon the right were less fortunate. The pressure both of the gas and the shells fell very severely upon them, and the few survivors were at last driven from their trenches, some hundreds of yards being lost, including the Shell-trap Farm. The Dublin Fusiliers, in the exposed flank of the 10th Brigade, were also very hard hit. Of these two gallant Irish regiments only a handful remained, and the Colonels of each, Moriarty and Loveband, fell with their men. Several of the regiments of the 10th Brigade suffered severely, and the 7th Argyll and Sutherland Highlanders were left with only 2 officers and 76 men standing. These two officers, by some freak of fate, were brothers named Scott, the sole hale survivors of thirty-six who had been attached to the battalion.

This misfortune upon the right left the rest of the 12th Brigade in a most perilous position, attacked on the front, the flank, and the right rear. No soldiers could be subjected to a more desperate test. The flank battalion was the 1st Royal Lancasters (Colonel Jackson), who lived up to the very highest traditions of the British Army. Sick and giddy with the gas, and fired into from three sides, they still stuck doggedly to their trenches. The Essex battalion stood manfully beside them, and these two fine battalions, together with the East Lancashires and Rifle Brigade, held their places all day and even made occasional aggressive efforts to counter-attack. At eight in the evening they were ordered to form a new line with the 10th Brigade, five hundred yards in the rear. They came back in perfect order, carrying their wounded with them. Up to this moment the Fourth Division had held exactly the same line which they had occupied from May 1.

To return to the events of the morning. The next unit from the north was the 85th Brigade (Chapman), which formed the left flank of the Twenty-eighth Division. Upon it also the gas descended with devastating effect. There was just enough breeze to drift it along and not enough to disperse it. The 2nd East Surrey, the flank battalion, held on heroically, poison-proof and heedless of the shells. Next to them, just south of the railway, the 3rd Royal Fusiliers were so heavily gassed that the great majority of the men were absolutely incapacitated. The few who could use a rifle resisted with desperate valour while two companies of the Buffs were sent up to help them, and another company of the same regiment was despatched to Hooge village, where the 9th Lancers and 18th Hussars of the 2nd Cavalry Brigade were very hard pressed. On the left of the cavalry, between Hooge and Bellewaarde, was the Durham Territorial Brigade, which was pushed forward and had its share of the gas and of the attack generally, though less hard pressed than the divisions of regular troops upon their left. In a war of large numbers and of many brave deeds it is difficult and perhaps invidious to particularise, but a few sentences may be devoted to one isolated combat which showed the qualities of the disciplined British soldier. Two platoons of the 7th Durhams, under two 19-year-old lieutenants, Arthur Rhodes and Pickersgill, were by chance overlooked when the front line was withdrawn 200 yards. They were well aware that a mistake had been made, but with a heroic if perhaps Quixotic regard for duty they remained waist-deep in water in their lonely trench waiting for their certain fate, without periscopes or machine guns, and under fire from their own guns as well as those of the enemy. Both wings were of course in the air. In the early morning they beat back three German attacks but were eventually nearly all killed or taken. Rhodes was shot again and again but his ultimate fate is unknown. Pickersgill was wounded, and the survivors of his platoon got him to the rear. The loss of such men is to be deplored, but the tradition of two platoons in cold blood facing an army is worth many such losses.

The Durham Territorial Artillery did excellent work in supporting the cavalry, though they were handicapped by their weapons, which were the ancient fifteen-pounders of the South African type. These various movements were all in the early morning under the stress of the first attack. The pressure continued to be very severe on the line of the Royal Fusiliers and Buffs, who were covering the ground between the railway line on the north and Bellewaarde Lake on the south, so the remaining company of the Buffs was thrown into the fight. At the same time, the 3rd Middlesex, with part of the 6th and 8th Durham Light Infantry, advanced to the north of the railway line. The German pressure still increased, however, and at mid-day the Buffs and Fusiliers, having lost nearly all their officers and a large proportion of their ranks, fell back into the wood to the south of the railway.

A determined attempt was at once made to recapture the line of trenches from which they had been forced. The 84th Brigade (Bowes), hitherto in reserve, was ordered to move along the south of the line, while the whole artillery of the Fifth Corps supported the advance. Meanwhile, the 80th Brigade (Fortescue) was pushed forward on the right of the 84th, with orders to advance upon Hooge and restore the situation there. It was evening before all arrangements were completed. About seven o'clock the 84th advanced with the

2nd Cheshires upon the left and the 2nd Northumberland Fusiliers upon the right, supported by the 1st Welsh, the Monmouths, and the feeble remains of the 1st Suffolks. Darkness had fallen before the lines came into contact, and a long and obstinate fight followed, which swayed back and forwards under the light of flares and the sudden red glare of bursting shells. So murderous was the engagement that the 84th Brigade came out of it without a senior officer left standing out of six battalions, and with a loss of 75 per cent of the numbers with which it began. The machine-gun fire of the Germans was extremely intense, and was responsible for most of the heavy losses. At one time men of the Welsh, the Suffolks, and the Northumberland Fusiliers were actually in the German trenches, but at dawn they were compelled to retire. Late in the evening the 3rd and 4th Brigades of Cavalry were pushed into the trenches on the extreme right of the British position, near Hooge, to relieve the 1st and 2nd Brigades, who had sustained heavy losses for the second time within ten days.

The general result of the attack of May 24 was that this, the most profuse emission of poison, had no more solid effect than the other recent ones, since the troops had learned how to meet it. The result seems to have convinced the Germans that this filthy ally which they had called in was not destined to serve them as well as they had hoped, for from this day onwards there was no further attempt to use it upon a large scale in this quarter. In this action, which may be known in history as the Battle of Bellewaarde, since it centred round the lake of that name, the British endured a loss of some thousands of men killed, wounded, or poisoned, but their line, though forced back at several points, was as firm as ever.

In all the fighting which forms the second half of this great battle one is so absorbed by the desperate efforts of regimental officers and men to hold on to their trenches that one is inclined to do less than justice to the leaders who bore the strain day after day of that uphill fight. Plumer, of the Second Army; Ferguson, of the Fifth Army Corps; Wilson, Snow, and Bulfin, of the Fourth, Twenty-seventh, and Twenty-eighth Divisions, De Lisle of the Cavalry these were the men who held the line in those weeks of deadly danger.

On May 25 the line was consolidated and straightened out, joining the French at the same point as before, passing through Wieltje, and so past the west end of Lake Bellewaarde to Hooge. At this latter village there broke out between May 31 and June 3 what may be regarded as an aftermath of the battle which has just been described. The château at this place, now a shattered ruin, was the same building in which General Lomax was wounded and General Monro struck senseless in that desperate fight on October 31. Such was the equilibrium of the two great forces that here in May the fight was still raging. Château and village were attacked very strongly by the German artillery, and later by the German infantry, between May 30 and June 3, but no impression was made. The post was held by the survivors of the 3rd Dragoon Guards, and the action, though a local one, was as fine an exhibition of tenacious courage as has been seen in the war. The building was destroyed, so to a large extent was the regiment, but the post remained with the British. of This narrative is a brief outline of the series of events which make up the second phase of that battle which, beginning in the north of the Allied lines upon April 22, was continued upon the north-eastern salient, and ended, as shown, at Hooge at the end of May. In this fighting at least 100,000 men of the three nations were killed or wounded. The advantage with which the Germans began was to some extent neutralised before the end, for our gallant Allies had never rested during this time, and had been gradually re-establishing their position, clearing the west of the canal, recapturing Steenstraate and Het Sas, and only stopping short of Pilken. On the other hand, the British had been compelled to draw in for two miles, and Ypres had become more vulnerable to the guns of the enemy. If any advantage could be claimed the balance lay certainly with the Germans, but as part of a campaign of attrition nothing could be devised which would be more helpful to the Allies. The whole of these operations may be included under the general title of the second Battle of Ypres, but they can be divided into two clearly separated episodes, the first lasting from April 22 to the end of the month, which may be called the Battle of Langemarck, and the second from May 4th to the 24th, with a long interval in the centre, which may, as already stated, be known as the Battle of Bellewaarde. In this hard-fought war it would be difficult to say that Ypres was more hard-fought than this, and it will survive for centuries to come if only in the glorious traditions of the Canadian Division, who first showed that a brave heart may rise superior to bursting lungs. These were the greatest of all, but they had worthy comrades in the Indians, who at the end of an exhausting march hurled themselves into so diabolical a battle; the Northern Territorial Division, so lately civilians to a man, and now fighting like veterans; the 13th Brigade, staggering from their exertions at Hill 60, and yet called on for this new effort; the glorious cavalry, who saved the situation at the last moment; and the much-enduring Fourth, Twenty-seventh, and Twenty- eighth Divisions of the line, who bore the bufferings of the ever-rising German tide. Their dead lie at peace on Ypres plain, but shame on Britain if ever she forgets what she owes to those who lived, for they and their comrades of 1914 have made that name a symbol of glory for ever.

It may help the reader's comprehension of the sequence sequence of events, and of the desperate nature of this second Battle of Ypres, if a short resume be here given of the happenings upon the various dates. A single day of this contest would have appeared to be a considerable ordeal to any troops. It is difficult to realise the cumulative effect when such blows fell day after day and week after week upon the same body of men. The more one considers this action the more remarkable do the facts appear.

April 22. Furious attack upon the French and Canadians. Germans gain several miles of ground, eight batteries of French guns, and four heavy British guns by the use of poison-gas. The Canadians stand firm.

April 23. Canadians hold the line. Furious fighting. French begin to re-form. Reserves from the Twenty-seventh and Twenty-eighth British Divisions, 13th Brigade, and cavalry buttress up the line.

April 24. Desperate fighting. Line pushed farther back, and Germans took about a thousand prisoners. Line never broken.

April 25. Battle at its height. 50th Northern Territorial Division come into the fight. 10th Regular Brigade come up. Canadians drawn out. The French advancing.

April 26. 11th Regular Brigade thrown into the fight. Also the Lahore Division of Indians. Trenches of Twenty-eighth Division attacked.

April 27. The French made some advance on the left. There was equilibrium on the rest of the line. Hard fighting everywhere.

April 28. The enemy still held, and his attack exhausted for the moment. French made some progress.

May 1. British 12th Brigade came into line.

May 2. Renewed German assault on French and British, chiefly by gas. Advance held back with difficulty by the Fourth Division.

May 3 and 4. Contraction of the British position, effected without fighting, but involving the abandonment of two miles of ground at the north- eastern salient.

May 5. German attack upon Fourth Division.

May 6. Attack still continued.

May 7. Artillery preparation for general German attack.

May 8. Furious attack upon Fourth, Twenty-eighth, and Twenty- seventh British Divisions. Desperate fighting and heavy losses. The British repulsed the attack on their left wing (Fourth Division), but sustained heavy loss on centre and right.

May 9. Very severe battle continued. British left held its ground, but right and centre tended to contract.

May 10. Fighting of a desperate character, falling especially upon the Twenty-seventh Division.

May 11. Again very severe fighting fell upon the Twenty-seventh Division on the right of the British line. Losses were heavy, and there was a slight contraction.

May 12. Readjustment of British line. Two divisions of cavalry put in place of Twenty-eighth Division. Furious artillery attack, followed by infantry advance. Cavalry and Twenty-seventh Division terribly punished. Very heavy losses, but the line held. Fourth Division fiercely engaged and held its line.

May 13. The Germans exhausted. The attack ceased. Ten days of mutual recuperation.

May 24. Great gas attack. Fourth Division on left had full force of it, lost heavily, but could not be shifted. In the evening had to retire five hundred yards for the first time since the fighting began. General result of a long day of furious fighting was some contraction of the British line along its whole length, but no gap for the passage of the enemy. This may be looked upon as a last despairing effort of the Germans, as no serious attempt was afterwards made that year to force the road to Ypres.

Such, in a condensed form, was the record of the second Battle of Ypres, which for obstinacy in attack and inflexibility in defence can only be compared with the first battle in the same section six months before. Taking these two great battles together, their result may be summed up in the words that the Germans, with an enormous preponderance of men in the first and of guns in the second, had expended several hundred thousand of their men with absolutely no military advantage whatever.

V. THE BATTLE OF RICHEBOURG FESTUBERT May 9-24

The new attack—Ordeal of the 25th Brigade—Attack of the First Division—Fateful days—A difficult situation — Attack of the Second Division—Attack of the Seventh Division — British success—Good work of the Canadians—Advance of the Forty- seventh London Division—The lull before the storm

Whilst this desperate fighting was going on in the north a very extensive and costly operation had been begun in the south, a great attack being made by the First Army, with the main purpose of engaging the bourg Festubert German troops and preventing them from sending help to their comrades, who were hard pressed by the French near Arras. In this the movement was entirely successful, but the direct gain of ground was not commensurate with the great exertions and losses of the Army. For some days the results were entirely barren, but the patient determination of Sir John French and of Sir Douglas Haig had their final reward, and by May 25, when the movement had been brought to a close, there had been a general advance of 600 yards over a front of four miles, with a capture of 10 machine guns and some 800 prisoners. These meagre trophies of victory may, however, hardly be said to compensate us for the severe and unavoidable losses which must always in the case of the attack be heavier than those of the bourg. This important attack was made upon May 9, over a front of about ten miles from the Laventie district in the north to that of Richebourg in the south. In the case of the northern attack it was carried out by Rawlinson's Fourth Corps, and was directed upon the sector of the German lines to the north-west of Fromelles at the point which is named Rouges Banes. The southern attack was allotted to the Indian Corps (Willcocks) and the First Corps acting together. These two efforts represented the real foci of activity, but a general action was carried on from one end of the line to the other in order to confuse the issue, and hold the enemy in his trenches.

Both in the north and in the south the special attack was opened by a sudden and severe bombardment, which lasted for about forty minutes. This had been the prelude to the victory of Neuve Chapelle, but in the case of Neuve Chapelle the British attack had been a complete surprise, whereas in this action of May 9 there is ample evidence that the Germans were well informed as to the impending movement, and were prepared for it. Their trenches were very deep, and more vulnerable to high explosives, in which we were deficient, than to shrapnel. None the less, the bombardment was severe and accurate, though, as it proved, insufficient to break down the exceedingly effective system of defence, based upon barbed wire, machine guns, and the mutual support of trenches.

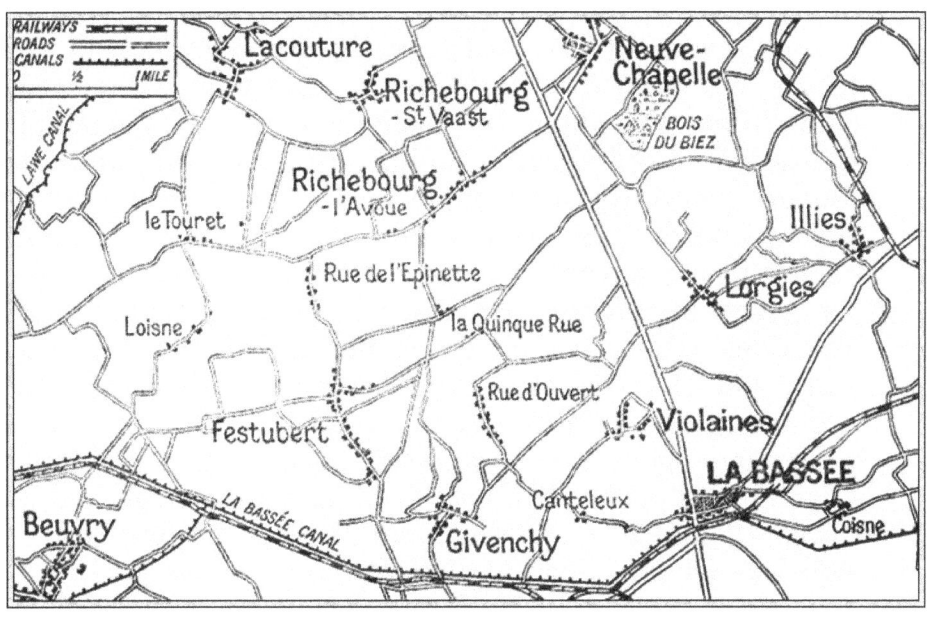

Richebourg District

The attack in the north was confided to Lowry-Cole's 25th Brigade, supported by the remainder of the Eighth Division. This brigade consisted of the 1st Irish Rifles, 2nd Berkshires, 2nd Rifle Brigade, 2nd Lincoln, and two Territorial battalions the 1st London and the 13th London (Kensington), The latter regiment was given a special task, which was to seize and hold a considerable mine-crater upon the left of the line. The rest of the brigade were ordered at 5:30 to charge the German trenches, which was done with the greatest dash and gallantry. Through a terrific fire of rifles and machine-guns the wave of men rolled forward, and poured into the trench, the 1st Irish Rifles and the 2nd Rifle Brigade leading the assault. It was found, however, that further progress could not be made. As the men sprang over the parapets they were mowed down in an instant. Long swathes of our dead marked the sweep of the murderous machine-guns. The Brigadier himself with his Brigade-major at his heels, sprang forward to lead the troops, but both were shot down in an instant, Lowry-Cole being killed and Major Dill badly wounded. It was simply impossible to get forward. No bravery, no perseverance, no human quality whatever could avail against the relentless sleet of lead. The 1st Londons coming up in support deployed and advanced over 400 yards of open with the steadiness of veterans, but lost nearly half their numbers. The Kensingtons in their crater had a similar experience, and could only hold on and endure a most pitiless pelting. For a long day, until the forenoon of the 10th, the ground which had been won was held. Then at last the bitter moment came when the enfeebled survivors, weakened by thirty-six hours of fighting, and fiercely attacked on all sides, were compelled to fall back upon their original lines. The retirement was conducted with a steadiness which verged upon bravado.

"These God-like fools!" was the striking phrase of a generous German who observed the thin ranks sauntering back under a crushing fire, with occasional halts to gather up their wounded. The casualty figures show how terrific was the ordeal to which the men had been exposed. The Irish Rifles lost the very heavy numbers of 9 officers killed, 13 wounded, and 465 men out of action. The total of the 2nd Rifle Brigade was even more terrible, working out as 21 officers and 526 men dead or wounded. The figures of the 2nd Berkshires and of the 2nd Lincolns were heavy, but less disastrous than those already quoted. The former lost 20 officers and 263 men, the latter 8 officers and 258 men. The 24th Brigade (Oxley) which, had supported the 25th, and had also reached the first trenches, endured losses which were almost as disastrous. The 2nd East Lancashires lost 19 officers and 435 men; the 1st Sherwood Foresters, 17 officers and 342 men; the 2nd Northamptons, 12 officers, and 414 men; the 5th Black Watch, 8 officers and 140 men. The losses of the 23rd Brigade, which remained in support, were by no means light, for the Scottish Rifles lost 12 officers and 156 men; while the 2nd Devons lost 7 officers and 234 men. Altogether the Eighth Division lost 4500 men, a single brigade (the 25th), accounting for 2232 of these casualties. Deplorable as they are, these figures must at least show that officers and men had done all that could be attempted to achieve the victory. When it is remembered that these were the same battalions which had lost so terribly at Neuve Chapelle just two months before, one can but marvel at the iron nerve which, enabled them once again to endure so searching a test.

It has been stated that the Kensingtons were given a separate mission of their own in the capture and bourg defence of a mine-crater upon the left of the British line. They actually carried not only the crater, but a considerable section of the hostile trenches, penetrating at one time as deep as the third line; but reinforcements could not reach them, their flanks were bare, and they were at last forced to retire. "It was bitter and damnable!" cries one of them out of his full heart. It was with the greatest difficulty that the remains of the gallant band were able to make their way back again to the British line of trenches. Nine officers were killed, 4 wounded, and 420 men were hit out of about 700 who went into action.

Such was the attack and bloody repulse which began the Battle of Richebourg. At the same hour the Indians and the

First Corps had advanced upon the German lines to the north of Givenchy with the same undaunted courage, the same heavy losses, and the same barren result. The events of May 9 will always stand in military history as among the most honourable, but also the most arduous, of the many hard experiences of the British soldiers in France.

In the case of the Indians, the attack was checked early, and could make no headway against the terribly arduous conditions. Their advance was upon the right of that already described of the Fourth Corps. Farther still to the right or to the south in the region of Richebourg l'Avoué was the front of the First Division, which was fated to be even more heavily punished than the Eighth had been in the north. In this case also there was a prelude of forty minutes' concentrated fire a period which, as the result L showed, was entirely inadequate to neutralise the many obstacles with which the stormers were faced.

During the night, the sappers had bridged the ditches between the front trenches and the supports, and had also crept out and thrown bridges over the ditches between the two lines. The 2nd Brigade (Thesiger), consisting of the 1st Northamptons, 2nd and 5th Sussex, 2nd Rifles, 1st North Lancashires, and 9th Liverpools, attacked upon the right indeed, they formed at that moment the extreme right of the whole British Army, save for the Forty-seventh London Division to the south. The weather was bright and clear, but the effect of the bombardment was to raise such a cloud of dust that two men from each platoon in the front line were able to carry forward a light bridge with which they gained a line about eighty yards from the enemy's parapet. The instant that the guns ceased, the infantry dashed forward, but were met by a withering fire. The 1st Northamptons and 2nd Sussex were in the lead, and the ground between the armies was littered with their bodies. In a second wave came the 2nd Rifles and the 5th Sussex, but human valour could do nothing against the pelting sleet of lead. The wire had been very imperfectly cut, and it was impossible to get through. The survivors fell back into the front trenches, while their comrades lay in lines and heaps upon the bullet-swept plain. The 5th Sussex Territorials had their baptism of fire, the first and last for many, and carried themselves like men. A line of German machine-guns was posted in a very close position almost at right angles to the advance, and it was these which inflicted the heaviest losses. Hardly a single man got as far as the German parapet. At 6:20 the assault was a definite failure.

On the left, the 3rd Brigade had kept pace with the 2nd, and had shared its trials and its losses. The van of the charging brigade was formed by the 2nd Munsters and the 2nd Welsh. The 1st Gloucesters, 1st South Wales Borderers, and 4th Welsh Fusiliers were in close support. Their attack was on the German line at the Rue des Bois, 300 yards away. They reached the trenches, though Colonel Richard of the Munsters and very many of his men were killed. This was the third Munster Colonel Charrier, Bent, Richard to be killed or disabled in the war. The men surged over the parapet, Captain Campbell-Dick standing on the crest of it, and whooping them on with his cap as if they were a pack of hounds. He fell dead even as they passed him. The trenches were taken, but could not be held, as there were no supports and the assault had failed on either side. Under cover of a renewed artillery fire the survivors came slowly and sullenly back. Once more, and for the third time, the 2nd Munsters were reduced to 200 rank and file. Three officers emerged unhurt from the action. A second attack was ordered for mid-day, the regiments being shifted round so as to bring the supports into the front line. It was soon found, however, that the losses had already been so heavy that it was impossible, especially in the 2nd Brigade, to muster sufficient force for a successful advance. The 1st Guards Brigade (Lowther) was therefore brought to the front, and after a renewed bombardment at 4 o'clock the two leading battalions the 1st Black Watch and the 1st Cameron Highlanders rushed to the assault over the bodies of their fallen comrades. It is on record that as the Highlanders dashed forward, a number of the wounded who had been lying in the open since morning, staggered to their feet and joined in the charge. It was a desperate effort, and the khaki wave rolled up to the trenches, and even lapped over them in places; but the losses were too heavy, and the advance had lost all weight before it reached the German line. At one point a handful of Black Watch got over the line, but it was impossible to reinforce them, and they were compelled to fall back. The 3rd Brigade on their flank had pushed forward the 1st Gloucester s and 1st South Wales Borderers. They found the enemy "standing 3 and 4 deep in their breastworks and fighting like demons." The British threw themselves down, and their guns showered shrapnel on the crowded German trenches. The enemy losses were great but the machine-guns were intact and no advance was possible. At 6 o'clock the survivors of both Brigades were back in their trenches once more. Late the same night the 5th Brigade of the Second Division was brought up to take over the line, and the remains of the First Division were withdrawn to the rear.

The losses of the 2nd Brigade were 70 officers and 1793 men, which might have been cited as possibly the highest number incurred in the same length of time up to that time, had it not been for the terrible figures of the 25th Brigade upon the same fatal day. The other two brigades of the Division were hard hit, the total losses of the Division amounting to nearly 5000 men. If the loss of the Indian Corps be included, the number of casualties in this assault cannot have been less than from 12,000 to 13,000 men;

while the losses to the enemy inflicted by the artillery could not possibly have approximated to this figure, nor had any advantage been obtained.

There are few single periods of the War so crowded with incident as from May 7 to 9, 1915. In the north the second Battle of Ypres was at its height. In the south the Battle of Richebourg had begun. But a third incident occurred upon the earlier date which struck the civilised world with a horror which no combat, however murderous, could inspire. It was the day when nearly 1200 civilians, with a considerable proportion of women and little children, were murdered by being torpedoed and drowned in the unarmed liner the *Lusitania*. Such incidents do not come within the direct scope of this narrative, and yet this particular one had an undoubted military bearing upon the War, since it hardened our resolve, stimulated our recruiting, and nerved our soldiers in a very marked degree, while finally removing any possibility of peace based upon compromise. No such crime against civilians has been committed in deliberate warfare since the days of Tamerlane or Timour the Tartar; yet it is dreadful to have to add that it was hailed as a triumph from one end of Germany to the other, that medals were struck to commemorate it, and that no protest appeared in the German Press. To such depths of demoralisation had this once Christian and civilised nation been reduced! Touch Germany where one would, on land or air, on the sea or under it, one came always upon murder.

It is impossible not to admire the tenacity of Sir John French under the very difficult circumstances in which he was now placed. His troops at Ypres were still fighting with their backs to the wall. Their position on May 10 was precarious. The only reinforcements they could hope for in case of disaster were from the south. And yet the south had itself received a severe rebuff. Was it best to abandon the attack there, and reassume the defensive, so as to have the men available in case there should come an urgent call from the north? A weaker general would have said so, and accepted his check at Festubert. Sir John, however, was not so easily to be deflected from his plans. He steadied himself by a day or two of rest, during which he not only prepared fresh forces for striking, but got the measure of the enemy's power at Ypres. Then it was determined that the action should proceed, but that it should be directed to the more southerly area of the British position, where it would be in closer touch with the French, and receive some support from their admirable artillery.

The centre of the British movement was still at Richebourg l'Avoué, but the direction of the advance was to the south and west. It had already been shown that the passage of open spaces under machine-gun fire was difficult and deadly by daylight, so it was determined that night should be used for the advance. Several successive nights were unfavourable, but the days were spent in a deliberate artillery preparation until the action was recommenced upon May 15. In the interval, the Second Division had taken the place of the First in the Givenchy sector, and the Seventh Division of the Fourth Corps had been brought round from the Laventie district, and was now upon the right of their comrades of the First Corps. The Canadian Division was brought up in support, while the Indian Corps still preserved its position upon the left. The general line of attack was from Richebourg by the Rue des Bois, and so south in front of Festubert. The advance was made by the Indians upon the left, and the Second Division upon the right at 11:30 on the night of May 15. The Indians were held up, Festubert and maintained from that time onwards a defensive position. When it is remembered that the Meerut Division had suffered heavily at Neuve Chapelle, that the Lahore Division had been very hard hit at Ypres, and that there was only a limited facility for replacing the losses of the native regiments, it is not to be wondered at that the Corps had weakened. The Second Division, however, would take no denial. The attack was in the hands of the 5th and 6th Brigades, with the 4th Guards Brigade in support. It was to sweep over the ground, which had been the scene of the repulse of the 9th, but it was to be screened by darkness. Soon after ten o'clock the men passed silently over the front trench, and lay down in four lines in the open waiting for the signal. At 11:30 the word was passed, and they advanced at a walk. The front line of the 5th Brigade was composed of the 2nd Worcesters upon the left, and the Inniskilling Fusiliers (taken from the 12th Brigade) upon the right. The leading battalions of the 6th Brigade were the 1st Rifles, the 1st King's Liverpools, 1st Berkshires, and upon the extreme right two companies (A and B) of the 7th King's Liverpools. Flares were suddenly discharged from the German trenches, and a ghostly flickering radiance illuminated the long lines of crouching men. There were numerous ditches in front, but the sappers had stolen forward and spanned them with rude bridges. The German fire was terrific, but the uncertain quivering light made it less deadly than it had been during the daytime, though very many fell. It was insufficient to determined rush of the British infantry. The rifles could not hold them back, and sweeping jets from machine-guns could not kill them fast enough: nothing but Death could hold that furious line. In three minutes they had swarmed across the open, and poured into the trenches, killing or taking all the Germans who were in the front line. The 2nd Worcesters on the left were held up by unbroken barbed wire, and were unable to get forward; but all the other battalions reached the trench, and cleared it for a considerable distance on either flank, the bombers rushing along it and hurling their deadly weapons in front of them. The remainder rushed down the communication trench, and seized the second line of defences some hundreds of yards behind the first. On the morning of Sunday, May 16, the Second Division had gained and firmly held about half a mile in breadth and a quarter of a mile in depth of the German trenches. There was still an open plain in the rear between the advanced troops and their supports, which as the light grew clearer was so swept by German fire that it was nearly impossible to get across it. About 8:30 in the morning, the remainder of the 7th King's Liverpools with some of their comrades of the 5th King's Liverpools endeavoured to join the others in front, but were shot to pieces in the venture. During the whole of the morning, however, single volunteers kept running forward carrying fresh supplies of bombs and bandoliers of cartridges for the men in front. The names of most of these brave men are to be found in the casualty lists, and their memory in the hearts of their comrades.

Four hours after this successful attack by the Second Division, at 3:30 on the morning of Sunday May 16 another assault was made some miles to the south, just to the north of Festubert. The attack bourg was made by the 20th Brigade (Heyworth) upon the left and the 22nd (Lawford) upon the right. The 2nd Borders and 2nd Scots Guards led the rush of the 20th, supported later by the 1st Grenadiers and 2nd Gordons; while the 1st Welsh Fusiliers and 2nd Queen's Surrey were in the van of the 22nd with the 2nd Warwicks, 8th Royal Scots, and 1st South Staffords behind them. The famous Seventh Division has never yet found its master in this campaign, and the Seventh Prussian Corps in the south could make no more of it than the Fifteenth had done in the north.

In the case of the 20th Brigade the Borders upon the left were held up for a time, but the Scots Guards advanced with a fury which took them far beyond the immediate objective, and was carried to such an extent that one company outdistanced all their comrades, and being isolated in the German position, were nearly all cut off. The rest of the Guards, however, having crossed the trench line, swung across, so that they were in the rear of the Germans who were holding up the Borders, so that the defenders were compelled to surrender. The 1st Grenadiers came up in support and the ground was made good. Meanwhile the 22nd Brigade upon the right had some desperate fighting. The 2nd Queen's Surrey had been temporarily stopped by heavy machine-gun fire, but two companies of the Welsh Fusiliers rushed the trenches opposite them and were quickly joined by the rest of the battalion. The Queen's Surrey refused to be rebuffed, and with the support of the 1st Staffords they again came forward, dashing through a sleet of bullets got to the bourg German line. Colonel Gabbett of the Fusiliers and Major Bottomley of the Queen's, one of the heroes of Gheluvelt, both met their death in this fine attack. On reaching the trenches the South Staffords sent their bombers under Lieutenant Hassell down the alleys of the Germans, gathering in many prisoners. A surprising feat was performed by Sergeant-Major Barter of the Welsh Fusiliers, while engaged in similar work, for he and seven men brought back 94 Germans, including 3 officers. The leading companies of the South Staffords under Major Lord and Captain Bearman got well forward into the enemy's ground, and held on there for three days under a terrible shell-fall, until they handed the position over to the 21st Brigade. Meanwhile, upon the left a mixed lot of men from the Welsh Fusiliers, Scots Guards, and Warwicks, all under Captain Stockwell, struggled along, actually swimming one ditch which was too deep to wade, and got into the Orchard which had been assigned as their objective. These men were afterwards withdrawn to the German front line trenches in order to escape from the very severe bombardment on the Orchard. Great difficulty was experienced in bringing in the wounded, owing to the space covered and to the incessant and extreme shelling. It is on record that the men of the field ambulance, under Lieutenant Greenlees of the Royal Medical Corps, were at work for thirty-six hours with three hours' break, always in the open and always under fire. These are the men who have all the dangers of war without its thrills, working and dying for the need of their comrades and the honour of their corps.

In this fine day's work, in which the Seventh Division lived up to its own reputation, Colonel Wood of the Borders and Colonel Brook of the 8th Royal Scots were killed, making four losses in one day among commanding officers of battalions.

On the night of May 16 the Germans made a counter-attack, which pushed back the extreme apex of the ground gained by the Seventh Division. All other points were held. The British had now cut two holes in the German front over a distance of about three miles; but between the two holes into which the heads of the Second and Seventh Divisions had buried themselves, there lay one portion of a thousand yards inviolate, strongly defended by intricate works and machine-guns. Desperate endeavours had been made upon the 16th to get round the north of this position by the Second Division, but the fire was too murderous, and all were repulsed. At half-past nine in the morning of the 17th the attempt was renewed from both sides with a strong artillery support. On the north the Highland Light Infantry and the 2nd Oxford and Bucks made a strong attack, while on the south the 21st Brigade pushed to the front. The 4th Camerons, a Gaelic-speaking battalion of shepherds and gillies, kept fair pace with the veteran regular battalions of the Brigade, but lost their gallant Colonel, Fraser. The fiery valour of the Camerons is shown by the fact that afterwards bodies of the fallen were found far ahead of any point reached that day by the main advance. Gradually the valiant defenders were driven from post to post, and crushed under the cross fire. About mid-day the position was in the hands of the British, 300 survivors having been captured. After this consolidation of their front, the two attacking divisions drove on together to the eastward, winning ground but meeting everywhere the same stark resistance. Farmhouse after farmhouse was carried. At one point a considerable body 'Of Germans rushed out from an untenable position; but on their putting up their hands and advancing towards the British, they were mowed down to the number of some hundreds by the rifles and cannon of their comrades in the rear. South of Festubert the thick spray of bombers and bayonet men thrown out by the Seventh Division into the German trenches were also making ground all day, and the enemy's loss in this quarter was exceedingly heavy. The 57th Prussian Regiment of Infantry, among others, is said to have lost more than two-thirds of their numbers during these operations.

By the evening of Monday, May 17, the hostile front had been crushed in for a space of over two miles, and the British Army had regained the ascendancy which had been momentarily checked upon May 9. If a larger tale of prisoners was not forthcoming as a proof of victory, the explanation lay in the desperate nature of the encounter. The sinking of the *Lusitania*, and the murders by poison-gas, were in the thoughts and on the lips of the assaulting infantry, and many a German made a vicarious atonement. At the same time the little mobs of men who rushed forward with white flags in one hand, and in many cases their purses outstretched in the other, were given quarter and led to the rear, safe from all violence save from their own artillery. There were many fierce threats of no quarter before the engagement, but with victory the traditional kindliness of the British soldier asserted itself once more.

On the evening of the 17th the men in the front Festubert line were relieved, Lord Cavan's 4th Guards Brigade taking over the advanced trenches in which the 1st King's Liverpools and other battalions of the 5th and 6th Brigades were lying. The Guards had to advance a considerable distance under very heavy fire to reach their objective, and there is a touch of other days in the fact that the Bishop of Khartoum stood by the trenches and blessed them as they passed. They lost many men from the terrible artillery fire, but in spite of this they at once advanced in a most gallant attack which won several hundred yards of ground. The Irish and 2nd Grenadiers were the attacking battalions with the Herts territorials in close support. The Irish Guards were especially forward and held the ground gained, but lost 17 officers and several hundred men. All day of the 18th the Guards held the advanced front line until relieved at midnight of that date by the advance of another Division.

The 18th saw the general advance renewed, but it was hampered by the fact that the heavy weather made it difficult to obtain the artillery support which is so needful where buildings have to be carried. The Indians upon the left sustained a heavy attack upon this day, the losses falling chiefly upon the Sirhind Brigade, and especially on the 1st Highland Light Infantry and the 15th Sikhs. It was in this action that Lieutenant Smyth and Private Lai Singh of the latter regiment saved the fight at a critical moment by bringing up a fresh supply of bombs. Ten men started on the venture, and only the two won home. The 19th was wet and misty. It was upon this date that the two hard-working and victorious Divisions, the Second and the Seventh, were relieved respectively by the Fifty-first Highland Territorial Division and by the Canadians, the guns of the two regular Divisions being retained. The operations which had hitherto been under Monro of the First Corps, were now confided to Alderson of the Canadians. At this time, the general level of the advance was the road which extends from La Quinque to Bethune. The change of troops did not entail any alteration in strategy, and the slow advance went forward. Upon the night of May 20-21 the Canadians continued the work of the Seventh Division, and added several fresh German trenches to the area already secured. From Richebourg to the south and east there was now a considerable erosion in the German position. The first objective of the Canadians was an orchard in the Quinque Rue position, which was assaulted by the 14th Montreal Regiment (Meighen) and the 16th Canadian Scottish (Leckie), after a gallant reconnaissance by Major Leckie of the latter regiment. The Canadians were thrust in between the 3rd Coldstream Guards of the Second Division upon their left, and the 2nd Wiltshires of the Seventh Division upon their right. The orchard was cleared in most gallant fashion, and a trench upon the flank of it was taken, but the Canadian loss was considerable in the battalions named and in the 13th Royal Canadian Highlanders in support. Another Canadian battalion, the 10th, had attacked the German line a mile to the south of the orchard, and had been repulsed. A heavy bombardment was organised, and the attempt was renewed upon the following day, two companies of the 10th, preceded by a company of grenade-throwers, carrying 400 yards of the trench at a very severe cost. It was partly recaptured by the Germans upon May 22, while part remained in the hands of the Canadians. Several counter-attacks were made upon the Canadians during this day, but all withered away before the deadly fire of the Western infantry.

On May 24 the Canadians were attacking once more at the position where the 10th Battalion had obtained a partial success upon the 22nd. It was a strongly fortified post, which had been named "Bexhill" by the British. The assault was carried out at daybreak by two companies of the 5th

Battalion under Major Edgar, with a company of the 7th British Columbians in support. Before six o'clock the position had been carried, and was held all day in face of a concentrated shell-fire from the German guns. It was a terrible ordeal, for the Brigade lost 50 officers and nearly 1000 men, but never their grip of the German trench. On the same night, however, another Canadian attack delivered by the 3rd Battalion (Rennie) with great fire, was eventually repulsed by the machine-guns.

This long-drawn straggling action, which had commenced with such fury upon May 9, was now burning itself out. Prolonged operations of this kind can only be carried on by fresh relays of troops. The Forty-seventh London Territorial Division was brought up into the front line, and found itself involved at once in some fierce fighting at the extreme right of the British line near Givenchy. The Forty-seventh Division (formerly the Second London Division) was in reality the only London division, since the battalions which composed the first, the Artists, Victorias, Rangers, Westminsters, etc., had already been absorbed by regular brigades. The division commanded by General Barter consisted of the 140th (Cuthbert), 141st (Thwaites), and 142nd (Willoughby) Brigades. On the evening of May 25 the latter Brigade, which occupied the front-line trench, was ordered to make an attack upon the German line opposite, whilst the 18th Battalion of the 141st Brigade made a strong feint to draw their fire. The first-line battalions were the 23rd and 24th (Queen's), of which the 23rd upon the left had some 300 yards of open to cross, while the 24th upon the right had not more than 150. Both battalions reached their objective in safety, and within three minutes had established telephonic communications with their supports of the 21st and 22nd Battalions. The capture of the trenches had not been difficult, but their retention was exceedingly so, as there was a ridge from which the German machine-guns commanded the whole line of trench. Each man had brought a sandbag with him, and these were rapidly filled, while officers and men worked desperately in building up a defensive traverse a labour in which Sergeant Oxman greatly distinguished himself. Three German counter-attacks got up within ten yards of the 24th, but all were beaten back. The German bombers, however, were deadly, and many officers and men were among their victims. The 21st Battalion had followed up the 23rd, and by 10:30 they were able to work along the line of the German trench and make good the position. All day upon May 26 they were exposed to a very heavy and accurate German fire, but that afternoon about 4 P.M. they were relieved by the 20th London from Thwaites' 141st Brigade. The line was consolidated and held, in spite of a sharp attack on the afternoon of May 28, which was beaten off by the 20th Battalion.

Whilst the London Division had been thrust into the right of the British line, the Canadian infantry had been relieved by bringing forward into the trenches the dismounted troopers of King Edward's and Strathcona's Horse, belonging to Seely's Mounted Canadian Brigade, who fought as well as their fellow-countrymen of the infantry a standard not to be surpassed. From this time onwards there was a long lull in this section of the British line. The time was spent in rearranging the units of the Army, and in waiting for those great reinforcements of munitions which were so urgently needed. It was recognised that it was absolutely impossible to make a victorious advance, or to do more than to hold one's ground, when the guns of the enemy could fire six shells to one. In Britain, the significance of this fact had at last been made apparent, and the whole will and energy of the country were turned to the production of ammunition. Not only were the old factories in full swing, but great new centres were created in towns which had never yet sent forth such sinister exports. Mr. Lloyd George, a man who has made atonement for any wrong that he did his country in the days of the Boer War by his magnificent services in this far greater crisis, threw all his energy and contagious enthusiasm into this vital work, and performed the same miracles in the organisation and improvisation of the tools of warfare that Lord Kitchener had done in the case of the New Armies. They were services which his country can never forget. Under Kitchener's inspiration the huge output of Essen and the other factories of Germany were equalled, and finally surpassed by the improvised and largely amateur munition workers of Britain. The main difficulty in the production of high explosives had lain in the scarcity of picric acid. Our Free Trade policy, which has much to recommend it in some aspects, had been pushed to such absurd and pedantic lengths that this vital product had been allowed to fall into the hands of our enemy, although it is a derivative of that coal tar in which we are so rich. Now at last the plants for its production were laid down. Every little village gasworks was sending up its quota of toluol to the central receivers. Finally, in explosives as in shells and guns, the British were able to supply their own wants fully and to assist their Allies. One of the strangest, and also most honourable, episodes of the War was this great economic effort which involved sacrifices to the time, comfort, and often to the health of individuals so great as to match those of the soldiers. Grotesque combinations resulted from the eagerness of all classes to lend a hand. An observer has described how a peer and a prize-fighter have been seen working on the same bench at Woolwich, while titled ladies and young girls from cultured homes earned sixteen shillings a week at Erith, and boasted in the morning of the number of shell cases which they had turned and finished in their hours of night shift. Truly it had become a National War. Of all its strange memories none will be stranger than those of the peaceful middle-aged civilians who were seen eagerly reading books upon elementary drill in order to prepare themselves to face the most famous soldiers in Europe, or of the schoolgirls and matrons who donned blue blouses and by their united work surpassed the output of the great death factories of Essen.

VI. THE TRENCHES OF HOOGE

The British line in June 1915—Canadians at Givenchy—Attack of 154th Brigade—8th Liverpool Irish Third Division at Hooge — 11th Brigade near Ypres—Flame attack on the Fourteenth Light Division —Victory of the Sixth Division at Hooge

The spring campaign may be said to have ended at the beginning of June. It had consisted, so far as the British were concerned, in three great battles.

The first was that of Neuve Chapelle. The second, and incomparably the greatest, was the second Battle of Ypres, extending from April 22 to the end of May, in which both sides fought themselves to a standstill, but the Germans, while gaining some ground, failed to reach their final objective. The third was the Battle of Bichebourg, from May 9 to May 18, which began with a check and ended by a definite but limited advance for the British. The net result of the whole operations of these three months was a gain of ground to the Germans in the Ypres section and a gain of ground to the Allies in the region of Festubert and Arras. Neither gain can be said to have been of extreme strategic importance, and it is doubtful if there was any great discrepancy between the losses of the two sides. There now followed a prolonged lull, during which the Germans were content to remain upon the defensive upon the west while they vigorously and successfully attacked the Russians in the east, combining their forces with those of Austria, and driving their half-armed enemy from the passes of the Carpathians right across Poland until the line of the Vistula had been secured. The Allies meanwhile pursued their ill-fated venture in the Dardanelles, while they steadily increased their numbers and, above all, their munitions of war in France and Flanders, having learned by experience that no bravery or devotion can make one gun do the work of six, or enable infantry who have no backing from artillery to gain ground from infantry which are well supported. For a long period to come the most important engagements were a series of fights upon June 16, July 30, and August 9, which may be looked upon as a single long-drawn-out engagement, since they were all concerned with the successive taking and retaking of the same set of trenches near Hooge, in the extreme northern section of the line. Before giving some account of these events it would be well to interrupt the narrative for a time in order to describe that vast expansion of the British Army which was the most unexpected, as it was the most decisive, factor in the war. Without entering into the question of the huge muster of men within the island, and leaving out of consideration the forces engaged in the Near East, the Persian Gulf, and the various Colonial campaigns, an attempt will be made to show the reader the actual battle-line in France, with the order and composition of the troops, during the summer of 1915.

The extreme left wing of the Allied Army consisted now, as before, of the Belgians and of a French corps, the right Moroccan Division of which was the neighbour of the British Army. The British line had been extended northwards as far as the village of Boesinghe.

If now the reader could for a moment imagine himself in an aeroplane, flying from north to south down the Imperial battle-line, he would see beneath him first Keir's Sixth Army Corps, which was composed of the Fourth Division (Wilson) and of the Sixth Division (Congreve). To the south of these lay the Forty- ninth West Riding Division of Territorials (Baldock). These three divisions, the Fourth, the Sixth, and the Forty-ninth, formed Keir's Sixth Army Corps, lying to the north of Hooge. Upon their right, in the neighbourhood of Hooge, holding the ground which had been the recent scene of such furious fighting, and was destined to be the most active section of the line in the immediate future, was Allenby's Fifth Corps. General Allenby had been taken from the command of the cavalry, which had passed to General Byng, and had filled Plumer's place when the latter took over Smith-Dorrien's Army at the end of April. Allenby's Corps consisted of the veteran Third Division (Haldane's) on the north. Then came, defending the lines of Hooge, the new Fourteenth Light Division (Couper). Upon its right was the Forty-sixth North Midland Division (Stuart-Wortley). These three divisions, the Third Regular, Fourteenth New, and Forty-sixth Territorial, made up the Fifth Corps.

The Second Army Corps (Ferguson) lay to the south of Hooge. Their northern unit was the old Regular Fifth Division (Morland). To its south was a second Regular division Bulfin's Twenty-eighth, of Ypres renown. On its right was the Fiftieth Northumbrian Division (Lindsay), consisting of those three gallant Territorial brigades which had done so splendidly in the crisis of the gas battle. The Third Army Corps (Pulteney's) came next in the line. This was the strongest corps in the whole Hooge. force, containing no fewer than four divisions. These were, counting as ever from the north, the Canadian Division (Alderson), the Twelfth New Division (Wing), the Twenty-seventh Division of Regulars (Snow), and the Eighth Division of Regulars (Davies). All these troops, the Sixth, Fifth, Second, and Third Corps, made up Plumer's Second

Army, which contained no fewer than thirteen divisions, or, approximately, 260,000 men.

The First Army, under Haig, which occupied the southern section of the British line, consisted of three Army Corps. To the north, in the Festubert region, was the hard-worked and depleted Indian Corps, which had fought under such extraordinary difficulties and shown such fine military qualities. Attached to them was the Fifty-first Highland Territorial Division (Bannatine-Allason). The first two brigades of this were pure Scottish, but the third contained three battalions from that nursery of British regiments, Lancashire. South of the Indians came the glorious old First Corps, and south of it the equally glorious Seventh Division (Capper), forming part of Rawlinson's Fourth Corps. Next to the Seventh Division was the new Ninth Division (Landon), composed of Scottish regiments a very fine unit. South of these, carrying the British line over the Bethune La Bassée Canal, and six miles towards Arras, were the Forty-seventh London Division (Barter) and the Forty-eighth South Midland Division (Fanshawe), drawn mostly from Warwick, Worcester, Gloucester, and Bucks. Altogether, Haig's First Army at the end of June contained nine divisions, or, roughly, 180,000 men. The whole great Army, then, which extended from north of Ypres to north of Arras, may have mustered in the line about 440,000 men, backed by an efficient field service, which may easily have numbered 120,000 more.

When one contemplates this magnificent force and remembers that ten months earlier the whole British Army at Mons had been four divisions, that at the Aisne there were six, that in the days of the first Ypres battle there were eight, and that now there were twenty-two, one marvels at the extraordinary powers of creation and organisation which had created so efficient and powerful a machine. It was rapidly made, and yet in no way was it crude or feeble. Particularly pleasing was it to note the names of the divisional commanders, and to see how many of the heroic leaders of brigades in those early classical conflicts Landon, Snow, Bulfin, Davies, Morland, Wing, Haldane, Wilson, and Congreve were now at the head of small armies of their own. Of the quality of this great force it is superfluous to speak. The whole of this chronicle is a record of it. One observation, however, should in justice be made. With that breadth and generosity of mind which make them the truly imperial people of the world, the English and the English press have continually extolled the valour of the Scots, Irish, Welsh, or men of the Overseas Dominions. There has hardly ever been a mention of the English as such, and the fact has given rise to some very false impressions. It is for the reader to bear in mind, none the less, that four-fifths of this great army was purely English, and that the English Divisions, be they North or South, have shown a sobriety of discipline and an alacrity of valour which place them in the very first place among fighting races. The New Army like the Old Fleet was in the main a triumph of England. Of its first thirty-three divisions all but five were predominantly English.

The men and the generals were there. The delay was still with the guns and the munitions. A heavy gun is not the product of a week or of a month, and before a great increase can be made in the output of shells the machinery for producing them has itself to be produced. But energetic minds and capable hands were busied with the problem from one end of Britain to the other, and the results were rapidly taking form. A considerable amount of the product was being despatched to Archangel to help our hard-pressed Russian Allies, and constant supplies were being despatched to the Dardanelles; but an accumulation was also being stored behind the lines in Flanders. The whole progress of the campaign depended upon this store being sufficient to sustain a prolonged attack, and the time had not yet come.

Before turning to the trenches of Hooge, where the greater part of the fighting occurred during this period of the war, some description must be given of a brisk action upon June 15, opposite Givenchy, immediately to the north of the La Bassée Canal, where the Canadian Division attacked with great gallantry and partly occupied a position which it was not found possible to retain. In this attack the Canadians displayed their usual energy and ingenuity by bringing up two eighteen-pounder field-pieces into their front trench, and suddenly opening fire point-blank at the German defences only seventy-five yards away. Captain Stockwell, with Lieutenants Craig and Kelly and their men, obviously took their lives in their hands, as their guns became the immediate mark of the German artillery, with the result that one was destroyed by a direct hit, and the crew of the other were put out of action by a shrapnel-burst. But before they were silenced the two guns did great damage to the German front-line defence, knocking out several machine-guns and cutting the barbed wire to pieces. After a quarter of an hour of glorious activity they were out of action; but they had smoothed the path for the infantry, who at six in the evening were over the parapet and into the trench opposite. The attack was made by the 1st Ontario Battalion (Hill), supported by the rest of the 1st Canadian Brigade. The storming-party was checked for a moment by the explosion of their own mine, which threw back with disastrous results, killing Lieutenant- Colonel Beecher and burying the bomb-store of the front line. Having seized the German trench, some remained to reverse the parapet, while others rushed on to the second trench, which they also carried. The supply of bombs ran short, however, and could not be replenished. Four messengers in succession rushing back for more were shot dead by the enemy's fire. A fort upon the left had not been taken, and the machine-guns from its loopholes swept down the captured trench and made it untenable. Slowly the Canadians were forced back, and before ten o'clock what was left of the Ontarios were back in their own trench once more. When it is stated that of 23 officers who took part in the advance 20 were killed or wounded, no further proof is needed of the stern insistence of the attack.

This gallant though fruitless attack of the Canadians at Givenchy was, as it appears, intended to Hooge coincide with an advance by the Seventh Division on their left, and of the Fifty-first upon the right of them. In the case of the Seventh Division there were two advances, one by day and one by night, in which single battalions were employed and no result achieved. In the second of these the 2nd Gordons lost heavily, having occupied a deserted trench which proved to be so commanded as to be untenable. Before regaining their own lines D Company was cut off and destroyed. On the right the Fifty-first Highland Territorial Division had an experience which was equally unsatisfactory. Hibbert's 154th Brigade made an advance which was bravely urged and bloodily repelled. The preparatory bombardment was answered by a very intense German fire, which was so heavy and accurate that it buried a number of men in the advance trenches, destroyed the bomb-stores, and made all communication nearly impossible. The secret of this extreme readiness of the Germans was divulged by a deserter who came over into the British trenches at the last moment, and said that they all knew that the attack was for six o'clock that day. It was at that very hour that the 6th Scottish Rifles and the 4th North Lancashires, of the Brigade, rushed the German position. Each battalion lost its commanding officer and its adjutant in the first few minutes, but the line of trenches was carried at one tiger-spring. The enemy's shell-fire was exceedingly heavy, and the losses were considerable. Having cleared the trench, the attacking line, especially the Scottish Rifles upon the left, came on unbroken wire, so they dug themselves in in the open and awaited supports. These for some reason were slow in coming up, and as the Germans were in force on either side, and the North Lancashires were also held up by wire, there was a danger lest the forward line might be cut off. It fell back, therefore, closely followed by the enemy, until an advance of the 4th Royal Lancasters helped them to form a line. The whole night was spent in a prolonged rifle duel, the two sides being at very close quarters, and the action resolving itself into a series of stubborn encounters by little groups of men holding shell-craters or fragments of trenches, and offering a sullen resistance to the considerable forces which were now pressing upon them. All order had been lost, the three battalions were hopelessly mixed together, and the command of each little group fell into the hands of any natural leader who won the confidence of the comrades round him. Slowly the ragged line retired, until they found themselves in the early morning back in the position from which they had started, having suffered and inflicted grievous losses, but with no gain of ground to justify them.

It might well have seemed that the attack had failed, or at least that another brigade would be needed to put matters right; but a reserve battalion had not yet gone into action, and to this unit was given the hard task of putting the Germans out once more from the trench which they had re-occupied. There have been days when the Liverpool Irish have proved themselves to be pugnacious in riotous times at home, but now they were to efface all such memories by their splendid bearing at this critical hour. It was 4 P.M. upon June 16, when, with a true Celtic yell, the 8th King's Liverpool, led by Major Johnson, dashed over the parapet and stormed through a hellish sleet of shrapnel to the Hooge. German trenches. "It was pattering like hail upon a window-pane." Officers and men went down in heaps, but nothing could stop the glorious impetuosity of the charge, delivered in the full light of a summer afternoon. "It's sure death, but remember we are Irish!" yelled a sergeant as he bounded on to the sand-bags. Next instant he had been blown to pieces. Captain Finegan, leading the rush, was shot down, as were the greater number of the regimental officers. Finegan's body was found afterwards at the extreme point of the advance, with twelve of his men lying round him. The Germans were swept out of the front trenches once more, and the Irishmen held desperately on to it for a long time against all the shell-fire of the enemy. It was a great day for Liverpool, July 16, when two of their citizen regiments, the 8th in the south and the 10th in the north, helped to stem the tide of two separate battles. The 8th King's lost nearly 500 men, and gained a reputation which will not easily die. The survivors were too few, however, to permanently hold the shell-raked trench which they had gained. The 153rd Brigade (Campbell), consisting of Gordons and Black Watch, relieved them in the front line, and the exhausted and decimated battalion was drawn off. In the meantime the 152nd Brigade, upon the left, had been unable to make progress. Of the attackers of the Fifty-first Division some 1500 men had fallen, and there was no permanent gain of ground.

On Wednesday, June 16, there occurred a brisk action to the immediate north of Hooge, at a point to the west and south-west of the Château, where the German line formed somewhat of a salient. This it was determined to straighten out in the familiar fashion, and a considerable force of artillery was secretly concentrated. The assault was assigned to the Third Division, and was carried out by Bowes' 8th Brigade on the left, and on the right by the 9th

Brigade, which consisted of the three Fusilier battalions and the Lincolns, together with the 10th Liverpool Scottish. The latter battalion had been seven months at the Front, doing every sort of hard work, but never getting an opportunity for distinction in action. The 9th Brigade, now commanded by General Douglas Smith, was in reserve near Poperinghe, but it was brought forward through Ypres for the assault. They marched through the shattered town on the Tuesday evening. "The sight of the ruined beauties of that once glorious old town did lots to make us just long to get at the Vandals who had done this wanton act of destruction." It was a longing which was soon to be appeased. By midnight the troops were in position, and at three in the morning of June 16 the bombardment began. It lasted with terrific intensity for about an hour, and was helped by the guns of the French Thirty-sixth Corps firing towards Pilken, whence the supports might come. Black and yellow clouds covered the whole line of the front German trench, which lay at the fringe of a wood, and out of this mist of death trees, sand-bags, and shattered human bodies flew high in the air. The barbed wire was shattered to pieces and the front parapets knocked to atoms.

Then, in an instant, the guns lifted on to the more distant support trenches, and the infantry, swarming over the low barricades, dashed in perfect order over the two hundred yards which separated them from the Germans.

It was an admirable advance, and could not have been better carried out. The front of the assault was about a quarter of a mile. The three Fusilier battalions in one long line, Northumberland Fusiliers on the left, Royals in the centre, and Scots on the right, rushed forward with terrific impetus, the rising sun glinting upon their lines of bayonets. They were over the lip of the front trench without a check, and rushed on for the second one. The supports, who were the Lincolns on the right and the Liverpool Scots on the left, followed closely after them, and seizing the German survivors, sent them to the rear, while they did what they could to reverse the parapet and prepare for a counter-attack. As they charged forward, it had been observed that one German trench upon the left was at right angles to the line of advance, and that it had been untouched by the bombardment. It was only about forty yards in length, but the fire from it was very murderous as it swept across the open ground. With quick decision the rear company of the Liverpool Scottish turned aside, and in spite of unbroken barbed wire carried the trench, capturing all the occupants.

Meanwhile the German artillery had opened with an intensity which was hardly inferior to that of the British, and they shelled with great accuracy the captured trench. The Fusiliers had dashed onwards, while the Liverpool Scots and Lincolns followed swiftly behind them, leaving the captured trench to the leading battalions of the 7th Brigade (Ballard), which was immediately in the rear of the attackers. So eager was everyone that the van of the supporting brigade was mixed with the rear of the attacking one. Thus the Honourable Artillery Company were exposed to a baptism of fire only second in severity to that of their Territorial comrades from Liverpool. They and the 3rd Worcesters, together with the 1st Wiltshires upon the flank, endured a very violent shelling, but held on for many hours to the captured positions. The Worcesters had over 300 casualties, including their colonel (Stuart), who had led them ever since Mons. The Honourable Artillery Company and Wiltshires suffered almost as heavily.

The advance still continued with great fury. It should have ended on the taking of the second line of trenches, but it was impossible to restrain the men, who yelled, "Remember the Lusitania!" to each other as they surged over the parapets and dashed once more at the enemy with bayonet and bomb. The third trench was carried, and even the fourth. But the assault had gone too far. The farther spray of stormers had got as far as the Bellewaarde Lake. It was impossible to hold these advanced positions. The assailants dropped sullenly back, and finally contented themselves by settling into the first line and consolidating their position there on a front of a thousand yards. The losses had been heavy, especially from the high-explosive shells, which, as usual, blew both trenches and occupants to pieces. Men died happy, however, with the knowledge that the days were past when no artillery answer could be made, and that now at least they had given the enemy the same intolerable experience which they had themselves so often endured. The Liverpool Scots suffered especially heavily, losing about 400 men and 20 officers. All the battalions of the 9th Brigade paid the price of victory, and the 8th Brigade, upon the left, sustained considerable losses, but these were certainly not larger than those of the Germans. Altogether, it was a very brisk little fight, and a creditable victory small, of course, when measured by the scale of Neuve Chapelle or Eichebourg, but none the less heartening to the soldiers. Two hundred prisoners and a quantity of material were taken. The trenches gained were destined to be retaken with strange weapons by the enemy upon July 30, and were again carried at the point of the bayonet by the British upon August 9. These actions will be described later. A pause of nearly three weeks followed, broken only by the usual bickerings up and down the line, where opposite trenches ran mines up to each other or exchanged fusillades of hand-bombs. There was no serious movement upon either side, the Germans being concentrated upon their great and successful Eastern advance; while the Allies in the West were content to wait for the day when they should have accumulated such a head of shell as would enable them to make a prolonged effort which would promise some definite result. More and more it had become clear, both from the German efforts and our own, that any coup de main was impossible, and that a battle which would really achieve a permanent gain must be an affair which would last a month or so, with steady, inexorable advance from day to day. This could only be hoped for by the storage of a very great quantity of ammunition. Hence the pause in the operations.

The The lull was broken, however, by a sharp fight upon July 6, in which Prowse's 11th Brigade of the Fourth Division took, and permanently held, a section of the German line. This considerable action was fought at the extreme northern end of the British line, where it joined on to the French Moroccan troops to the north of Ypres. The sudden and swift advance of the 1st Rifle Brigade, the leading British battalion, seems to have taken the Germans by surprise, and, dashing forwards, they seized two lines of trenches and established themselves firmly within them. The 1st Somerset Light Infantry shared the credit and the losses of the charge. They were in immediate support of the Rifle Brigade, their task being to dig a communication trench. A hundred prisoners and a number of mortars and machine-guns were the immediate trophies. Three times during the day did the Germans counter-attack in force, and three times they were driven back with heavy loss. Their total casualties certainly ran into a thousand. On the other hand, both the Rifle Brigade and the Somersets suffered severely, partly from flanking machine-gun fire in the attack, but chiefly, as usual, from heavy shell-fire afterwards. Indeed, it may be said that a victorious battalion was too often an exhausted battalion, for since the German guns had the precise length of the captured trench, the more heroically it was held the heavier the losses. Until the artillery of the Allies should be able to dominate that of the enemy, it was difficult to see how ground could be gained without this grievous after-price to be paid. On this occasion it was paid to the full, but the ground was permanently occupied, and a heavy blow was struck at the Bavarians and Prussians who held that portion of the line.

Part of the 12th Brigade (Anley) took over some of the captured trenches from the 11th, and came in for some of the German anger in consequence. The 2nd Lancashire Fusiliers were very heavily shelled, losing their commanding officer, Colonel Griffin, the machine-gun officer, and the adjutant on the morning of July 7. A sap ran up to the trench, and this was the scene of desperate bomb-fighting, the Fusiliers expending eight thousand bombs in two days. So great was the pressure that part of the 1st Warwicks came up in support. There were several infantry advances of the enemy, which were all crushed by the British fire. No dervishes could have shown more devoted courage than some of the Germans. In one rush of sixty men all were shot down, which did not prevent another forty from emerging later from the same trench. Gradually they learned that their task was impossible, and the position remained with the British. Altogether the Lancashire Fusiliers lost 8 officers and 400 men in this action.

The succession of British successes which have been recorded in their order was broken at this point by a temporary reverse, which involved no permanent loss of ground, but cost many valuable lives. It is a deplorable thing that, when fighting against men who are usually brave and sometimes heroic, we are obliged continually to associate any success which they may obtain with some foul breach of the ancient customs of war. With the Germans no trick was too blackguardly or unsoldierly for them to attempt. At the end of April, as already shown, they nearly snatched an important victory by the wholesale use of poison. Now, at the end of July, they gained an important local success by employing the cruel expedient of burning petrol. These different foul devices were hailed by the German Press at the time as various exhibitions of superior chemical methods; whereas in fact they were exhibitions of utter want of military chivalry and of that self-restraint which even in the fiercest contest prevents a civilised nation from sinking to such expedients. It is the most pressing objection to such methods that if they are once adopted the other side has no choice but to adopt them also. In the use of gas devices, both aggressive and offensive, the British engineers soon acquired an ascendency, but even if the Germans learned to rue the day that they had stooped to such methods the responsibility for this unchivalrous warfare must still rest with them.

The attack fell upon that section of trench which had been taken by the British in the Hooge district on June 16. It was held now by a brigade of the Fourteenth Light Infantry Division (Couper), which had the distinction of being the first unit of the New Army to be seriously engaged. Nothing could have been more severe indeed, terrific than the ordeal to which they were subjected, nor more heroic than the way in which it was borne. Under very desperate conditions, all the famous traditions of the British rifle regiments were gloriously upheld. They were destined for defeat but such a defeat as shows the true fibre of a unit as clearly as any victory.

Nugent's 41st Brigade, which held this section of trench, consisted of the 7th and 8th King's Royal Rifles, with the 7th and 8th Rifle Brigade. The position was a dangerous little salient, projecting Hooge right up to the German line.

It is clear that the Germans mustered great forces, both human and mechanical, before letting go their attack. For ten days before the onset they kept up a continuous fire, which blew down the parapets and caused great losses to the defenders. On July 29 the 7th King's Royal Rifles and the 8th Rifle Brigade manned the front and supporting trenches, taking the place of their exhausted comrades. They were just in time for the fatal assault. At 3:20 in the morning of July 30 a mine exploded under the British parapet, and a moment afterwards huge jets of flame, sprayed from their diabolical machines, rose suddenly from the line of German trenches and fell in a sheet of fire into the front British position. The distance was only twenty yards, and the effect was complete and appalling. Only one man is known to have escaped from this section of trench. The fire was accompanied by a shower of aerial torpedoes from the Minenwerfer, which were in themselves sufficient to destroy the garrison. The Germans instantly assaulted and occupied the defenceless trench, but were held up for a time by the reserve companies in the supporting trenches. Finally these were driven out by the weight of the German attack, and fell back about two hundred yards, throwing themselves down along the edges of Zouave and Sanctuary Woods, in the immediate rear of the old position. What with the destruction of the men in the front trench and the heavy losses of the supports, the two battalions engaged had been very highly tried, but they still kept their faces to the foe, in spite of a terrific fall of shells. The British artillery was also in full blast. For many hours, from dawn onwards, its shells just skimmed over the heads of the front British line, and pinned the Germans down at a time when their advance might have been a serious thing, in the face of the shaken troops in front of them. It is said that during fourteen hours only five of their shells are known to have fallen short, though they fired from a distance of about three miles, and only a couple of hundred yards separated the lines a testimony to the accuracy of the munition-workers as well as of the gunners.

The position gained by the Germans put them behind the line of trenches held upon the British right by two companies of the 8th Rifle Brigade. These brave men, shot at from all sides and unable to say which was their parapet and which their parados, held on during the whole interminable July day, until after dusk the remains of them drew off into the shelter of the prophetically- named Sanctuary Wood. Another aggressive movement was made by the German stormers down the communication trenches, which enabled them to advance while avoiding direct fire; but this, after hard fighting, was stopped by the bombers of the Riflemen.

The two battalions of the 41st Brigade, which had just been relieved and were already on their way to a place of rest, were halted and brought back. They were the 8th King's Royal Rifles and the 7th Rifle Brigade. These two battalions had been eight days under incessant fire in the trenches, with insufficient food, water, and sleep. They were now hurried back into a hellish fire, jaded and weary, but full of zeal at the thought that they were taking some of the pressure on their comrades. An order for an instant counter-attack had been given, but it was recognised that two brigades at least were necessary for such a task, and that even then, without a very thorough artillery preparation, the affair was desperate, since the Germans had already consolidated the position, and their artillery, large and small, was very masterful. For some reason, however, instead of a brigade, only two fresh battalions could be spared. These were the 9th King's Royal Rifles, of the 42nd Brigade, and the 6th Cornwalls, of the 43rd. Of these the 9th King's Royal Rifles attacked, not from the wood, but from the Menin road upon the left.

There had been three-quarters of an hour of intense bombardment before the attack, but it was not successful in breaking down the German resistance. At 2:45 P.M. the infantry advance began from the wood, all four units of the 41st Brigade taking part in it. It is difficult to imagine any greater trial for troops, since half of them had already been grievously reduced and the other half were greatly exhausted, while they were now asked to advance several hundred yards without a shadow of cover, in the face of a fire which was shaving the very grass from the ground. "The men behaved very well," says an observer, "and the officers with a gallantry no words can adequately describe. As they came out of the woods the German machine-gun fire met them and literally swept them away, line after line. The men struggled forward, only to fall in heaps along the edge of the woods." The Riflemen did all that men could do, but there comes a time when perseverance means annihilation. The remains of the four battalions were compelled to take shelter once more at the edge of the wood. Fifty officers out of 90 had fallen. By 4 P.M. the counter-attack had definitely failed.

The attack of the 9th King's Royal Rifles, along the Menin road, led by Colonel Chaplin, had rather better success, and was pushed home with great valour and corresponding loss. At one time the stormers reached the original line of trenches and took possession of one section of it. Colonel Chaplin was killed, with many of his officers and men, by a deadly machine-gun fire from the village of Hooge. A gallant lad, Lieutenant Geen, with a handful of men, charged into this village, but never emerged. The attack was not altogether unproductive, for, though the advanced position was not held, the 9th retained trenches which linked up the Menin road with the left of the Zouave Wood. With the darkness, the wearied and thinned ranks of the 41st Brigade were withdrawn into reserve.

It was not destined, however, that Nugent's hard-worked brigade should enjoy the rest that they needed so badly. They had left the 10th Durham Light Infantry and the 6th Cornwall Light Infantry to defend the wood, but at 2:20 in the morning the Germans renewed their diabolical tactics with liquid fire, which blazed over the trenches and scorched the branches overhead. This time the range was farther and the effect less deadly. An attack was evidently impending, and the Riflemen were hurried back to reinforce the two battalions left in possession. There was a night of alarms, of shell-fire, and of losses, but the German infantry advance was not serious, and those who reached the woods were driven out again.

For some days afterwards there was no change in Hooge. the general situation. Sixty officers and 2000 men were the terrible losses of the 41st Brigade during this action. The 9th battalion, in its flank attack, lost 17 officers and 333 of the ranks. The 43rd Brigade (Cockburn) endured considerable losses whilst in support of the 41st, especially the 6th Cornwalls, who bore the brunt of the fighting. This battalion had only seven officers left when it returned to Ypres, and by the unfortunate mischance of the fall of a ruined house, they lost immediately afterwards four more, including Major Barnett, the temporary chief, and the adjutant Blagrove. These officers perished whilst endeavouring to save their men who were buried among the ruins.

This difficult and trying action was fought under the immediate supervision of General Nugent, of the 41st Brigade, who was with the firing- line in the woods during the greater part of it. When the brigade, or the shattered remains of it, were withdrawn upon August 1, General Nugent remained behind, and consulted with General Cockburn, of the 43rd Brigade, as to the feasibility of a near attack. The consultation took the form of a reconnaissance conducted on hands and knees up to a point close to the enemy line. After this inspection it was determined that the position was far too formidable for any merely local attempt. It was determined that General Congreve, of the Sixth Division, should take the matter over, that several days should be devoted to preparatory bombardment, and that the whole division should be used for the assault.

All foul advantages, whether they be gas, vitriol, Hooge or liquid fire, bring with them their own disadvantages. In this case the fall of their comrades filled the soldiers with a righteous anger, which gave them a fury in the assault which nothing could withstand. The preparations were completed in a week, and the signal was given in the early morning of August 9. Artillery had been concentrated during the interval, and the bombardment was extraordinarily intense and accurate. So perfect was the co-ordination between the infantry and the guns, that the storming battalions dashed out of the trenches whilst the German lines were still an inferno of exploding shells, with the certain conviction that the shell-fire would have ceased before they had actually got across the open. The cease-fire and the arrival of the panting, furious soldiers were practically simultaneous. On the left, some of our men ran into our own shrapnel, but otherwise all went, to perfection.

The infantry assault had been assigned to the Sixth Division, who advanced at 3:15, with two brigades in front and one in support. The 18th Brigade (Ainslie) was upon the right. Colonel Towsey was in immediate command. The 2nd Durham Light Infantry were in the lead, and got across two companies in front with little loss; while the 2nd Sherwood Foresters, who followed, were caught in shell-fire and had very many casualties. The attack on this flank was supported by the 1st East Yorks and the Westminsters, who lay in the woods to the rear, the East Yorks being speedily engaged. The wave of infantry were over the German parapet in an instant. All resistance was vain, and those who stood were bayoneted, while the fugitives were pelted with bombs from traverse to traverse wherever they attempted to make head against their pursuers. So sudden had been the British rush that many of the Germans were found in the dug-outs and in the old mine-crater, from which they had not time to emerge and to meet the assault for which they were waiting. Over a hundred of these were taken prisoners. The whole place was a perfect charnel-house, for there were 200 German dead in the crater, 300 in front of the line, and a great number also of the Riflemen who had been killed nine days before.

On the left of the line a no less dashing attack had been made by the 16th Brigade (Nicholson), and the trenches were carried in line with those now held by the 18th. This successful advance was carried out by the 1st Shropshires, the 1st Buffs, and the 2nd York and Lancasters, with the 1st Leicesters in support. The distance between the lines at this point was very much less than on the right, which partly accounts for the smaller casualties.

When the trenches had been taken, the sappers, with their usual cool disregard of danger, sprang forward into the open and erected barbed wire. The gains were rapidly consolidated, men were sent back to avoid overcrowding, and protective cover raised against the heavy shelling which always follows swiftly upon the flight of the German infantry. It came in due course, and was succeeded by an attempt at a counter-attack. "At about 10 o'clock the enemy was observed creeping in four parties towards us. They were very near us, and came forward on their hands and knees, laden with bombs and hand-grenades. We opened fire with rifles and machine-guns. Our bomb-throwers worked like machines, and did work they did. The Germans were all mowed down and blown to atoms, or else ran for their lives." Many of our prisoners were killed by German shells before they could be removed. In spite of the failure of the German infantry, the artillery fire was very deadly, both the Durhams and the Sherwood Foresters being hard put to it to hold on to their trenches. At 4:30 in the afternoon the Sherwood Foresters fell back to the edge of the wood, some of their trenches having entirely ceased to exist.

There were several German infantry attempts during the day, but all of them met the same fate as the first. The loss of the enemy, both in the attack and in the subsequent attempts at recapture, was very heavy, running certainly into some thousands of dead or wounded; while the British losses in the actual attack, owing to the admirable artillery arrangements, were very moderate. Some hundreds of prisoners were taken, sixty of whom by a strange freak surrendered to an unarmed observation officer named Booth. It was a fair revenge for the setback of July 30, and it was won in honest, virile fashion by the use of the legitimate weapons of civilised warfare.

During the long day the Germans strove hard, by an infernal shell-fire, raking all the trenches from the direction of Hill 60, to drive the infantry from the captured position. They clung desperately to what they had won, but they were cut off from all supplies. Many of the Westminsters lost their lives in heroically bringing up water and food to the advanced line. For fourteen hours the men were under a murderous fire, and for the same period the British artillery worked hard in supporting them. Men can endure punishment far more cheerfully when they hear the roar of their own shells overhead and know that the others are catching it also. "The guns put heart into us," said one of the survivors. Finally, night put an end to the slaughter and the uproar. Under the shadow of darkness relieving troops crept to the front, and the weary, decimated, but triumphant brigades were drawn off to the rear.

Some of the more forward of the troops had got right across the Menin road and established themselves in positions so far in advance that for some time no orders could reach them; nor was their situation known until desperate messengers came back from them clamouring for cartridges and bombs. These men were only drawn in on the morning of the 10th, after enduring nearly thirty hours of desperate fighting, without food, water, or help of any kind.

The losses were, as usual, far heavier in holding the trenches than in winning them. The 16th Brigade lost 400 and the 18th 1300 men. The 2nd Durhams were the chief sufferers, with 12 officers and 500 men out of action; but the Shropshires lost no fewer than 19 officers with 250 men. The 2nd Sherwoods, 1st East Yorkshires, 1st Buffs, and 2nd York and Lancasters were all hard hit.

A considerable change in the general arrangement of the Army was carried out early in August. This consisted in the formation of a third army under General Monro, an officer whose rapid rise was one of the phenomena of the war. This army consisted of the Seventh Corps (Snow) and the Tenth Corps (Morland). The rearrangement would be of little importance, since most of the units have already been mentioned, but it was accompanied by a large extension of the British line. Up to this date it had joined the French about six miles south of the La Bassée Canal. Now the Tenth French Army (Foch) was left in position before Lens, and the British took up the line again upon the farther side of them, carrying it from the south of Arras to the neighbourhood of Albert, thus adding a dozen miles or so to the British region, and bringing the total to about fifty a small proportion, it is true, but a very vital sector, and the one most free from any natural feature of protection. There was at this time an ever-thickening flow of reinforcements, as well as of munitions, from across the Channel, but the new movements of Germany in the Near East made it very evident that their use would not be confined to the lines of Flanders. It was towards the end of this summer that the length of the war and the increasing pressure of the blockade began to interfere with the food-supplies of the German people. It had been pretended that this was so before, but this was an attempt by the German Government to excite sympathy in neutrals. There is no doubt, however, that it was now a fact, and that it continued to slowly tighten from month to month, until it finally became extreme. There are few Britons who feel satisfaction at such a method of warfare, but so long as armies represent the whole manhood of a nation, it is impossible to make any provision by which food shall reach the civilian and not the soldier. It is always to be borne in mind that the British, with an almost exaggerated chivalry, considering the many provocations which they had received, did not exert their full power of blockade for many months. It was only when Germany declared the British Islands to be blockaded as from February 18, 1915, and that food-ships would be destroyed, that the British in retaliation, by an Order of Council in March of the same year, placed German food upon the index. Thus by one more miscalculation the Germans called down trouble upon their own heads, for whereas their decree proved to be worthless, that of Britain was ever more effective. It is curious to remember that only forty-five years before, the Germans, without one word of protest from any of their people, had starved the two millions of Paris, while Bismarck, in his luxurious rooms at Versailles, had uttered his brutal jest about roast babies. They are not so very slow those mills of God!

Before passing on to an account of the great Battle of Loos, which terminated the operations upon the British front for this year, a few words may be said of those happenings elsewhere which do not come within the immediate scope of this narrative, but which cannot be entirely omitted since every failure or success had an indirect influence upon the position in France. This is particularly true of the naval campaign, for the very existence of our Army depended upon our success in holding the command of the sea. This was fully attained during the year 1915 by the wise provisions of Admiral Jellicoe, who held back his Grand Fleet in such a manner that, far from the attrition upon which the German war-prophets had confidently counted, it was far stronger at the end of the year than at the beginning, while its influence had been such that the German High Sea Fleet might as well have never existed for all the effect which it had upon the campaign. In spite of the depredations of German submarines, which were restrained by no bonds of law or humanity, British commerce flowed in its double tide, outwards and inwards, with a volume which has seldom been surpassed, and the Channel crossing was guarded with such truly miraculous skill that not a transport was lost. It was a task which the Navy should never have been called upon to do, since the need of a Channel tunnel had for years been obvious; but granting that it had to be done, nothing could exceed the efficiency with which it was carried out. The success, however, cannot blind us to the waste of merchant tonnage or of convoying cruisers absorbed in this vital task, nor to the incessant delays and constant expense due to the want of foresight upon the part of those who opposed this necessary extension of our railway system. There was little naval fighting during the year, for the simple reason that our sailors had nothing to fight. Upon January 24 a German squadron of battle-cruisers attempted a repetition of the Scarborough Raid, but was nearly intercepted by a British squadron of greater power under Admiral Beatty. In a running fight which only came to an end when the Germans had gained the protection of their mine-fields considerable punishment was inflicted upon them, which included the loss of the 15,000-ton armoured cruiser *Blücher*. There were 123 survivors out of a crew of 800. Some damage was inflicted upon the Lion, but the British casualties were slight and no vessel was lost, save in the Berlin papers.

Upon February 20 the adventure of the Dardanelles was begun by a bombardment of the outer forts by the Allied Fleets. The British ships engaged in these operations were pre-Dreadnought battleships, with the notable exception of the new cruiser *Queen Elizabeth*. On March 18, in an attempt to force the Straits, the *Ocean* and the *Irresistible* were lost by floating torpedoes. On May 13 we lost in the same locality the *Goliath*, which was also torpedoed in a very gallant surface attack delivered at night by a Turkish or German boat. On the 26th the *Triumph* fell a victim to a submarine in the same waters. The other naval events of the year include numerous actions of small craft with varying results, and the final destruction of the *Dresden*, the *Königsberg*, and every other German warship left upon the face of the waters. The British anti-submarine devices in home waters reached a high point of efficiency, and the temporary subsidence of submarine warfare is to be attributed rather to the loss of these vessels than to any remonstrances upon the part of neutrals.

Some allusion should be made to the Zeppelins which were malevolently active during the year, but whose efficiency fortunately fell very far short of either the activity or the malevolence. Instead of proving a blessing to mankind, the results of the energy and ingenuity of the aged German inventor were at once turned to the most devilish use conceivable, for their raids effected no possible military object, but caused the death or mutilation of numerous civilians, including a large number of women and children. The huge bombs were showered down from the airships with no regard at all as to whether a legitimate mark lay beneath them, and the huge defenceless city of London was twice attacked on the plea that the possession of munition works made the whole of it a fortress. The total result of all the raids came to about 1500 killed and wounded. It is probable that the destruction of the invading of airships in 1916 killed more German fighting adults than were killed in England by all their raids combined. They effected nothing decisive save the ignominy of the murderers who used them.

Of the Dardanelles Campaign nothing need be said, since it will be fully treated in many separate accounts, save that our general position was greatly weakened by the large number of vessels needed for the conduct of these operations, nor did we profit much by their abandonment since the call of Salonica soon became equally insistent. We were able during the year to continue the absorption of the German Colonial Empire, none of which, save East Africa, remained intact at the end of it. Egypt was successfully defended against one or two half-hearted advances upon the part of the Turks. The Mesopotamian Campaign, however, had taken at the close of the year a sinister turn, for General Townshend, having pushed forward almost to the gates of Bagdad with a very inadequate force, was compelled to retreat to Kut, where he was surrounded and besieged by a considerable Turkish army. The defence was a heroic one, and only ended in the spring of 1916, when the starving survivors were forced to surrender.

As to the affairs of our Allies, some allusion will be made later to the great French offensive in Champagne, which was simultaneous with our own advance at Loos. For the rest there was constant fighting along the line, with a general tendency for the French to gain ground though usually at a heavy cost. The year, on the other hand, had been a disastrous one for the Russians who, half-armed and suffering terrible losses, had been compelled to relinquish all their gains and to retreat for some hundreds of miles. As is now clear, the difficulties in the front were much increased by lamentable political conditions, including treachery in high places in the rear. For a time even Petrograd seemed in danger, but thanks to fresh supplies of the munitions of war from Britain and from Japan they were able at last to form a firm line from Riga in the north to the eastern end of the Romanian frontier in the south.

The welcome accession of Italy upon May 23 and the lamentable defection of Bulgaria on October 11 complete the more salient episodes of the year.

VII. THE BATTLE OF LOOS

The First Day—September 25

General order of battle—Check of the Second Division — Advance of the Ninth and Seventh Divisions—Advance of the First Division—Fine progress of the Fifteenth Division—Capture of Loos—Work of the Forty-seventh London Division

Whilst the Army had lain in apparent torpidity during the summer a torpidity which was only broken by the sharp engagements at Hooge and elsewhere great preparations for a considerable attack had been going forward. For several months the sappers and the gunners had been busy concentrating their energies for a serious effort which should, as it was hoped, give the infantry a fair chance of breaking the German line. Similar preparations were going on among the French, both in Foch's Tenth Army to the immediate right of the British line, and also on a larger scale in the region of Champagne. Confining our attention to the British effort, we shall now examine the successive stages of the great action in front of Hulluch and Loos the greatest battle, both as to the numbers engaged and as to the losses incurred, which had ever up to that date been fought by our Army.

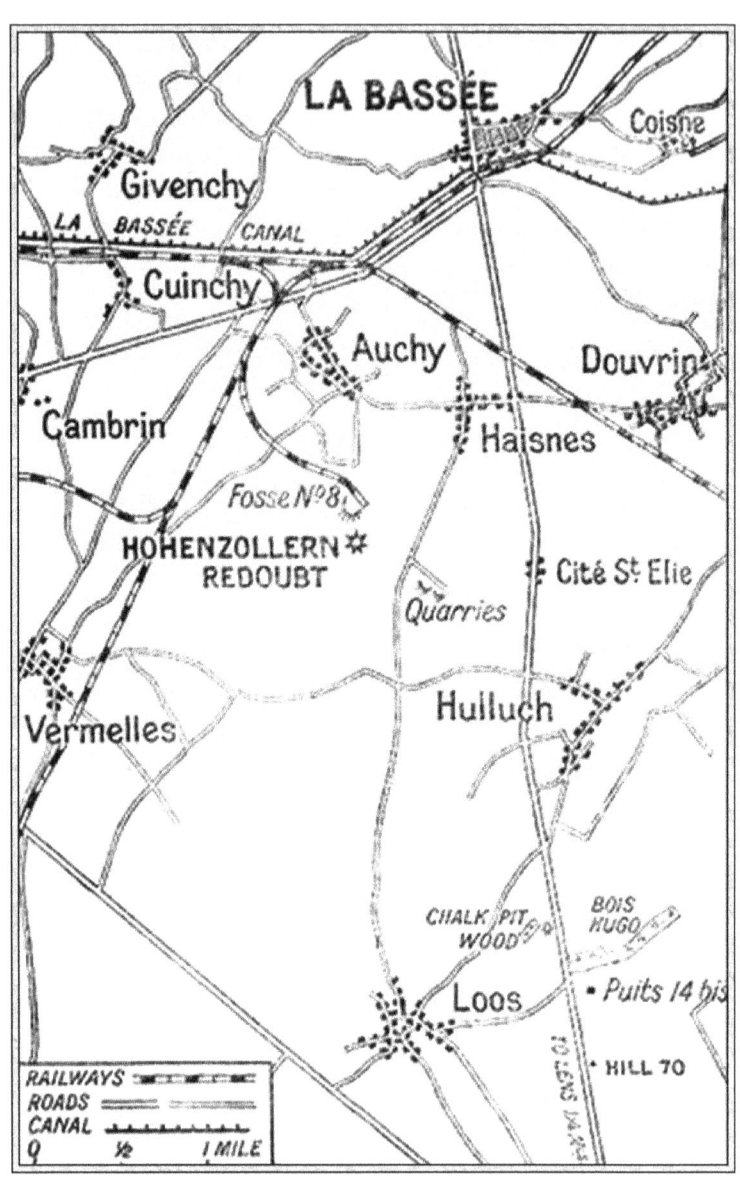

Loos District

The four days which preceded the great attack of September 25 were days of great activity. An incessant and severe bombardment was directed upon the German lines along the whole front, but especially in the sector to the immediate south of the La Bassée Canal, where the main thrust was to be made. To this severe fire the Germans made hardly any reply, though whether from settled policy or from a comparative lack of munitions is not clear. On each of the days a feint attack was made upon the German line so far as could be done without actually exposing the men. The troops for the assault were gradually brought into position, and the gas-cylinders, which were to be used for the first time, were sunk in the front parapets.

The assault in the main area was to extend from the La Bassée Canal in the north to the village of Grenay in the south, a front of about seven miles, and it was to be supported and supplemented by many subsidiary attacks along the whole line up to the Ypres salient, and northwards still to where the monitors upon the coast held the German coastguards to their sand-dunes. For the moment we will deal only with the fortunes of the main attack. This was to be delivered by two army corps, both belonging to Haig's First Army, that tempered blade which has so often been the spear-head for the British thrust. The corps were the First (Hubert Gough's) and the Fourth (Rawlinson's). It will be remembered that a British army corps now consisted of three divisions, so that the storming line was composed of six divisions, or about seventy thousand infantry.

The line of the advance was bisected by a high road from Vermelles to Hulluch. This was made the boundary line between the two attacking corps. To the left, or north of this road, was the ground of the First Corps; to the right, or south, of the Fourth.

The qualities of the Regular and Territorial regiments had already been well attested. This was the first occasion, however, when, upon a large scale, use was made of those new forces which now formed so considerable a proportion of the whole. Let it be said at once that they bore the test magnificently, and that they proved themselves to be worthy of their comrades to the right and the left. It had always been expected that the new infantry would be good, for they had in most cases been under intense training for a year, but it was a surprise to many British soldiers, and a blow to the prophets in Berlin, to find that the scientific branches, the gunners and the sappers, had also reached a high level. "Our enemy may have hoped," said Sir John French, "not perhaps without reason, that it would be impossible for us, starting with such small beginnings, to build up an efficient artillery to provide for the very large expansion of the Army. If he entertained such hopes he has now good reason to know that they have not been justified by the result. The efficiency of the artillery of the new armies has exceeded all expectations." These were the guns which, in common with many others of every calibre, worked furiously in the early dawn of Saturday, September 25, to prepare for the impending advance. The high explosives were known to have largely broken down the German system of defences, but it was also known that there were areas where the damage had not been great and where the wire entanglements were still intact. No further delay could be admitted, however, if our advance was to be on the same day as that of the French. The infantry, chafing with impatience, were swarming in the fire trenches. At 5.40 A.M. the gas-cylinders were turned on. At 6:30 A.M. the guns ceased fire, and the ardent soldiers Regulars, New, and Territorials dashed forward upon their desperate venture.

The following rough diagram of the action will help the reader to understand the order in which the six divisions attacked, and in a very rough way the objectives in front of them. It is impossible to describe simultaneously the progress of so extended a line.

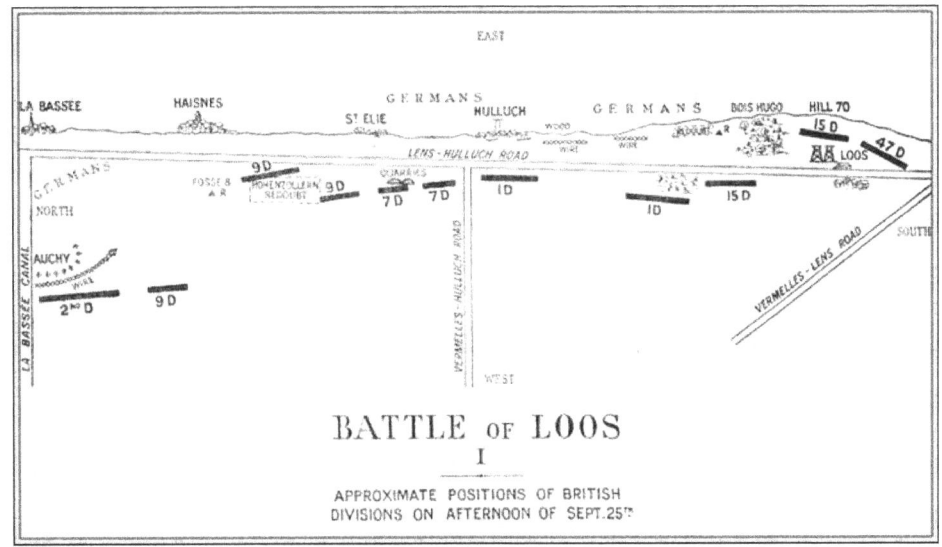

Battle of Loos

It will be best, therefore, to take the various divisions from the northern end, and to follow the fortunes of each until it reached some definite limit. Afterwards an attempt will be made to co-ordinate these results and show their effects upon each other.

The second regular division (Home), acting upon the extreme left of the main attack, had two brigades north of the La Bassée Canal and one to the south. The most northern was the 5th (Cochrane's), and its operations really formed part of the subsidiary attacks, and will be treated under that head. South of it was the 6th (Daly's), to the immediate north of the canal. The gas, drifting slowly up the line before a slight southern breeze, had contaminated the air in this quarter, and many of the men were suffering from the effects. None the less, at half-past six the advance was made in a most dashing manner, but the barbed wire defences were found to be only partially damaged and the trenches to be intact, so no progress could be made. The 2nd South Staffords and 1st King's Liverpools on the left and right reached the German position, but in face of a murderous fire were unable to make good their hold, and were enduring heavy losses, shared in a lesser degree by the 1st Rifles and 1st Berks in support. Upon their right, south of the canal, was the 19th Brigade (Robertson). The two leading regiments, the 1st Middlesex and 2nd Argylls, sprang from the trenches and rushed across the intervening space, only to find themselves faced by unbroken and impassable wire. For some reason, probably the slope of the ground, the artillery had produced an imperfect effect upon the defences of the enemy in the whole sector attacked by the Second Division, and if there is one axiom more clearly established than another during this war, it is that no human heroism can carry troops through uncut wire. They will most surely be shot down faster than they can cut the strands. The two battalions lay all day, from morning till dusk, in front of this impenetrable obstacle, lashed and scourged by every sort of fire, and losing heavily. Two companies of the 2nd Welsh Fusiliers, who gallantly charged forward to support them, shared their tragic experience. It was only under the cover of dusk that the survivors were able to get back, having done nothing save all that men could do. Their difficult situation was rendered more desperate by the fact that the wind drifted the gas that filthy and treacherous ally over a portion of the line, and some of our soldiers were poisoned by the effects. The hold-up was the more unfortunate, as it left the Germans the power to outflank the whole advance, and many of the future difficulties arose from the fact that the enemy's guns were still working from Auchy and other points on the left rear of the advancing troops. In justice to the Second Division, it must be remembered that they were faced by the notoriously strong position called "the railway triangle," and also that it is on the flanking units The that the strain must especially fall, as was shown equally clearly upon the same day in the great French advance in Champagne.

The advance of the next division, the Ninth Scottish Division (Thesiger's) of the new armies, was of a most energetic nature, and met with varying fortunes according to the obstacles in their path. The valour and perseverance of the men were equally high in each of its brigades. By an unfortunate chance, General Landon, the officer who had played so essential a part on the fateful October 31, 1914, and who had commanded the Ninth Division, was invalided home only two days before the battle. His place was taken by General Thesiger, who had little time in which to get acquainted with his staff and surroundings. The front to be assaulted was of a most formidable nature. This Hohenzollern Redoubt jutted forward from the main German line, and was an enclosure seamed with trenches, girdled with wire, and fringed with machine- guns. Behind and to the north of it lay the slag-heap Fosse 8. The one favourable point lay in the fact that the attacking infantry had only a hundred yards to cross, while in the other parts of the line the average distance was about a quarter of a mile.

The attack of the Ninth Division was carried out with two brigades, the 26th (Ritchie) and 28th (Dickens), with the 27th (Bruce) in close support.

Continuing the plan of taking each unit from the north, we will follow the tragic fortunes of the 28th Brigade on the left. This brigade seems to have been faced by the same unbroken obstacles which had held up their neighbours of the Second Division upon the left, and they found it equally impossible to get forward, though the attack was urged with all the constancy of which human nature is capable, as the casualty returns only too clearly show.

The most veteran troops could not have endured a more terrible ordeal or preserved a higher heart than these young soldiers in their first battle. The leading regiments were the 6th Scottish Borderers and the 11th Highland Light Infantry. Nineteen officers led the Borderers over the parapet. Within a few minutes the whole nineteen, including Colonel Maclean and Major Hosley, lay dead or wounded upon the ground. Valour could no further go. Of the rank and file of the Borderers some 500 out of 1000 were lying in the long grass which faced the German trenches. The Highland Light Infantry had suffered very little less. Ten officers and 300 men fell in the first rush before they were checked by the barbed wire of the enemy. Every accumulation of evil which can appal the stoutest heart was heaped upon this brigade not only the two leading battalions, but their comrades of the 9th Seaforths and 10th H.L.I, who supported them. The gas hung thickly about the trenches, and all of the troops, but especially the 10th H.L.I., suffered from it. Colonel Graham of this regiment was found later incoherent and half unconscious from poisoning, while Major Graham and four lieutenants were incapacitated in the same way. The chief cause of the slaughter, however, was the uncut wire, which held up the brigade while the German rifle and machine-gun fire shot them down in heaps. It was observed that in this part of the line the gas had so small an effect upon the enemy that their infantry could be seen with their heads and shoulders clustering thickly over their parapets as they fired down at the desperate men who tugged and raved in front of the wire entanglement. An additional horror was found in the shape of a covered trench, invisible until one fell into it, the bottom of which was studded with stakes and laced with wire. Many of the Scottish Borderers lost their lives in this murderous ditch. In addition to all this, the fact that the Second Division was held up exposed the 28th Brigade to fire on the flank. In spite of every impediment, some of the soldiers fought their way onwards and sprang down into the German trenches; notably Major Sparling of the Borderers and Lieutenant Sebold of the H.L.I, with a handful of men broke through all opposition. There was no support behind them, however, and after a time the few survivors were compelled to fall back to the trenches from which they had started, both the officers named having been killed. The repulse on the left of the Ninth Division was complete. The mangled remains of the 28th Brigade, flushed and furious but impotent, gathered together to hold their line against a possible counter-attack. Shortly after mid-day they made a second attempt at a forward movement, but 50 per cent of their number were down, all the battalions had lost many of their officers, and for the moment it was not possible to sustain the offensive.

A very different fate had befallen the 26th Brigade upon their right. The leading battalions of this brigade were the 5th Camerons on the left, gallantly led by Lochiel himself, the hereditary chieftain of the clan, and the 7th Seaforths on the right. These two battalions came away with a magnificent rush, closely followed by the 8th Gordons and the 8th Black Watch. It was a splendid example of that *furor Scoticus* which has shown again and again that it is not less formidable than the Teutonic wrath. The battalions were over the parapet, across the open, through the broken wire, and over the entrenchment like a line of Olympic hurdlers. Into the trenches they dashed, seized or killed the occupants, pressed rapidly onwards up the communications, and by seven o'clock had made their way as far as Fosse 8, a coal-mine with a long, low slagheap lying in the rear of the great work, but linked up to it in one system of defences. It was a splendid advance, depending for its success upon the extreme speed and decision of the movement. Many officers and men, including Lord Sempill, the gallant Colonel of the Black Watch, were left upon the ground, but the front of the brigade rolled ever forwards. Not content with this considerable success, one battalion, the 8th Gordons, with a handful of the Black Watch, preserved sufficient momentum to carry it on to the edge of the fortified village of Haisnes, in the rear of the German position. The reserve brigade, the 27th, consisting of the 11th and 12th Royal Scots, 10th Argyll and Sutherland Highlanders, and 6th Scots Fusiliers, swept onwards in support of this movement. This brigade had varying fortunes, part of it being held up by wire. It did not get so far forward as the brigade upon its left, but it reached and took Fosse Alley, to the immediate west of the Lens-Hulluch road. This position it held against bombing attacks upon each flank until the morning of Monday the 27th, as will be described later. The Highlanders upon their left, who had got nearly to Haisnes, dropped back when they found themselves unsupported, and joined the rest of their brigade in the neighbourhood of Fosse 8.

It should be mentioned that the field-guns of the 52nd Brigade E.F.A. pushed up in the immediate rear of the firing line of the Ninth Division, and gave effective support to the infantry. The fact that they could do this across the open tends to show that infantry supports could be pushed up without being confined unduly to the communication trenches. The spirited action of these guns was greatly appreciated by the infantry.

For the moment we will leave the Ninth Division, its left held up in line with the Second Division, its right flung forward through the Hohenzollern Redoubt and Fosse 8 until the spray from the wave had reached as far as Haisnes. Let us turn now to the veterans of the Seventh Division, the inheritors of the glories of Ypres, who filled the space between the right of the Ninth Division and the road from Vermelles to Hulluch which divided Gough's First and Rawlinson's Fourth Corps. This division was constituted as before, save that the 8th and 9th Devons of the New Army had taken the place of the two Guards battalions in the 20th Brigade. Upon receiving the word to advance, "Over the top and the best of luck!" the men swarmed on short ladders out of the fire trenches and advanced with cool, disciplined valour over the open ground. On reaching the German wire the leading brigades the 22nd on the left with the 2nd Warwicks and 1st South Staffords in the lead, the 20th on the right with the 2nd Gordons and 8th Devons in the place of honour lay down for a short breather, while each soldier obeyed instructions by judging for himself the point at which the broken, tangled mass of writhing strands could most easily be penetrated. Then once more the whistles blew, the men rushed forward, and, clearing the wire, they threw themselves into the front trench. The garrison of 200 men threw their arms down and their hands up with the usual piteous but insincere cry of "Kameraden!" Flooding over the line of trenches, the division pushed rapidly on without a check until they reached the Quarries, a well-marked post in front of the village of Hulluch. Here more prisoners and eight field-guns were taken by the 20th Brigade. From the Quarries to the village is roughly half a mile of uphill ground, devoid of cover. The impetus of the advance carried the men on until they were at the very edge of the village, where they were held up by the furious fire and by a line of barbed wire, which was bravely cut by Private Vickers of the 2nd Warwicks and other devoted men. Another smaller village, Cité St. Élie, to the north of Hulluch, was also reached, the 2nd Queen's Surrey making good the western edge of it. At both these points the division had reached its limit, but still farther to the north its left-hand brigade was at the southern outskirts of Haisnes in touch with-the gallant men of the Ninth Division, who were to the west of that important village. These advanced lines could not be held without supports; the 21st Brigade had already been absorbed farther back, and the men of the Seventh Division fell back about 4 P.M. as far as the Quarries, where for a time they remained, having lost many officers and men, including Colonel Stansfeld of the 2nd Gordons, a gallant officer who was hit by a shell in the first advance, but asked only that he should be let lie where he could see his men. Colonel Heath of the Surreys was also killed after the return to the Quarries.

Such was the advance of the First Army Corps, ending in a bloody repulse upon the left of the line and a hardly less bloody success upon the right. Across the Vermelles-Hulluch high road, the Fourth Army Corps had been advancing on the same line, and its fortunes had been very similar to those of its neighbour. The First Division was operating on the left of the corps, with the Fifteenth Scottish Division (New) in the centre and the Forty-seventh Territorial (London) on the right. Thus the First Division was advancing upon Hulluch on the immediate right of the Seventh Division, so that its operations are the next to be considered.

The attack of this division was carried out by the 1st Brigade upon the left and by the 2nd upon the right, while the 3rd was in support. Two battalions, the 9th King's Liverpool and the London Scottish, acted as a small independent unit apart from the brigades. The respective objectives for the two leading brigades were the Chalk Pit and Fosse 14 for the

2nd, while the 1st was to aim at Hulluch. These objectives were somewhat diverging, and the two Territorial battalions, forming what was called Green's Force, were to fill up the gap so occasioned, and to prevent any German counter-attack coming through.

Both brigades soon found great difficulties in their path. In the case of each the wire was but imperfectly cut, and the German trenches were still strong.

We will first follow the fortunes of the 1st Brigade. Their rush was headed by two brave battalions of the New Army, the 8th Berkshires on the left and the 10th Gloucesters on the right. Both of these units did extraordinarily well, and after bearing down a succession of obstacles got as far as the edge of Hulluch, capturing three lines of trenches and several guns upon the way. The 1st Camerons pressed close at their heels, lending them the weight to carry them over each successive difficulty. The advance took some time and was very costly. The Berkshires alone in the course of the day lost 17 officers and 400 men, and were led by a young sub-lieutenant (Lawrence) at the close. The Gloucesters and Camerons suffered almost as heavily.

The experience of the 2nd Brigade to the immediate south was still more trying, and it was held up to an extent which had a serious bearing upon the fortunes of the day. The German trenches near Lone Tree, which faced the brigade, were found to be intact and strongly covered by wire. They were attacked by the 2nd Rifles and 1st North Lancashires, with the 2nd Sussex in immediate support, but no progress could be made. The 1st Northamptons threw themselves into the fight, but still the trench was held at a time when it was vital that the 2nd Brigade should be at its post in the general scheme of advance. The ground was taken, however, on each flank of the Lone Tree position, and Green's Force, whose function had been to link up the diverging operations of the two brigades, was brought up for the attack. The two battalions advanced over six hundred yards by platoon rushes under heavy gusts of fire. As they reached a point within fifty yards of the German line, a few grey-clad, battle-stained infantrymen clambered slowly on to the parapet with outstretched hands. Upon the British ceasing their fire a party of 3 officers and 400 men were marched out of the trenches and gave themselves up. Their stout resistance is a lesson in the effect which a single obstinate detachment can exert in throwing a large scheme out of gear.

The 1st Brigade had now got through upon the left, and the 2nd was able to follow them, so that the whole force advanced as far as the Lens-Hulluch road, getting in touch with the 20th Brigade of the Seventh Division on the left. Here the resistance was strong and the fire heavy. The division had lost very heavily. Of the 9th King's Liverpool only Colonel Ramsay, 4 subalterns, and 120 men were left, while many of the other battalions were almost as hard hit. It was now raining and the light was failing. The men dug themselves in near the old German trenches, the 3rd Brigade coming up and taking its position on the right flank, where late that night it connected up by means of its outer unit, the 2nd Welsh, with the Twenty-fourth Division, which had come up in support.

The temporary check to the advance of the First Division had exposed the left flank of its neighbour to the south, the Fifteenth (M'Cracken's) Scottish Division of the New Army. The two divisions were to have met at Fosse 14, but the Fifteenth Division arrived there some hours before the others, for the reason already stated. In spite of this a very fine advance was made, which gained a considerable stretch of ground and pierced more deeply than any other into the German line. The 46th Brigade was on the left, consisting of the 7th Scots Borderers and 12th Highland Light Infantry in front, with the 8th Borderers and 10th Scottish Rifles behind them. It was upon the parapet in front of this brigade that Piper Laidlaw marched up and down before the attack under a heavy fire, warming the blood of the crouching men with the maddening scream of his war-pipes. Not until he was shot down did this gallant man cease to urge forward his comrades. The 46th Brigade dashed forward at the signal, and with a fine fury flooded over the German trenches, which they carried at a rush, storming onwards across the Lens road and up the long slope of Hill 70, taking Fosse 14 upon the way, and eventually reaching the summit of the incline. The 45th supporting Brigade came along after them, detaching, as they passed, 100 bombers of the 6th Camerons to help the First Division to get forward. These brave Highlanders held the advanced line for some hours under heavy fire from the Lens batteries.

The 44th Brigade upon the right of the 46th had made an advance which was equally fiery and successful. In this brigade the 9th Black Watch and 8th Seaforths were in the lead, with the 7th Camerons and 10th Gordons behind. This brigade dashed into the main street of Loos, where they met the Londoners of Barter's Forty-seventh Division. They helped to consolidate this flank and to clear the houses of Loos, while some of them pushed forward towards Hill 70. When they reached the crest of the hill they found the remains of the 46th Brigade, consisting of remnants of the 12th H.L.I., 7th Scots Borderers, and 10th Scottish Rifles, upon their left. It is possible that they could have dug in and held their own, but the objective as given in the original orders had been the village of St. Augustine, and with heroic perseverance these brave men would be contented with nothing less than the full performance or death in the attempt. Alas! for many of them it was the latter. Gathering themselves together, they flung themselves forward over the crest. On the other side was a long, low slope with isolated houses at the bottom, the suburbs of the village of St. Laurent, which they mistook for St. Augustine. These crackled at every window with machine-gun fire. Of the devoted band who rushed forward none reached the houses. The few survivors fell back upon the crest, and then, falling back about one hundred and fifty yards, they dug in upon the slope on the west side of it. Their position was an extraordinarily dangerous one, for they had no protection upon the left flank, where lay a thick wood the Bois Hugo through which a German attack might come which would cut them off from the Army. Colonel Purvis, of the Highland Light Infantry, with quick foresight, built up a thin line of resistance upon this side from Fosse 14 in the south to the advanced left point, manning it with a few of his own men under Lieutenant M'Neil. A welcome reinforcement of the 6th Camerons and 7th Scots Fusiliers from the 45th Brigade were thrown in to strengthen this weak point. This was done about 1 P.M. It was only just in time, for in the afternoon the German infantry did begin to debouch from the wood, but finding organised resistance they dropped back, and their advance on this line was not renewed until the next morning, when it fell upon the Twenty-first Division. For a time the pressure was very great, but the men rallied splendidly round a tattered flag bearing the Cameron tartan, and, though it was impossible to get forward, they still, in a mixed and straggling line with hardly any officers, held firmly to their ground. Late in the evening the 13th Royal Scots and the 11th Argyll and Sutherlands came up to thicken the line.

Leaving the Fifteenth Division holding on desperately to that advanced position where, as Captain Beith has tersely said, a fringe of Jocks and Sandies lie to mark the farthest point of advance, we turn to the remaining division upon the right the Forty-seventh London, under General Barter. This division upheld splendidly upon this bloody day the secular reputation of the Cockney as a soldier. With a keen, quick brain, as well as a game heart, the Londoner, like the Parisian, has proved that the artificial life of a great city does not necessarily dull the primitive qualities which make the warrior. The cream of the London Territorial regiments had already been distributed among regular brigades, and had made themselves an individual name, but this was the first occasion upon which a whole division was engaged in a really serious operation.

The left of the division was formed by Thwaites' 141st Brigade with the 18th London Irish in the front line and the 20th Blackheath Battalion in immediate support. To their right was Cuthbert's 140th Brigade, which formed the extreme right of the whole attack, a position which caused them to think as much of their flank protection as of their frontal advance. This brigade had the 6th and 7th Londons in the van, with the 8th and 15th (Civil Service) in support. The 142nd Brigade (Willoughby) was in the second line.

The advance of the 141st Brigade was a splendid one. At the whistle the 18th London Irish, with a fighting yell, flooded over the parapet with their regimental football kicked in front of them, and were into the German trench like a thunderbolt. A few minutes later they were followed by the Blackheath men, who passed the captured trench, rushed on to the second, and finally won the third, which opened for them the road to Loos. Into the south end of Loos they streamed, while the 44th Brigade of the Fifteenth Division rushed the north end, turning out or capturing the 23rd Silesians, who held the post. The 19th St. Pancras Battalion followed up the attack, while the 17th (Poplar) were in reserve. Meanwhile, the 140th Brigade had done most useful work by making a lodgment on the Double Grassier, formidable twin slag-heaps which had become a German fort. The ground to the immediate south of Loos was rapidly seized and consolidated by the Londoners, several guns being captured in the chalk pits near the village. This operation was of permanent importance, as the successful British advance would inevitably form a salient projecting into the hostile lines, which would be vulnerable if there were not some good defensive position on the flank. The work of the Forty-seventh Division assured such a line in the south.

By mid-day, as has been shown, the British advance had spent its momentum, and had been brought to a standstill at all points. The German lines had been almost but not quite shattered. A map of the photographed trenches shows that beyond the point reached by the advanced troops there was only the last line which held them up. To the east of that was open country. But the German reserves were hurrying up from all quarters in their rear, from Roulers, from Thielt, from Courtrai and Menin and Douai. At the latter place was a division of Guards just brought across from the Russian front. These also were hurried into the fight. The extreme British line was too thin for defence, and was held by exhausted men. They were shelled and bombed and worn down by attack after attack until they were compelled to draw slowly back and re-form on interior lines. The grand salient which had been captured with such heroic dash and profuse loss of life was pared down here and contracted there. The portion to the south held by the Londoners was firmly consolidated, including the important village of Loos and its environs. An enormous mine crane, three hundred feet high, of latticed iron, which had formed an extraordinarily good observation point, was one of the gains in this direction. The Fifteenth Division had been driven back to the western side of Hill 70, and to the line of the Lens-Hulluch-La Bassée road. The Seventh and Ninth

Divisions had fallen back from Haisnes, but they still held the western outskirts of Hulluch, the edge of St. Élie, the Quarries, and Fosse 8. It was at this end of the line that the situation was most dangerous, for the failure of the Second Division to get forward had left a weak flank upon the north, which was weaker because the heavily-gunned German position of Auchy lay to the north-west of it in a way that partially enfiladed it.

The struggle was particularly desperate round the slag-heaps which were known as Fosse 8. This position was held all day by the 5th Camerons, the 8th Black Watch, and the 7th Seaforths of the 26th Brigade, the remaining battalion of which, the 8th Gordons, were with the bulk of the 27th Brigade in the direction of Haisnes. These three battalions, under a murderous fire from the Auchy guns and from the persistent bombers, held on most tenaciously till nightfall. When the welcome darkness came, without bringing them the longed-for supports, the defenders had shrunk to 600 men, but their grip of the position was not relaxed, and they held it against all attacks during the night. About five next morning the 73rd Brigade of the Twenty-fourth Division a unit straight from home pushed up to their help under circumstances to be afterwards explained, and shared their great dangers and losses during the second day of the fighting.

The battalions of the Ninth Division which had got as far as the outskirts of Haisnes held on there until evening. By that time no reinforcements had reached them and they had lost very heavily. Both their flanks were turned, and at nightfall they were driven back in the direction of the Quarries, which was held by those men of the Seventh Division (mostly of the 22nd Brigade) who had also been compelled to fall back from Hulluch. During the night this position was wired by the 54th Company of Royal Engineers, but the

Germans, by a sudden and furious attack, carried it, driving out the garrison and capturing some of them, among whom was General Bruce, the Brigadier of the 27th Brigade. After the capture of the Quarries, the flanks of the 27th Brigade were again turned, and it was compelled to return as far as the old German front line. The 20th Brigade had fallen back to the same point. These misfortunes all arose from the radically defective position of the northern British line, commanded as it was by German guns from its own left rear, and unprotected at the flank.

Whilst this set-back had occurred upon the left of the attack, the right had consolidated itself very firmly. The position of the Forty-seventh Division when darkness fell was that on their right the 140th Brigade had a strong grip of part of the Double Grassier. On their left the 19th Battalion (St. Pancras), which had lost its Colonel, Collison-Morley, and several senior officers, was holding South-east Loos in the rear of the right flank of the Fifteenth Division. The 20th was holding the Loos Chalk Pit, while the 17th and 18th were in the German second-line trenches.

There is reason to believe that the rapid dash of the stormers accomplished results more quickly than had been thought possible. The Twenty first and Twenty-fourth Divisions were now brought up, as Sir John French clearly states in his dispatch, for a specific purpose: "To ensure the speedy and effective support of the First and Fourth Corps in the case of their success, the Twenty-first and Twenty-fourth Divisions passed the night of the 24th and 25th on the line of Beuvry Noeux-les-Mines."

Leaving the front line holding hard to, or in some cases recoiling from, the advanced positions which they had won, we will turn back and follow the movements of these two divisions. It is well to remember that these divisions had not only never heard the whistle of a bullet, but they had never even been inside a trench, save on some English down-side. It is perhaps a pity that it could not be so arranged that troops so unseasoned in actual warfare should occupy some defensive line, while the older troops whom they relieved could have marched to battle. Apart, however, from this inexperience, which was no fault of their own or of their commanders, there is no doubt at all that the men were well-trained infantry and full of spirit. To bring them to the front without exciting attention, three separate night marches were undertaken, of no inordinate length, but tiring on account of the constant blockings of the road and the long waits which attended them. Finally they reached the point at which Sir John French reported them in his dispatch, but by ill-fortune their cookers came late, and they were compelled in many cases to move on again without a proper meal. After this point the cookers never overtook them, and the men were thrown back upon their iron rations. Providence is not a strong point of the British soldier, and it is probable that with more economy and foresight at the beginning these troops would have been less exhausted and hungry at the end. The want of food, however, was not the fault of the supply services.

The troops moved forward with no orders for an instant attack, but with the general idea that they were to wait as a handy reserve and go forward when called upon to do so. The 62nd Brigade of the Twenty-first Division was sent on first about eleven o'clock, but the other brigades were not really on the road till much later. The roads on which they moved those which lead through Vermelles to Hulluch or to Loos were blocked with traffic: guns advancing, ambulances returning, troops of all sorts coming and going, Maltese carts with small-arm ammunition hurrying forward to the fighting-line. The narrow channel was choked with the crowd. The country on either side was intersected with trenches and laced with barbed wire. It was pouring with intermittent showers. The soldiers, cold, wet, and hungry, made their way forward with many stoppages towards the firing, their general direction being to the centre of the British line.

"As we got over this plain," writes an officer, "I looked back, and there was a most extraordinary sight; as far as you could see there were thousands and thousands of our men coming up. You could see them for miles and miles, and behind them a most colossal thundercloud extending over the whole sky, and the rain was pouring down. It was just getting dark, and the noise of our guns and the whole thing was simply extraordinary."

Early on the march the leading brigade, the 73rd, was met by a staff officer of the First Army, who gave the order that it should detach itself, together with the 129th Field Company of Sappers, and hasten to the reinforcement of the Ninth Division at Fosse 8. They went, and the Twenty-fourth Division knew them no more. The other two brigades found themselves between 9 and 10 P.M. in the front German trenches. They had been able to deploy after leaving Vermelles, and the front line were now in touch with the 63rd Brigade of the Twenty-first Division upon the right, and with the 2nd Welsh Regiment, who represented the right of the 3rd Brigade of the First Division, upon their left. The final orders were that at eleven o'clock next day these three divisions First, Twenty-fourth, and Twenty-first were to make a united assault past Hulluch, which was assumed to be in our hands, and on to the main German line. This, then, was the position of the reserves on the night of September 25-26.

It was a nightmare night in the advanced line of the Army. The weather had been tempestuous and rainy all day, though the men had little time to think of such matters. But now they were not only tired and hungry, but soaked to the skin. An aggressive enemy pelted them with bombs from in front, and their prospects seemed as black as the starless sky above them. It is, however, at such a time that the British soldier, a confirmed grumbler in his hours of ease, shows to the best advantage. The men knew that much ground had been gained. They had seen prisoners by hundreds throwing up their hands, and had marked as they rushed past them the vicious necks of the half-buried captured cannon. It was victory for the Army, whatever might be their own discomfort. Their mood, therefore, was hilarious rather than doleful, and thousands of weary Mark Tapleys huddled under the dripping ledges of the parapets. "They went into battle with their tails right up, and though badly mauled have their tails up still." So wrote the officer of a brigade which had lost more than half its effectives.

VIII. THE BATTLE OF LOOS

The Second Day—September 26

Death of General Capper—Retirement of the Fifteenth Division— Advance of the Twenty-fourth and Twenty-first Divisions—Heavy losses — Desperate struggle—General retirement on the right—Rally round Loos—Position in the evening

Sunday the 26th was a day of hard fighting and of heavy losses, the reserves streaming up from the rear on both sides, each working furiously to improve its position. From early in the day the fighting was peculiarly bitter round Fosse 8 in the section carried and held by the Ninth Division. It has been already mentioned that three battalions, the 5th Camerons, 7th Seaforths, and 8th Black Watch of the 26th Brigade, held this place all the evening of the 25th and all night, until reduced to less than the strength of a regiment. It has also been stated that the 73rd Brigade had been detached from the Twenty-fourth Division to their aid. These men, with no preliminary hardening, found themselves suddenly thrust into one of the very hottest corners of a desperate fight. Under these circumstances it is all to the credit of these troops that they were able to hold their position all day, though naturally their presence was not of the same value as that of a more veteran brigade.

The 73rd Brigade were put into German trenches to the east of Fosse 8, their order from the left being 7th Northamptons, 12th Royal Fusiliers, and 9th Sussex, with the 13th Middlesex echeloned on their right rear. They were constantly attacked, but were suffering more from cold, hunger, and exhaustion than from the Germans. All day they and the remains of the Scots held the place against intermittent assaults, which occasionally had some partial success, but never quite enabled the enemy to re-establish his position. It was not, however, until the morning of the 27th, as will afterwards be narrated, that their most severe ordeal was to come.

Close to Fosse 8, and on the south of it, was the Death of position of the Quarries, from which the 22nd Brigade (Capper) of the Seventh Division had been driven by a sudden rush of the Germans during the night. After an abortive but expensive attack by the 9th Norfolks next morning, there was a more serious effort by a body of mixed troops, led by Captain Carter and including several units of the Second Division, notably the 2nd Worcesters and 1st Rifles. These battalions pushed their way up to the Quarries, and although they were unable to evict the Germans they established themselves firmly close to the south-western edge and there awaited events. To the south of them the 20th Brigade of the Seventh Division held firmly to their line. It was on this day that they lost their heroic leader, Sir Thomson Capper, the fine soldier who had so often braced by word and example their ever-thinning lines during the black days of Ypres, with which his name and that of his division will be eternally associated. There was no more valiant or trusted leader in the Army. He was shot through the lungs, was carried to the rear, and died in hospital next day. "We are here to do the impossible" was one of the fiery aphorisms which he left to the Army.

On the southern front of the British there was also an inclination to contract the line upon the morning of the 26th. The fact that the French attack upon the right on the day before had not had much success rendered that wing very open to a flank attack. The Fifteenth Scottish Division still held on hard to the slopes of Hill 70, but early in the day their line had been driven somewhat to the westward. At nine o'clock they had renewed their attack upon Hill 70, supported by some reinforcements. They were not strong enough, nor was their artillery support sufficiently powerful to enable them to carry the crest of the hill. When their advance was checked the Germans returned upon them with a series of counter-attacks which gradually drove them down the hill. In the desperate series of rallies in which they made head against the Germans it is difficult to distinguish regiments, since the men fought for the most part in a long, scattered fringe of mixed units, each dour infantryman throwing up his own cover and fighting his own battle. The 6th Camerons preserved their cohesion, however, and particularly distinguished themselves, their gallant leader, Douglas Hamilton, falling at their head in the thick of the fight. "I must get up! I must get up!" were his last words before he expired. The final effect of these episodes was to drive the British off the greater part of the slope of Hill 70, and down towards the village of Loos.

It will be remembered that the weary Twenty-fourth Division (Ramsay), with its comrade the Twenty-first (Forestier-Walker) upon its right and the Regular First Division upon its left, had received its orders to advance at eleven o'clock. It had been supposed that Hulluch was in British hands, but this was found not to be so. The orders, however, still held good. The Twenty-fourth Division had already been stripped of the 73rd Brigade, and now it was further denuded by two battalions of the 71st, the 9th Norfolks and 8th Bedfords, who were told off to help to retake the Quarries. The Norfolks made an attack upon a strong position, and lost 200 men and officers in the attempt. The Bedfords, who were in support, lost touch both with their own division and with the one that they were helping, so that they were not strongly engaged during the day.

The hour had now come for the general advance. General Mitford with the 72nd Brigade was leading, with two battalions of the 71st Brigade behind, and his pioneer battalion in support. On his left was the 2nd Welsh, and, as he imagined, the whole of the First Division. On his right was the 63rd Brigade and the rest of the Twenty-first Division, less the 62nd Brigade, as afterwards explained. It formed a solid wall of 20,000 infantry which might well turn the tide of a great battle.

We shall follow this advance of the Twenty-fourth Division upon the left, who were compelled to go forward with their flank exposed on account of some delay in the attack by the First Division. Afterwards we shall return to consider the movements of the Twenty-first Division on their right. The leading brigade, the 72nd, moved forward with the 8th West Kents upon the left, and the 9th East Surreys upon the right. Behind them were the 8th Queen's Surreys (left) and the 8th Buffs (right), with the pioneer battalion, the 12th

Sherwood Foresters, in support. They were followed by the two remaining battalions of the 71st Brigade, the 9th Suffolks and the 11th Essex. As the advance continued the second line joined with the first, and the 11th Essex from behind also pushed its way abreast of the foremost. The line of advance was to the south of Hulluch, and this line was preserved. As matters turned out, the numerous guns in the south of that village were all available for defence against the advance of the Twenty-fourth Division. This caused them very heavy losses, but in spite of them they swept onwards with an unfaltering energy which was a monument to those long months of preparation during which Sir John Ramsay had brought his men to a high state of efficiency. Under every possible disadvantage of hunger, cold, exhaustion, and concentrated fire, they behaved with a steadiness which made them worthy of the honoured names which gleamed upon their shoulder- straps. One platoon of the Essex diverged into Hulluch in a vain attempt to stop the machine-guns and so shield their comrades. Hardly a man of this body survived. The rest kept their eyes front, took their punishment gamely, and pushed on for their objective. The breadth of the attack was such that it nearly covered the space between Hulluch in the north and the Bois Hugo in the south. About mid-day the Twenty-fourth Division had reached a point across the Lens-Hulluch road which was ahead of anything attained in this quarter the day before. They were up against unbroken wire with an enfilade rifle and machine- gun fire from both flanks and from Hulluch on their left rear, as well as a heavy shell-fire of asphyxiating shells. A gallant attempt was made to pierce the wires, which were within fifty yards of the German position, but it was more than flesh and blood could do. They were driven back, and in the retirement across the long slope which they had traversed their losses were greatly increased. Their wounded had to be left behind, and many of these fell afterwards into the hands of the

Germans, receiving honourable treatment from them. The losses would have been heavier still had it not been that the Suffolks in support lined up in a sunken road three hundred yards south of Hulluch, and kept down the fire of the machine-guns. Some of these raw battalions endured losses which have never been exceeded in this war before they could finally persuade themselves that the task was an impossible one. The 8th West Rents lost their Colonel, Vansittart, 24 officers, and 556 men; the 8th Buffs their Colonel, Homer, 24 officers, and 534 men; the other battalions were nearly as hard hit. These figures speak for themselves. Mortal men could not have done more. The whole brigade lost 78 officers and 2000 men out of about 3600 engaged in the attack. When these soldiers walked back and there is testimony that their retirement was in many cases at a walk they had earned the right to take their stand with any troops in the world. The survivors resumed their place about 1:30 in the German trenches, where for the rest of the day they endured a very heavy shelling. The movements of the Twenty-first Division upon the right were of a very much more complex nature, and there is a conflict of evidence about them which makes the task of the historian a peculiarly difficult one. The great outstanding fact, however, which The story presents itself in the case of each of the three brigades is that the men in nearly every instance behaved with a steady gallantry under extraordinarily difficult circumstances which speaks volumes for their soldierly qualities. Sir Edward Hutton, who raised them, and General Forestier-Walker, who led them, had equal cause to be contented with the personnel. "The men were perfectly magnificent, quite cool and collected, and would go anywhere," says one wounded officer. "The only consolation I have is the memory of the magnificent pluck and bravery shown by our good men. Never shall I forget it," cries another. It is necessary to emphasise the fact, because rumours got about at the time that all was not as it should be rumours which came from men who were either ignorant of all the facts or were not aware of the tremendous strain which was borne by this division during the action. These rumours were cruel libels upon battalions many of which sustained losses in this their first action which have seldom been matched during the war. We will follow the fortunes of each brigade in turn, holding the balance as far as possible amid evidence which, as already stated, is complex and conflicting.

The 62nd Brigade (Wilkinson), consisting of the 8th East Yorks, 10th Yorks, 12th and 13th Northumberland Fusiliers, with the 14th Northumberland Fusiliers as pioneer battalion, was hurried away separately and taken to the south and east of Loos to reinforce the Fifteenth Division, which had sustained such losses on the 25th that they could not hold both the front and the flank.

The 62nd pushed on, reached the point of danger The as early as the night of the 25th, and occupied a line of slag-heaps to the south-east of Loos, where there was a gap through which the enemy could penetrate from the flank. It was a prolongation of the same general defensive line which had been established and held by the Forty-seventh Division, and it was the more important as the French advance upon our right had not progressed so far as our own, leaving our right flank in the air, exactly as our left flank had been left open by the holding up of the Second Division. The 62nd Brigade was only just in time in getting hold of the position, for it was strongly attacked at five in the morning of the 26th. The attack fell mainly upon the 8th East Yorkshires and the 10th Yorkshires, who were driven back from the farther side of the great dump which was the centre of the fight, but held on to the Loos side of it with the support of the 13th Northumberland Fusiliers. This line was held all day of the 26th. So stem was the fighting that the

Fusiliers lost 17 officers and 400 men, while the 8th East Yorkshires at the slag-heaps lost the same heavy proportion of officers and 300 men. More than once the fighting was actually hand to hand, especially with the East Yorkshires. Colonel Hadow, together with Majors Noyes and Dent, all of the 10th Yorkshires, were killed, while Colonel Way of the East Yorkshires was wounded. It will be noted, then, that the 62nd Brigade was working independently of the rest of the Twenty-first Division on one flank, as the 73rd of the Twenty-fourth Division was upon the other.

The main attack of the division was carried out by the 63rd and 64th Brigades, the only ones which The remained under the command of General Forestier-Walker. A formidable line of obstacles faced them as they formed up, including the Chalk Pit and the Chalk Pit Wood, and on the other side of the Lens-Hulluch road, upon their right front, Fosse 14 and the Bois Hugo, the latter a considerable plantation full of machine-guns and entanglements. The original plan had been that the advance should be simultaneous with that upon the left, but the enemy were very active from an early hour upon this front, and the action seems, therefore, to have been accelerated. Indeed, the most reasonable view of what occurred seems to be that the enemy had themselves planned a great attack at this point at that hour, that the bickerings of the morning were their preliminary bombardment, and that the British attack became speedily a defensive action, in which the 63rd Brigade was shattered by the weight of the enemy attack, but inflicted such loss upon it that it could get no farther, and ceased to endanger the continuity of our line. It is only on this supposition of a double simultaneous attack that one can reconcile the various statements of men, some of whom looked upon the movement as an attack and some as a defence.

The 63rd Brigade (Nicholls) moved forward with the 8th Lincolns upon the right and the 12th Yorkshires upon the left. These regiments advanced to a point just east of the Lens-Hulluch road. In support, on the immediate west of the road, lining the Chalk Pit Wood, were the 10th Yorks and Lancasters, with the 8th Somersets. For several hours this position was maintained under a heavy and deadly fire.

"The shells ploughed the men out of their shallow trenches as potatoes are turned from a furrow," says an officer. Two companies of the 8th Somersets, however, seem to have lost direction and wandered off to Hill 70, where they were involved in the fighting of the Fifteenth Division. Two companies of the Yorks and Lancasters were also ordered up in that direction, where they made a very heroic advance. A spectator watching them from Hill 70 says: "Their lines came under the machine-guns as soon as they were clear of the wood. They had to lie down. Many, of course, were shot down. After a bit their lines went forward again and had to go down again. They went on, forward a little and then down, and forward a little and then down, until at last five gallant figures rose up and struggled forward till they, too, went down... The repeated efforts to get forward through the fire were very fine."

These four companies having left, there remained only two of the Somersets and two of the Yorks and Lancasters in the wood. Their comrades in advance had in the meantime become involved in a very fierce struggle in the Bois Hugo. Here, after being decimated by the machine-guns, they met and held for a time the full force of the German attack. The men of Yorkshire and of Lincolnshire fought desperately against heavy masses of troops, thrown forward with great gallantry and disregard of loss. For once the British rifle-fire had a chance, and exacted its usual high toll. "We cut line after line of the enemy down as they advanced." So rapid was the fire that cartridges began to run low, and men were seen crawling up to their dead comrades to ransack their pouches.

The enemy was dropping fast, and yet nothing could stop him. Brigadier Nicholls walked up to the firing line with reckless bravery and gave the order to charge. Bayonets were actually crossed, and the enemy thrown back. The gallant Nicholls fell, shot in the thigh and stomach, and the position became impossible. The Lincolns had suffered the appalling loss of all their officers and 500 men. The Yorkshires were in no better case. The survivors fell back rapidly upon the supports.

Fortunately, these were in close attendance. As the remains of the Lincolns and the West Yorkshires, after their most gallant and desperate resistance to the overwhelming German attack, came pouring back with few officers and in a state of some confusion from the Bois Hugo and over the Lens-Hulluch road, the four companies under Majors Howard and Taylor covered their retreat and held up for a time the German swarms behind them, the remains of the four battalions fighting in one line.

One party of mixed Lincolns and Yorkshires held out for about seven hours in an advanced trench, which was surrounded by the enemy about eleven, and the survivors, after sustaining very heavy losses—"the trench was like a shambles"—did not surrender until nearly six o'clock, when their ammunition had all been shot away. The isolation of this body was caused by the fact that their trenches lay opposite the south end of the Bois Hugo. The strong German attack came round the north side of the wood, and thus, as it progressed, a considerable number of the Lincolns and some of the West Yorks, still holding the line upon the right, were entirely cut off. Colonel Walter of the

Lincolns, with Major Storer, Captains Coates and Stronguist, and three lieutenants, are known to have been killed, while almost all the others were wounded. A number of our wounded were left in the hands of the Germans. There is no doubt that the strength of the German attack and the resistance offered to it were underrated by the public at the time, which led to the circulation of cruel and unjust rumours.

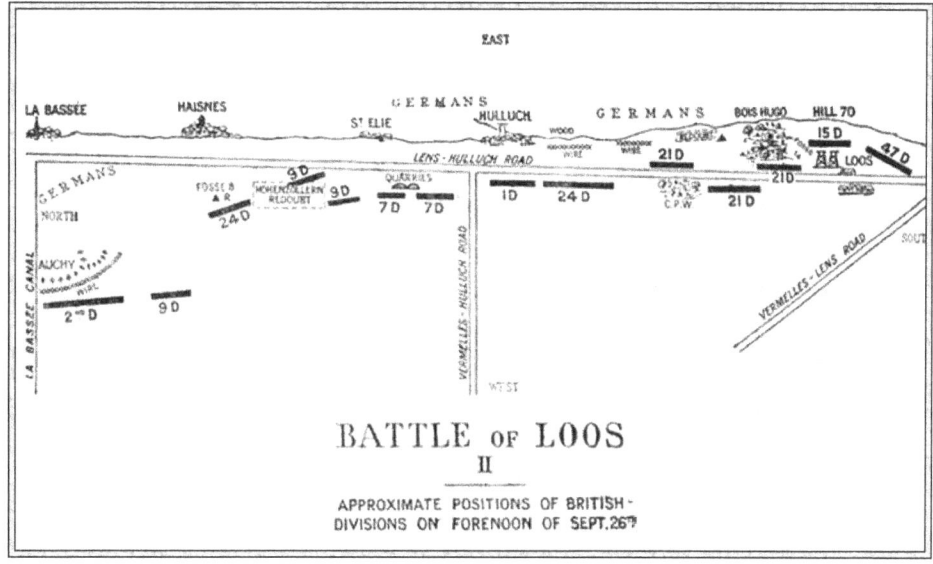

Battle of Loos 2

The 64th Brigade (Gloster) was in support some little distance to the right rear of the 63rd, covering the ground between the Lens-Hulluch road and Loos. About noon a message was received by them to the effect that the 63rd was being very strongly pressed, and that help was urgently needed. The 14th Durham Light Infantry was moved forward in support, and came at once under heavy fire, losing its Colonel (Hamilton), 17 officers, and about 200 men. The 15th Durham Light Infantry was then thrown into the fight, and sustained even heavier losses. Colonel Logan, 18 officers, and 400 men were killed or wounded. About one o'clock the two Durham battalions were in the thick of the fight, while Captain Liebenrood, machine-gun officer of the 64th Brigade, did good work in keeping down the enemy fire. The two battalions of Yorkshire Light Infantry (9th and 10th) were held in reserve. About 2:30 the pressure upon the front of the 63rd Brigade had become too great, and both it and the two Durham battalions were driven back. Their resistance, however, seems to have taken the edge off the dangerous counter-attack, for the Germans did not come on past the line of the road and of the Chalk Pit Wood.

It will be remembered that when the two advanced brigades of the Fifteenth Division established themselves in hastily-dug trenches upon the western slope of Hill 70, they threw back their left flank obliquely down the hill towards Fosse 14 in order to avoid being at the mercy of any force which endeavoured to get behind them on this side. Only a very thin line of men could be spared for this work, under a young Australian subaltern named M'Neil. These soldiers held the post for twenty-four hours, but when the heavy German attack which drove in the Twenty-first Division and cut off the Lincolns struck up against them, they were all killed or wounded, including their gallant leader, who managed, with several bullets in him, to get back to the British line. This led to the final retirement down Hill 70 of the men of the Scotch Division, who dug themselves in once more at the foot of the hill, not far from the village of Loos.

The losses. It may be noted that the losses of the two supporting divisions were about 8000 men. Their numbers in infantry were about equal to the British troops at Waterloo, and their casualties were approximately the same. Mention has already been made of the endurance of

Mitford's 72nd Brigade. The figures of the 63rd and their comrades of the 64th are little inferior. Of these troops more than 40 per cent of the rank and file, 65 per cent of their officers, and 75 per cent of their commanders lay upon the field of battle. When one recollects that 33 per cent was reckoned a high rate of loss by the greatest authorities upon warfare, and when one remembers that these were raw troops fighting under every discomfort and disadvantage, one feels that they have indeed worthily continued the traditions of the old Army and founded those of the new. There were isolated cases of unordered retirement, but in the main the regiments showed the steadiness and courage which one would expect from the good North-country stock from which they came.

The divisional artillery of the Twenty-first Division had come into action in the open behind the advancing infantry, and paid the price for their gallant temerity. The 94th Brigade E.F.A. lost especially heavily, eight of its guns being temporarily put out of action. Major Dobson of this brigade was among the killed. It is to be feared that the guns did not always realise the position of the infantry, and that many of the 64th Brigade especially were hit by their own shrapnel. Such painful incidents seem almost inseparable from modern warfare. The artillery kept its place, and afterwards rendered good service by supporting the advance of the Guards.

Whilst this advance and check had taken place in the centre and right centre of the British position, the London Division, upon the extreme right, was subjected rather to bombardment than to assault. A heavy fall of asphyxiating shells was experienced a little after 9 A.M., and many men were gassed before they were able to put on their helmets. The second German line of captured trenches was held very firmly by General Thwaites with the rest of the 141st

Brigade, while the 140th retained a defensive flank, the whole forming a strong *point d'appui* for a rally and reorganisation. Men of the Twenty-first Division re-formed upon this line, and the battle was soon re-established. This re-establishment was materially helped by the action of the 9th and 10th Yorkshire Light Infantry battalions previously mentioned of the Twenty-first Division, who had become a divisional reserve. These two battalions now advanced and gained some ground to the east of Loos on the enemy's left flank. It may be mentioned that one of these battalions was ordered to discard its packs in order to ease the tired soldiers, and that on advancing from their trenches these packs were never regained. Their presence afterwards may have given the idea that equipment had been abandoned, whereas an actual order had been obeyed. The movement covered the reorganisation which was going on behind them. One small detachment under Captain Laskie of the 10th Y.L.I, did especially good work. The Yorkshiremen were aided by men of the Northumberland Fusiliers of the 62nd Brigade, who held on to the trenches to the east of Loos. A cavalry detachment from Campbell's 6th Cavalry Brigade, under Campbell himself, had also appeared about 4 P.M. as a mobile reserve and thrown itself into Loos to strengthen the defence.

The evening of this day, September 26, found the British lines contracted as compared with what they had been in the morning. The Forty-seventh Division had, if anything, broadened and strengthened their hold upon the southern outskirts of Loos. The western slope of Hill 70 was still held in part. Thence the line bent back to the Loos-La Bassée road, followed the line of that road for a thousand yards, thence onwards to near the west end of the village of Hulluch, and then as before. But the exchanges would seem to have been in favour of the Germans, since they had pushed the British back for a stretch of about a mile from the Lens-Hulluch road, thus making a dent in their front. On both sides reserves were still mustering. The Guards' Division had been brought up by Sir John French, and were ready for operations upon the morning of the 27th, while the Twenty-eighth Division was on its way. The Germans, who had been repeatedly assured that the British Army extension was a bluff, and that the units existed only upon paper, must have found some food for thought as the waves rolled up.

IX. THE BATTLE OF LOOS

From September 27 to the End of the Year

Loss of Fosse 8—Death of General Thesiger—Advance of the Guards—Attack of the Twenty-eighth Division—Arrival of the Twelfth Division—German counter-attacks—Attack by the Forty-sixth Division upon Hohenzollern Redoubt—Subsidiary attacks —General observations—Return of Lord French to England

The night of September 26 was a restless and tumultuous one, the troops being much exhausted by their long ordeal, which involved problems of supply unknown in any former wars. The modern soldier must be a great endurer as well as an iron fighter.

The Germans during the night were very pushful in all directions. Their reserves are said to have been very mixed, and there was evidence of forty- eight battalions being employed against the British line, but their attacks were constant and spirited. The advanced positions were, however, maintained, and the morning of the 27th found the attackers, after two days of incessant battle, still keeping their grip upon their gains.

The main part of the day began badly for the British, however, as in the early morning they were pushed off Fosse 8, which was an extremely important point and the master-key of the whole position, as its high slag-heap commanded Slag Alley and a number of the other trenches to the south of it, including most of the Hohenzollern Redoubt. The worn remains of the 26th Brigade were still holding the pit when morning dawned, and the units of the 73rd Brigade (Jelf) were in a semicircle to the east and south of it. These battalions, young troops who had never heard the whiz of a bullet before, had now been in close action for thirty-six hours, and had been cut off from all supplies of food and water for two days. Partly on account of their difficult tactical position, and partly because they were ignorant of how communications are kept up in the trenches, they had become entirely isolated. It was on these exhausted troops that the storm now broke. The northern unit consisted of the 7th Northamptons, whose left wing seems to have been in the air. Next to them were the 12th Royal Fusiliers. There had been several infantry attacks, which were repulsed during the night. Just at the dawn two red rockets ascended from the German lines, and at the same moment an intense bombardment opened upon Fosse 8, causing great loss among the occupants. It was at this time that General Thesiger, Commander of the Ninth Division, together with his Staff- Major, Burney, was killed by a shell. Colonel Livingstone, Divisional C.O. of Engineers, and Colonel Wright, of the 8th Gordons, were also hit. In the obstinate defence of the post the 90th Company R.E. fought as infantry, after they had done all that was possible to strengthen the defences.

A strong infantry attack had immediately followed the bombardment. They broke in, to the number of about a thousand, between the Northamptons and Fusiliers. By their position they were now able to command Fosse 8, where the 9th Sussex had been, and also to make untenable the position of the 27th Brigade, which occupied trenches to the south which could be enfiladed. In "The First Hundred Thousand" will be found a classical account of the straits of these troops and their retirement to a safer position. General Jelf telephoned in vain for the support of heavy guns, and even released a carrier pigeon with the same urgent request. Seeing that Fosse 8 was lost, he determined to hold on hard to the Hohenzollern Redoubt, and lined its trenches with the broken remains of his wearied brigade. The enemy at once attacked with swarms of well- provided bombers in the van, but were met foot to foot by the bombers of the 73rd Brigade, who held them up. The 26th Brigade endeavoured to counter-attack, but were unable to get forward against the machine-guns, but their bombers joined those of the English brigade and did splendid work. The ground was held until the troops, absolutely at the limit of human endurance, were relieved by the 85th Brigade of the Twenty-eighth Division, as will be described later. The trench held by the Sussex was commanded from above and attacked by bombers from below, so that the battalion had a very severe ordeal. Lieutenant Shackles defended a group of cabarets at one end of the position until he and every man with him was dead or wounded. Having taken that corner, the Germans bombed down the trench. Captain MacIvor with thirty men on that flank were all killed or wounded, but the officer leading the bombers was shot by Captain Langden and the position saved. Nineteen officers and 360 men fell in this one battalion.

"We gained," said one of them, "two Military Crosses and many wooden ones." It had been an anxious day for all, and most of all for General Jelf, who had been left without a staff, both his major and his captain having fallen.

Up to mid-day of the 27th the tide of battle had The set against the British, but after that hour there came into action a fresh force, which can never be employed without leaving its mark upon the conflict. This was the newly-formed division of Guards (Lord Cavan), consisting of the eight battalions which had already done such splendid service from Mons onwards, together with the newly-formed Welsh Guards, the 3rd and 4th Grenadier Guards, the 2nd Coldstream, and the 2nd Irish.

On September 25 the Guards reached Noeux-les-Mines, and on September 26 were at Sailly-la-Bourse. On the morning of the 27th they moved forward upon the same general line which the previous attack had taken that is, between Hulluch on the left and Loos on the right and relieved the two divisions which had suffered so heavily upon the previous day. The general distribution of the Guards was that the 1st Brigade (Fielding), consisting of the 2nd Grenadiers, 2nd and 3rd Coldstream, and 1st Irish, were on the left. They had taken over trenches from the First Division, and were now in touch upon their left with the Seventh Division. On the right of the 1st Guards' Brigade was the 2nd (Ponsonby), consisting of the 3rd Grenadiers, 1st Coldstream, 1st Scots, and 2nd Irish. On their right again, in the vicinity of Loos, was the 3rd Brigade (Heyworth), the 1st and 4th Grenadiers, 2nd Scots, and 1 st Welsh. These last two brigades, upon which the work fell for the 1st Brigade remained in a holding position were operating roughly upon the same ground as the Twenty-first Division had covered the Before, and had in their immediate front the same wood—the Chalk Pit Wood—from which we had been driven, and the Chalk Pit near the Lens-Hulluch road, which we had also lost, while a little more to the right was the strong post of Fosse 14 and the long slope of Hill 70, the whole of which had passed back into the hands of the enemy. These formidable obstacles were the immediate objective of the Guards. During the night of the 26th-27th many stragglers from the Twenty-first and Twenty-fourth Divisions passed through the Guards, informing them that their front was practically clear of British troops, and that they were face to face with the enemy.

At 2:30 P.M. the British renewed their heavy bombardment in the hope of clearing the ground for the advance. There is evidence that upon the 25th the enemy had been so much alarmed by the rapid advance that they had hurriedly removed a good deal of their artillery upon the Lens side. This had now been brought back, as we found to our cost. At four o'clock the heavy guns eased off, and the two brigades of Guards (2nd and 3rd) advanced, moving forward in artillery formation that is, in small clumps of platoons, separated from each other.

The 2nd Irish were given their baptism of fire by being placed in the van of the 2nd Brigade with orders to make good the wood in front. The 1st Coldstream were to support them. Advancing in splendid order, they reached the point without undue loss, and dug themselves in according to orders. As they lay there their comrades of the 1st Scots passed on their right under very heavy fire in salvos of high-explosive shells, and carried Fosse 14 by storm in the most admirable manner, while the Irish covered them with their rifle-fire. Part of the right-hand company of the Irish Guards got drawn into this attack and rushed forward with the Scots. Having taken Fosse 14, this body of men pushed impetuously forward, met a heavy German counter-attack, and were driven back. Their two young leaders, Lieutenants Clifford and Kipling, were seen no more. The German attack came with irresistible strength, supported by a very heavy enfilade fire. The remains of the Scots Guards were driven with heavy losses out of Fosse 14, and both they and the

Irish were thrown back as far as the line of the Loos-Hulluch road.

The remains of the shaken battalions were joined by two companies of the 2nd Coldstream and reformed for another effort. In this attack of the 2nd Brigade upon Fosse 14, the Scots were supported by two companies of the 3rd Grenadiers, the other two being in general reserve. These two companies, coming up independently somewhat later than the main advance, were terribly shelled, but reached their objective, where they endured renewed losses. The officers were nearly all put out of action, and eventually a handful of survivors were brought back to the Chalk Pit Wood by Lieutenant Ritchie, himself severely wounded.

Captain Alexander, with some of the Irish, had succeeded also in holding their ground in the Chalk Pit Wood, though partly surrounded by the German advance, and they now sent back urgently for help. A fresh advance was made, in the course of which the other two companies of Coldstreamers pushed forward on the left of the wood and seized the Chalk Pit. It was hard soil and trenching was difficult, but the line of the wood and of the pit was consolidated as far as possible. A dangerous gap had been left between the 1st Coldstream, who were now the extreme left of the 2nd Brigade, and the right of the 1st Brigade. It was filled up by 150 men, hastily collected, who frustrated an attempt of the enemy to push through. This line was held until dark, though the men had to endure a very heavy and accurate shelling, against which they had little protection. In the early morning the 1st Coldstream made a fresh advance from the north-west against Fosse 14, but could make no headway against the German fire. The line of Chalk Pit Wood now became the permanent line of the Army.

The 3rd Brigade of Guards had advanced at the same time as the 2nd, their attack being on the immediate right on the line of Fosse 14 and Hill 70. It may indeed be said that the object of the 2nd Brigade attack upon Fosse 14 was very largely to silence or engage the machine-guns there and so make it easier for the 3rd Brigade to make headway at Hill 70. The Guardsmen advanced with great steadiness up the long slope of the hill, and actually gained the crest, the Welsh and the 4th Grenadiers in the lead, but a powerful German redoubt which swept the open ground with its fire made the summit untenable, and they were compelled to drop back over the crest line, where they dug themselves in and remained until this section of the line was taken over by the Twelfth Division.

The Guards had lost very heavily during these operations. The 2nd Irish had lost 8 officers and 324 men, while the 1st Scots and 1st Coldstream had suffered about as heavily. The 3rd Brigade had been even more severely hit, and the total loss of the division could have been little short of 3000. They continued to hold the front line until September 30, when the 35th and 36th Brigades of the Twelfth Division relieved them for a short rest. The Fifteenth Division had also been withdrawn, after having sustained losses which had probably never been excelled up to that hour by any single division in one action during the campaign. It is computed that no fewer than 6000 of these gallant Scots had fallen, the greater part upon the blood-stained slope and crest of Hill 70. Of the 9th Black Watch little more than 100 emerged safely, but an observer has recorded that their fierce and martial bearing was still that of victors.

The curve of the British position presented a perimeter which was about double the length of the arc which marked the original trenches. Thus a considerably larger force was needed to hold it, which was the more difficult to provide as so many divisions had already suffered heavy losses.

The French attack at Souchez having come to a standstill, Sir John French asked General Foch, the Commander of the Tenth Army, to take over the defence of Loos, which was done from the morning of the 28th by our old comrades of Ypres, the Ninth Corps. During this day there was a general rearrangement of units, facilitated by the contraction of the line brought about by the presence of our Allies. The battle-worn divisions of the first line were withdrawn, while Bulfin's Twenty-eighth Division came up to take their place.

The Twenty-eighth Division, of Ypres renown, had reached Vermelles in the early morning of Monday the 27th—the day of the Guards' advance. The general plan seems to have been that it should restore the fight upon the left half of the battlefield, while the Guards' Division did the same upon the right. General Bulfin, the able and experienced Commander of the Twenty-eighth, found himself suddenly placed in command of the Ninth also, through the death of General Thesiger. The situation which faced him was a most difficult one, and it took cool judgment in so confused a scene to make sure where his force should be applied. Urgent messages had come in to the effect that the defenders of Fosse 8 had been driven out, that as a consequence the whole of the Hohenzollern Redoubt was on the point of recapture, and that the Quarries had been wrested from the Seventh Division by the enemy. A very strong German attack was surging in from the north, and if it should advance much farther our advance line would be taken in the rear. It was clear that the Twenty-eighth Division had only just arrived in time. The 85th Brigade under General Pereira was hurried forward, and found things in a perilous state in the Hohenzollern Redoubt, where the remains of the 26th and 73rd Brigades, driven from Fosse 8 and raked by guns from the great dump, were barely holding on to the edge of the stronghold. The 2nd Buffs dashed forward with all the energy of fresh troops, swept the enemy out of the redoubt, pushed them up the trench leading northwards, which is called "Little Willie" ("Big Willie" leads eastward), and barricaded the southern exit. Matters were hung up for a time by the wounding both of General Pereira and of his Brigade-Major Flower, but Colonel Roberts, of the 3rd Royal Fusiliers, carried on. The Royal Fusiliers relieved the Buffs, and the 2nd East Surrey took over the left of the line.

An attack was organised upon the powerful position at Fosse 8, but it had to be postponed until the morning of September 28. At 9 A.M. the 2nd Buffs delivered a very strong assault. The 3rd Middlesex were to have supported them, but came under so heavy a fire in their trenches that they were unable to get forward. The Buffs, in the face of desperate opposition, scrambled up the difficult sides of the great dump a perfect hill self-erected as a monument of generations of labour. They reached the summit, but found it swept by gusts of fire which made all life impossible. Colonel Worthington and fifteen of his officers were killed or wounded in the gallant venture. Finally, the remains of the battalion took cover from the fire in Dump Trench at the bottom of the hill. It was in this trench that the Middlesex men had been held. Their Colonel, Neale, had also been killed. From this time onwards Fosse 8 was left in the hands of the Germans, and the action of the Twenty-eighth Division became more of a defensive one to prevent any further whittling away of the ground already gained.

As the pressure was still great from the direction of Fosse 8, two battalions of the 83rd Brigade, the 1st York and Lancasters and 1st Yorkshire Light Infantry, were sent up to reinforce the line. On the 29th they helped to repel two attacks all along the front of the redoubt, one in the morning and one in the afternoon, when the Germans came on to the surface only to be shot back into their burrows again. On the same day the 83rd and 84th Brigades relieved the weary Seventh Division in the Quarries. Whilst these operations had been carried on upon the north half of the field of battle, to the left of the bisecting road, the Twelfth Division, a South England unit of the New Army, had moved forward into the space to the right of the road, taking over the trenches held by the Guards, and connecting up with the French at Loos. Save in the sector occupied by the Twenty-eighth Division the action had died down, and the British, aided partly by those pioneer battalions which had been formed out of ordinary infantry regiments to do work usually assigned to the sappers, strengthened their hold upon the ground that they had won, in the sure conviction that they would soon have to defend it. The shell-fire continued to be heavy upon both sides, and in the course of it General Wing, of the Twelfth Division, was unfortunately killed, being struck by a shell outside his divisional headquarters. He had been one of the artillery officers who had most to do with the fine handling of the guns of the Second Corps at Le Cateau, and was a very rising soldier of the most modern sort. Three divisional generals killed Capper, Wing, and Thesiger and one brigadier a prisoner! Such losses in the higher ranks are hardly to be matched in our history. To equal them one has to go back a hundred years to that supreme day when Picton, De Lancy, Ponsonby, and so many others died in front of their troops upon the historic plateau of Waterloo.

On October 1, at eight in the evening, Bulfin's men were hard at work once more. It will be remembered that the "Little Willie" Trench had been plugged at the southern end by the Buffs three days before. The Germans still held the main line of it, but could not get down it into the

Hohenzollern Redoubt. It was now charged most brilliantly and carried by the 1st Welsh, of the 84th Brigade, but after holding it for a day they lost so heavily that they were compelled to resume their old position once more. The 1st Suffolk tried to win the ground back, but without success.

Upon the afternoon of Sunday, October 3, the fighting, which had died down, broke out once more. The front line at this date was formed by the Ninth French Corps, our splendid comrades of Ypres, upon the right, occupying Loos and that portion of the slopes of Hill 70 which had remained in our hands. On their left was the Twelfth British Division up to the Vermelles-Hulluch road, and to their left Bulfin's Twenty-eighth Division, holding the northern area, including the Hohenzollern Redoubt. For several days the bombing parties of the enemy had been eating their way into this fortress, and upon the 3rd the greater part of it reverted into their hands, the enemy driving in the 84th Brigade. These attacks were based upon their strong positions in the north, and supported by the machine-guns of Fosse 8 and the heavy artillery of Auchy. On the same day a strong force advanced against the right of the Twenty-eighth Division between the Quarries and the Vermelles-Hulluch road, but this attack was repulsed with heavy loss.

On October 4 and 5 the Twenty-eighth Division was withdrawn, and the Guards, after three days' rest, were called upon once more, the 3rd Guards Brigade taking its position at the section of the Hohenzollern Redoubt which we held, while the 1st was on their right, and the 2nd in reserve at Vermelles. At the same time the First Division moved to the front on the right of the Guards, relieving the Twelfth Division. All these troops were keenly alive to the fact that the Germans were unlikely to sit down under their defeat, and that the pause was only the preliminary to a great counter-attack. All efforts were therefore made to consolidate the ground. The great The expectations were fulfilled, for upon October 8 the enemy brought up their reserves from far and near, determined to have back the ground that they had lost. The British and French were no less inexorable in their grip of that which had cost them so much to win. It is the attacker in modern warfare who pays the price. Sometimes he gets the value of his blood, sometimes he pays it freely and gets nothing whatever in exchange. So it was in this instance. Along the whole long curve of the defence, from the southern trenches of the Hohenzollern Redoubt in the north to the French position in the south, the roar of the battle went up. On the left of the French was the First Division, on their left the Twelfth, on theirs the Guards, on theirs the Seventh, stout fighters all. The Germans rushed on boldly, swarms of bombers in front, lines of supporting infantry behind. Everywhere they were cut down and brought to a stand by the sleet of bullets. It was the British machine-gunner who now crouched under cover and spread death fan-wise before him, while it was the German infantryman who rushed and tripped and rose and fell in the desperate effort to carry out the plans of his chiefs. All honour to him for the valour of his attempt.

To appreciate the nature of a great deal of this fighting one must remember that the whole scene of it was intersected by a perfect maze of trenches which belonged to the original German third line of defence, and were therefore familiar to them, while they were strange to those British troops who now occupied them. All along these zigzag lines the two parties were only from thirty to fifty yards apart, so that the broad, deserted plain was really intersected with narrow runways of desperately active life. Attacks developed in an instant, bombing parties sprang forward at any moment, rifles were used at point-blank range, so that an exposed bayonet was often snapped off by a bullet. "Close to the bombers' keep fifty small bayonet periscopes, four bayonets, and five foresights of rifles were shot off in an hour and a half," says an officer present. Over traverses men pelted each other with anything that was deadly, while above their heads the great shells for ever screamed and rumbled.

A great effort was made against the trench called "Big Willie," running out from the Hohenzollern Redoubt, which had been taken over by the Guards. In the afternoon of the 8th, after a heavy bombardment had flailed the position for four hours, there was a determined rush of bombers upon these trenches, the Germans, our old friends of the Seventh Westphalian Corps, coming on in three battalions, each of them down a different communication trench. The general direction of the attack was from the north and east. The trenches assaulted were held by the 1st and 2nd Brigades of Guards, both of which were heavily engaged. The riflemen, however, were useless, as only a bomber can meet a bomber. At first the stormers had some success, for, pushing along very valiantly and with great technical precision, they broke into the section of trench held by the 3rd Grenadiers, putting out of action most of the bombers and machine-gunners of that corps. "Our fellows were being bombed back from traverse to traverse, and we could just see the top of the Boche helmets going along The the trench." Lieut. Williams, with a machine-gun, stopped the rush, but was soon shot through the head. General Ponsonby, commanding the 2nd Brigade, called, however, for the bombers of the 3rd Coldstream, who swept down the trench, pelted the Germans out of it, and gloriously avenged the prostrate Grenadiers. The 2nd Coldstream had themselves been driven back, and their bomb- store was temporarily captured, but they came back and regained it after some stark face-to-face fighting, in which Sergeant Brooks, a British berserker, won his V.C. The remains of the 3rd Grenadiers also came back, led by Lieut. Geoffrey Gunnis, and cleared the last corner of what they had lost.

The Guards lost 100 men in this action, many of them blown to pieces by the bombs, but they entirely cleared the trenches and regained every inch of lost ground. The fight lasted for two hours and a half, in the course of which 9000 bombs were thrown by the British.

Another focus of strife upon October 8 was the Chalk Pit upon the Lens-Hulluch road, that tragic spot which had seen in turn the advance of the Fifteenth Division, of the Twenty-first, and of the Guards. It had now been taken over by the First Division, who had come back into the line after a rest. Across that road of death, the Loos Hulluch highway, lay the ill-omened Bois Hugo, which offered a screen for the German advance. Twelve battalions were attacking, and as many more on the line held by the French. Here the Germans lost very heavily, going down in heaps before the rifle-fire of the 1st Gloucesters, 2nd Munster Fusiliers, 9th King's Liverpool, and other battalions in the First Division firing line. The French 75's had been equally deadly and successful. Between the position held by the Guards near the Hohenzollern Redoubt on the left and that of the First Division at the Chalk Pit on the right, the ground was held by the Twelfth Division, the 37th Brigade of which (Fowler) was briskly engaged. The 6th Buffs of this brigade was immediately to the right of the Vermelles-Hulluch road, with the 6th Royal West Kent continuing the line northwards down to the Quarries. The 6th Queen's Surrey and 7th East Surrey were in support. Somewhat to the right front of this brigade was a position one hundred and fifty yards wide, called Gun Trench, which was one of the scattered forts which the enemy still held to the west of the Loos-Hulluch road. An attack was organised upon this position by Colonel Venables of the West Kents, who was badly wounded in the venture. The British, led by Captain Margetts, reached the trench in spite of terrific fire and corresponding losses, including the whole crew of a machine-gun of the East Surreys which had been most gallantly rushed to the front by Lieutenant Gibson. Half the trench was cleared, but the Germans had themselves been on the point of attacking, and the communications leading eastwards were stuffed with men a prolongation, no doubt, of the same attack which was breaking to the north upon the Guards. The weak spray of British stormers could make no progress against the masses in the supporting trenches, and were bombed back to their own position. It was a brave but fruitless attempt, which was destined to be renewed with greater success a few days later, when Gun Trench passed completely into the hands of the British. The West Kents lost 200 killed and wounded in this affair. At night the whole line of the French and British defences was inviolate, and though there was an acute controversy between the official accounts as to the number of German casualties, it is certain that, whatever they may have been, they had nothing to show in return, nor is it a sign of military virtue to recoil from an enterprise with little loss. The German fighter is a tougher fellow than the cutters-down of his casualty lists will allow. British losses were comparatively small.

Though the Germans had gained no ground upon the 8th, the British were averse from allowing them to remain in undisputed possession of that which they had won upon the 3rd. It was especially upon the Hohenzollern Redoubt that the British fighting line fixed a menacing gaze, for it had long been a centre of contention, and had now passed almost completely into the possession of the enemy. It was determined to make a vigorous attempt to win it back. The Forty- sixth North Midland Territorial Division (Stuart-Wortley), who were veterans of nine months' service at trench warfare, but had not yet been heavily engaged, were brought up from the rear, and upon October 12 they relieved the Guards Division on the left of the front line. At the same time it was planned that there should be an attack of the First Division to the west of Hulluch, and of the Twelfth Division in the region of the Quarries. Of these we shall first describe the attack of the Territorials upon the Hohenzollern Redoubt.

On October 13, at noon, a severe bombardment was opened which concentrated upon the enclosure of the redoubt, and the space between that and Fosse 8.

This bombardment for some reason does not seem to have been effective, and even while it went on the sniping and machine-guns were active in the enemy line. An hour later there was an emission of gas, borne by a brisk breeze towards the German trenches, and later still a smoke-cloud was sent out to cover the advance. At two o'clock the troops dashed over the parapet, the 138th Brigade, consisting of men of Lincoln and Leicester, upon the left, while the 137th, the men of Stafford, were on the right. In immediate support was the 139th, a Sherwood Forester Brigade. The line upon the left was headed by the 4th Leicesters and 5th Lincolns, the men, with that light-hearted courage which is so intolerable to the heavier German spirit, singing, "Here we are, here we are, here we are again!" as they vaulted out of their trenches. The attack upon the right was led by the 5th North and 5th South Staffords. The advance was splendidly executed, and won the critical admiration of some of the Guards who were privileged to see it. In the face of a murderous fire the attacking line swept, in an order which was only broken by the fall of stricken men, up to the front-line trench, two hundred yards in front. Here, however, the attack was held up by an overwhelming fire. The 5th North Staffords, whose objective was "Big Willie," were exterminated for all immediate military purposes, their losses being 19 officers and 488 men. The gallant survivors succeeded in getting as far as a communication trench which led to "Big Willie," and held on there. The advance of the 5th South Staffords upon the right was conditional upon the success of their comrades to the left. The officer commanding the left companies saw that little progress had been made, and exercised his discretion in holding back his men. The officer on the right of the South Staffords could not see what was going on, and advanced his company, with the result that they ran into the same fatal fire, and lost terribly. The two reserve companies coming up were only able with very great difficulty to reach the British frontline trenches, dropping half their number in the venture. The result of all this slaughter, which seems to have been entirely due to inadequate artillery preparation, was that the second line of attack upon the right, consisting of the 6th North and 6th South Staffords, could do no more than garrison the frontline trenches, and lost very heavily in doing so.

On the left, however, things had gone better, for at that part our guns seemed to have made more impression. The advance of the 4th Leicesters and 5th Lincolns swept over the Hohenzollern Redoubt and carried the whole of this formidable work up to Fosse Trench. About a hundred yards short of this point the advance was held up by concentrated machine-gun fire. The losses had been very heavy, especially in officers. The rear companies won forward to the front none the less, and the 4th Lincolns came up also to thicken the attenuated firing-line. They held their ground with difficulty, but were greatly helped by their pioneer battalion, the 1st Monmouths, veterans of Ypres, who rushed forward with rifle and with spade to consolidate the captured ground.

Bombing parties had been sent out by the British, those on the right to reach and bomb their way down " Big Willie," those on the left to clear Fosse Trench. The parties upon the right, drawn from the various Stafford regiments, got into "Big Willie," and stuck to their work until they were all destroyed, officers and men. The enemy bombers then counter-attacked, but were met by Lieutenant Hawkes with a party of the 5th South Staffords, who drove them back again. The pressure was very severe, however, until about four in the afternoon, when the action upon the right died down into a duel of heavy guns upon either side. On the left, however, where the gallant Territorial infantry held hard to its gains, the action was very severe. The bombing attacks went on with varied fortunes, a company of the 5th Leicesters bombing its way for more than two hundred yards up "Little Willie" Trench before its supplies ran out and it had to retire. At three o'clock there was a fresh infantry advance, the 7th Sherwood Foresters of the reserve 139th Brigade endeavouring to get forward, but losing so many in crossing the redoubt that they were unable to sally out from the farther side. The redoubt was now so crowded with mixed units all under heavy fire that there might have been a Spion Kop but for the steadiness of all concerned. At one time the men, finding themselves practically without officers, began to fall back, but were splendidly rallied by Colonel Evill of the 1st Monmouths and a few other survivors. The advent of two companies of the 5th Leicesters retaining their disciplined order helped to avert the danger, and the line was formed once again along the western face of the redoubt. During this movement the 7th Sherwood Foresters who remained in the north-east of the redoubt were cut off, but with splendid pertinacity they held their ground, and made their way back when darkness fell. In the early morning of the 14th, Captain Checkland, with a company of the 5th Sherwood Foresters, pushed an advance up to the place where their comrades of the 7th Battalion had been, and found Captain Vickars of that regiment, who, with a bravery which deserves to be classical, defended almost single-handed a barrier, while he ordered a second one to be built behind him, cutting him off from all succour. He was desperately wounded, but was brought back by his comrades.

The 8th Sherwood Foresters had also come to the front, and made a spirited attack in the early morning of the 14th, driving the enemy from the western side of the redoubt and firmly establishing the British gains in that quarter. This gain was permanent, though it proved to be rather a visible prize for valour than a useful strategic addition to the line. So long as the sinister, low-lying dump of Fosse 8 overlooked it and was itself untaken, it was impossible to make much use of the redoubt. For forty-eight hours the advanced line was held by the 139th Brigade against several brisk counter- attacks. At the end of that time the position was handed over to the safe custody of the Guards, while the Forty-sixth North Midland Division withdrew from that front line which was of their own creation. Colonel Martin of the 4th Leicesters, who was shot through the knee, but refused to move until he saw the result of the attack, Colonel Fowler of the 8th Sherwoods, Colonel Sandall of the 5th Lincolns, Major Cooper of the 4th Lincolns, and nearly 4000 officers and men, were among the casualties during the forty-eight hours of exposure.

The action was a very desperate one, and nothing could have been finer than the conduct of all engaged. "It was not the actual advance, but the holding of the position afterwards, that was dreaded, as the Germans are so quick at counter-attacking." So wrote one of the combatants. The dread was well founded, for the Germans proved to be very numerous and aggressive, and there can be little doubt that at this period their bombers had a technical proficiency which was superior to our own, whether their opponents were Guards or Territorials. It is characteristic of the unique warfare now prevailing that the contending parties had practically abandoned rifles, save as so many pikes, and that each man carried a pouch full of projectiles, the size of a duck's egg, and capable of disabling a dozen in a single burst. It may be added that both sides wore leathern helmets, sometimes with the visors up and sometimes with the face entirely concealed, so that it appeared to be a murderous strife of the strange, goggle-eyed, mask-faced creatures of a nightmare. Such were the extraordinary products of modern European warfare. Could all the ground taken have been permanently held, this would have been a fine little victory. So constant has been the phenomenon that the extreme point cannot be held that it could now be stated as an axiom for either side, and seemed to suggest that the methods of attack should be in some way modified. Each successive line of resistance has decreased the momentum of the stormers and has helped to lessen their store of bombs, while the farther they have advanced the more difficult it is for fresh men or supplies to reach them. Then, again, their diminished numbers have caused a contraction and bunching of the line, so enabling the counter-attack to get round their flanks. Add to this the physical exhaustion caused by extreme exertions while carrying a considerable weight, and one has the factors which always produce the same result, and which led eventually to the more fruitful tactics of the limited objective.

When the Forty-sixth Midland Division advanced upon the Hohenzollern Redoubt on October 13, there was a brisk attack also by the Twelfth Division upon their right, and by the First Division on the right of the Twelfth. In the case of the Twelfth Division, now commanded by General Scott, the 37th Brigade (Fowler) was heavily engaged. The 7th East Surreys of this brigade carried and permanently held the Gun Trench, a position which had cost them the lives of many officers and men upon the 8th. Attacking the same line of trenches to the left, the 6th Buffs lost heavily under oblique fire, without any appreciable gain. Of three companies who went out, 11 officers and 400 men were left upon the ground, and a photograph has revealed the perfect alignment of the dead. The 35th Brigade (Straubensee) had a similar experience to the left near the Quarries, the losses falling most heavily upon the 5th Berkshires and the 7th Norfolks.

At the same hour the First Division, with a smoke and gas screen before them, had broken in upon the German lines to the south-west of Hulluch, near the Hulluch-Lens road. About a thousand yards of trenches were taken, but the shell-fire was so murderous that it was found to be impossible to retain them. On the whole, it must be admitted that, although ground was gained along the whole line from the Hohenzollern Redoubt to Hulluch by this very desperate fighting, the losses were so heavy and the results so barren that there was no adequate return for the splendid efforts of the men. The attack was urged by Territorials upon the left, New Army men in the centre, and Regulars upon the right, and at all points it was equally gallant. The operations at the main seat of action, the Loos sector, have been treated continuously in order to make a consecutive narrative, but we must now return to consider the subsidiary attacks along the line upon September 25.

While the First and Fourth Corps, supported by subsidiary the Eleventh, had been delivering this great attack between La Bassée and Grenay, a series of holding actions had been fought from the coast downwards, so as to pin the Germans so far as possible to their places. Some of these attacks were little more than demonstrations, while others in less serious times would have appeared to be considerable engagements.

The Second Regular Division (Horne), acting upon the extreme left of the main attack, was astride of the La Bassée Canal. The most northern brigade, the 5th (Cochrane's), was opposite to Givenchy, and its advance seems to have been intended rather as a distraction than as a serious effort. It took place half an hour or so before the general attack in the hope of misleading them as to the British plans. At the signal the three leading regiments, the 1st Queen's Surrey, the 2nd Oxford and Bucks, and the 2nd Highland Light Infantry, dashed forward and carried the trench line which faced them. The 9th Glasgow Highlanders advanced upon their right. The attack was unable to make any further progress, but the fight was sustained for several hours, and had the desired effect of occupying the local forces of the enemy and preventing them from detaching reinforcements to the south.

The same remark would apply to the forward movement of the 58th Brigade of the Nineteenth Division to the immediate north of Givenchy. This division of the New Army is mainly English in composition, but on this their first serious engagement the work fell chiefly upon two Welsh battalions, the 9th Welsh and the 9th Welsh Fusiliers. Both these corps sustained heavy losses, but sacrificed themselves, as so many others were obliged to do, in keeping up the appearance of an attack which was never seriously intended.

Taking the subsidiary attacks from the south upwards, we come next to that of the Indians in the vicinity of Neuve Chapelle. This was a very brilliant affair, carried out with the true Indian tiger spring. Had it been possible to support by adequate reserves of men and an unrestricted gun-fire, it had in it the possibility of a fine victory. The attack was carried out by the Meerut Division, with the Garhwali Brigade on the right and the Bareilly upon the left, the

Dehra Dun being in reserve. On the right the Garhwalis were partly held up by wire, but the Bareillys came through everything and swept into the front-line trenches, taking 200 unwounded prisoners of the Seventh Westphalian Corps. Two battalions of the Black Watch, the 2nd and 4th, with the 69th Sikhs, were in the lead, a combination which has broken many a battle line before. The 58th Rifles (Vaughan's) and a second Sikh regiment, the 33rd, thickened the attack, and they swept forward into the second-line trenches, which they also cleared. They were now half a mile within the enemy's position, and both their flanks were open to attack. The reserve brigade was hurried up, but the trenches were blocked with wounded and prisoners, so that progress was very difficult. The German counter-attack was delivered with great energy and valour. It took the form of strong bombing parties acting upon each exposed flank. The 8th Gurkhas, who had been the only battalion which succeeded in breaking through on the right, linked up with the 4th Black Watch, holding back the flank advance to the south, but to the north the Germans got so far forward that the advanced Indians were practically cut off. The immediate neighbours of the Indians to the north were the 60th Brigade of the Twentieth Division, another English division of the New Army. Two battalions of this brigade, the 12th Rifle Brigade and the 6th Shropshires, were thrown into the fight, and covered the threatened flank until their supply of bombs more and more an essential of modern warfare was exhausted. It was clearly necessary that the advanced troops should be drawn back, since the reserves could not be got up to support them, and the need was becoming very great. In a little they might be attacked on front and rear with the chance of disaster. The Sikhs and Highlanders fell back, therefore, with great steadiness, but enduring heavy losses. In the end no ground was gained, but considerable punishment was inflicted as well as suffered, the German trenches being full of their dead. The primary purpose of holding them to their ground was amply fulfilled. It cannot be denied, however, that in this, as in so many other episodes of the Battle of Loos, the German showed himself to be a stubborn fighter, who rises superior to temporary defeat and struggles on while there is still a chance of victory. His superior supply of bombs had also a good deal to do with the success of his counter-attack.

Whilst this very sharp conflict had been raging on the Indian line, the Eighth Division to the north was engaged in a very similar operation in the region of Bois-Grenier. The course of events was almost exactly the same in each instance. The attack of the Eighth Division was carried out by the 25th Brigade (Stephens). The 2nd Rifle Brigade were on the right, the 2nd Berks in the centre, and the 2nd Lincoln upon the left. The front trench was carried, and 120 men of the Sixth Bavarian Reserve Division fell into the hands of the stormers. Part of the second line was also captured. The positions were held for the greater part of the day, and it was not until four in the afternoon that the increasing pressure of the counter-attack drove the British back to their original line. Here again the object of detention had been fully achieved.

The most important, however, of all the subsidiary attacks was that which was carried out to the extreme north of the line in the district of Hooge. This attack was made by the Fifth Corps, which had changed both its general and its divisions since the days of its long agony in May. It was now commanded by General Allenby, and it consisted of the Third Regular Division (Haldane), the Fourteenth Light Infantry Division of the New Army (Couper), and the Forty-sixth Division of Midland Territorials (Stuart-Wortley), the fine work of which at a later stage of the operations has already been described. The first two of these units bore the brunt upon September 25. The advance, which was across the old bloody ground of Bellewaarde, was signalled by the explosion of a large mine under the German position in the trenches immediately south of that Via Dolorosa, the Ypres-Menin road.

The attack upon the left was made by the 42nd Brigade (Markham), all four battalions, the 5th Oxford and Bucks, 5th Shropshires, 9th Rifle Brigade, and 9th Rifles being strongly engaged. The German trenches were reached and occupied, but after some hours the counter-attack proved to be too strong, and the brigade fell back to its original line.

Two brigades of the Third Division attacked in the centre in the direction of Bellewaarde Lake. The 7th Brigade upon the left ran into unbroken wire, before which the leading regiments, the 2nd Irish Rifles and the 2nd South Lancashire, sustained heavy losses while making no progress. The 8th Brigade to the south of them had better fortune, however. This brigade, strengthened by the 1st Scots Fusiliers, made a fine advance immediately after the great mine explosion. Some 200 prisoners and a considerable stretch of trench were captured. A redoubt had been taken by the 4th Gordons, and was held by them and by the 4th Middlesex, but the bombardment in the afternoon was so terrific that it had to be abandoned. By evening the original line had been reoccupied, the division having certainly held the Germans to their ground, but at very heavy cost to themselves. As these various attacks from the 5th Brigade at the La Bassée Canal to the Fourteenth Division at Ypres never entered into the scheme of the main fight, it is not to be wondered at that they ended always as they began. Heavy loss of life was doubtless incurred in nearly every case. Sad as it is that men should die in movements which are not seriously intended, operations of this kind must be regarded as a whole, and the man who drops in an attack which from the beginning has been a mere pretence has enjoyed as heroic an end as he who falls across the last parapet with the yell of victory in his dying ears.

A modern battle is a sudden furious storm, which may blow itself out in two or three days, but leaves such a tempestuous sea behind it that it is difficult to say when the commotion is really over. In the case of the Battle of Loos, or of Loos Hulluch, it may be said to have begun with the British advance upon September 25, and to have ended with the establishment of an equilibrium on the northern flank of our salient on October 13. From that time onwards for many weeks comparative peace rested upon this sector. A time therefore, has come when the operations may be reviewed as a whole. The net result was a gain to the British of nearly seven thousand yards of front and four thousand of depth, though if one be asked what exact advantage this gain brought, save as a visible sign of military virtue, it is hard to find an answer. Had the gain gone to that farther distance which was hoped for and aimed at, the battle might, as in the case of the French in Champagne, have been a considerable victory. As it was, the best that we can claim is that one or two more such advances in the same neighbourhood would bring the valuable French coal-fields back to their rightful owners. The most substantial proofs of victory were 3000 prisoners, including 57 officers, 26 field-guns, and 40 machine-guns. On the other hand, in the mixed fighting of the 26th we lost not fewer than 1000 prisoners, including a brigadier-general. Altogether the losses to the Army during the three weeks of fighting were not less than 50,000 men and 2000 officers. A large proportion of these were wounded.

There are some consolations for our limited success in this venture. Having started to endeavour to break the German line in one movement, it was natural to persevere, but now that we can see from how strong a hand our enemy played, we may well ask ourselves whether a more successful advance upon the 26th and 27th might not have led to grave troubles. The French had been held on the right; the Second Division was stationary upon the left. Therefore we were advancing from a contracted base, and the farther the advance went the more it resembled a long, thin tongue protruded between the jaws of the enemy. There was considerable danger that the enemy, closing in on either flank while holding the advance in front, might have bitten it off, for we know for certain that we had none of those successive rolling waves of reinforcement coming up which would turn an ebb to a flood. However, as it was we had much for which to be thankful. When one thinks of the almost superstitious reverence with which the German army used to be regarded an army which had never once been really beaten during three European campaigns it is surely a just cause for sober satisfaction that a British force, half of which consisted of new formations, should have driven such an enemy with loss of prisoners and guns out of a triple line of fortifications, strengthened by every device of modern art, and should afterwards have permanently held the greater part of the field against every effort at reconquest.

The account of this great battle, a battle in which from first to last no fewer than twelve British divisions were engaged in the Loos area alone, cannot be concluded without a word as to the splendid French success won in Champagne during the same period. There is a great similarity between the two operations, but the French attacked with at least three times as many men upon a threefold broader front. As in our own case, their best results were gained in the first spring, and they were able to continue their gains for several days, until, like ourselves, they found that the consolidating defence was too strong for the weakening attack. Their victory was none the less a very great one, yielding 25,000 prisoners and 125 captured cannon. It is impossible to doubt that both French and British if they duly learned their lessons, and if they continued to accumulate their resources, were now on the path which would lead them to final victory.

Before settling down into the inactivity enforced by the Flemish mud, there was one further brisk skirmish upon October 20 in that old battle-ground, the Hohenzollern Redoubt. This was a bombing attack, organised by the 2nd Irish Guards and led by Captain Hubbard. The Irishmen were new to the game, and somewhat outclassed at first by the more experienced Germans, but under the gallant encouragement of Lieutenant Tallents, who rallied them after being himself badly wounded, they turned the tide, and, aided by the Coldstream, made good the section attacked. Lieutenant Hamilton was killed and 60 men killed or wounded in this brisk encounter.

Coming of So, for a second time, wet, foggy winter settled down upon the water-logged, clay-bottomed trenches. Little did those who had manned them at Christmas of 1914 imagine that Christmas of 1915 would find them in the same position. Even their brave hearts would have sunk at the thought. And yet a move back of a couple of miles at Ypres, and a move forward of the same extent in the south, were all that either side could show for a year's hard work and the loss of so many thousand lives. Bloch, the military prophet of 1898, had indeed been justified of his wisdom. Far off, where armies could move, the year had seen great fluctuations. The Russians had been pushed out of Poland and far over their own borders. Serbia had been overrun. Montenegro was on the verge of utter destruction. The great attempt upon the Dardanelles had been made and had failed, after an epic of heroism which will surely live forever in our history and in that of our brave Australian and New Zealand brothers. We had advanced in Mesopotamia to within sight of the minarets of Bagdad, and yet again we had been compelled to leave our task unfinished and our little force was besieged at Kut. The one new gleam of light in the whole year had been the adhesion of Italy to the cause of Freedom. And yet, though nearly every detail had been adverse to us, our deepest instincts told us that the stream did in truth move with us, however great and confusing might be the surface current. Here on the long western line, motionless, but not passive, locked in a vast strain which grew ever more tense, was the real war. All others were subsidiary. And here in this real war, the one theatre where decisive results could be looked for, our position was very different in the opening of 1916 to that which 1915 had shown us. In the year our actual Army in France had grown three and fourfold. The munitions had increased in far greater proportions. The days had gone for ever when a serious action meant three months of shell economy before the fight and three months of recuperation after it. To the gunners it was like an evil dream to look back to the days when three shots per day was the allowance, and never save on a definite target. Now, thanks to the driving power of Lloyd George and his admirable band of assistants, there would never again be a dearth, and no attack should ever languish for want of the means to follow it up. Our guns, too, were clustering ever more thickly and looming ever larger. Machine-guns were pouring forth, though there, perhaps, we had not yet overtaken our enemy. Above all, our Fleet still held the seas, cries of distress or at least of discomfort from within Germany rose ever more clearly, and it was certain that the sufferings which she had so wantonly and wickedly inflicted upon others were beginning to be repaid to her. "Gott" does indeed "strafe," and needs no invocation, but now, as always, it is on the guilty that the rod falls. The close of 1915 found the Empire somewhat disappointed at the past, but full of grim resolution for the future.

One event had occurred in the latter end of the year which cannot be allowed to pass without comment. This was the retirement of Sir John French, and his return as Lord French to take command of the home forces. It is a difficult matter to get the true proportion, either of events or of characters, in so great an epoch as this. It will be years before the true scale will gradually be found. At the same time it can be said now with absolute certainty that the name of John French will go down to history for the sterling work that he has done during sixteen months of extreme military pressure. Nothing which the future could bring, however terrific our task, could be charged with the same possibilities of absolute disaster as those operations of the past through which he and his brilliant subordinates had successfully brought the Army. His was the preparation of the troops before the campaign, his the responsibilities of mobilisation, and his the primary credit that they were in the fighting line by August 22, 1914—they who, upon August 4, had been scattered without their reserves or full equipment over a dozen garrison towns. This alone was a great feat. Then came the long, desperate fight to make head against a superior foe, the rally, the return, the fine change of position, the long struggle for the coast, the victory saddened by the practical annihilation of the old Regular Army, the absorption and organisation of the new elements, the resumption of the offensive, and that series of spirited actions which, if they never attained full success, were each more formidable than the last, and were all preparatory exercises for the great Somme battles of 1916. This was the record which Lord French took back with him to the Horse Guards, and it is one which can never be forgotten by his fellow-countrymen.

Sir Douglas Haig, who succeeded to the chief command, was the leader who would undoubtedly have been called to the vacant post by both Army and public had leaders been chosen in the old Pretorian fashion. From the beginning he and Smith-Dorrien had been the right and left hands of the Chief, and now that ill- health had unhappily eliminated the latter, Haig's claim was paramount. Again and again he had borne the heaviest part in the fighting, and had saved the situation when it seemed desperate. He was a man of the type which the British love, who shines the brighter against a dark background. Youthful for so high a command, and with a frame and spirit which were even younger than his years, with the caution of a Scotchman and the calculated dash of a leader of cavalry, he was indeed the ideal man for a great military crisis. No task might seem impossible to the man who had held back the German tide at Ypres. With Haig in command and with an Army which was ever growing in numbers, in quality, and in equipment, the British waited with quiet confidence for the campaign of 1916.

Arthur Conan Doyle wrote 6 volumes in his Great War Series and all are available.

Arthur Conan Doyle – A Short Biography

The Scottish physician and writer Sir Arthur Ignatius Conan Doyle's name is inseparable from the phenomenon of Sherlock Holmes, undoubtedly his greatest character and the eponymous meticulous, deductive and frankly genius hero of crime fiction. However, his prolific writing was in more than just the crime fiction genre; alongside the 56 short stories and 4 novels of Sherlock Holmes he explored science fiction and fantasy as well as plays, historical novels and poetry. Another of Conan Doyle's notable characters is Professor Challenger, whose aggression and dominance serves as the antithesis of Holmes, and demonstrates Conan Doyle's capacious imagination and dramatic skill. Returning to his name, it is worthy of note that there is uncertainty surrounding his surname; while he is often referred to as Conan Doyle, where Conan and Doyle are treated as a compound surname, the entry at his baptism records Arthur Ignatius Conan as first names, and Doyle as a solitary last. Indeed, his father's name was simply Doyle. Moreover, the catalogues of the British Library and the Library of Congress insist of Doyle as his surname. Regardless, he began to refer to himself as Conan Doyle and his second wife would take this as her surname, so he will herein be referred to as Conan Doyle, in accordance with his apparent preference.

He was born in Edinburgh at 11 Picardy Place on 22nd May 1859 to his parents Charles Altamont Doyle, an Englishman of Irish descent, and Mary (née Foley), an Irishwoman, who had married in 1855. He had a brother named Innes. Charles was developing an alcohol dependence which would become incompatible with family life, and they dispersed in 1864 at which point the children were temporarily housed at various addresses across Edinburgh. They reunited in 1867, only to live together at 3 Sciennes place in a squalid tenement flat. Fortunately for the children, they had wealthy uncles who were willing to support them by paying for education and clothing. Accordingly at the age of nine Conan Doyle was sent to Hodder Place, Stonyhurst, a Roman Catholic Jesuit preparatory school. He was here for the two years between 1868 and 1870 at which point he went on to Stonyhurst College where he stayed until 1875 when he went for a year to Stella Matutina, Jesuit school in Feldkirch, Austria.

This school education set him up for a place at the University of Edinburgh, where he studied medicine between 1876 and 1881. Part of his course involved placements in Aston, (now a suburb of Birmingham, though at the time it was its own town),

Sheffield and in Ruyton-XI-Towns, an unusually named village in Shropshire which acquired its numeral when, in the twelfth century, a castle was built there which became the focus of eleven small and disparate communities. It was during this study that he began writing short stories, with the successful submission of 'The Haunted Grange of Goresthorpe' to Blackwood's Magazine arguably his greatest literary achievement at the time. As well as this recognition, he saw his first published piece 'The Mystery of the Sasassa Valley', a story set in South Africa, printed on 6th September 1879 in Chambers's Edinburgh Journal, and only 17 days later his first non-fiction article was published in the British Medical Journal on 20th September, entitled 'Gelsemium as poison'. Having finished his studies he took an appointment as a Doctor on the Greenland whaler Hope of Peterhead in 1880 and then, following his graduation, he assumed the role of ship's surgeon on the SS Mayumba during its 1881 voyage to the West African coast.

1882 saw his move to Plymouth where he joined the medical practice of former classmate George Turnavine Budd, though they had a difficult professional relationship and Conan Doyle left shortly thereafter in order to set up his own independent practice. Having arrived in Portsmouth in June of that year and disembarked the SS Mayumba with a mere £10 (£700 today) to his name, he proceeded to establish his practice at 1 Bush Billas in Elm Grove, Southsea, a seaside town in the country of Hampshire. He was not met with initial success, and in order to pass the time between visits from patients he resumed his story writing. During this period he completed his first novel, The Mystery of Cloomber, though it was not published until 1888, and the unfinished Narrative of John Smith, which only recently saw publication in 2011. Alongside these longer works was the steady production of a portfolio of short stories which included 'The Captain of the Pole-Star' and 'J. Habakuk Jephson's Statement', both inspired by the time he spent at sea. Meanwhile, in 1885 he completed a doctorate on the subject of tabes dorsalis, the slow degradation and demyelination of the sensory neurons that carry afferent information. He also married Louisa Hawkins, who was the sister of one of his patients, that same year. However, two years after this marriage he met and fell in love with Jean Elizabeth Leckie, though he maintained a platonic relationship with her out of respect for and loyalty to his wife for whom he still had great affection.

Though he struggled to find a publisher for the stories he wrote in these stretches of inactivity, his literary career would take an historic turn in 1886 when, on 20th November, Ward Lock & Co offered Conan Doyle £25 for all rights to A Study In Scarlet. The first and one of the most famous of the Sherlock Holmes franchise, it introduced the public to a new, empirical and methodical mode of crime fiction, and indeed criminality itself, by the combination of a perspicacious, brilliantly observant and data-driven detective whose army doctor companion Watson provided further scientific support as well as a means of observing and narrating Holmes's processes and adventures. The novel was a success; a letter from Robert Louis Stevenson who had acquired a copy of the novel in Samoa, wrote with "[his] compliments on your very ingenious very interesting adventures of Sherlock Holmes", while noting the similarity between Holmes's methods and a certain Joseph Bell, upon whom Holmes was based. Conan Doyle even wrote to Bell explaining so, and that "round the centre of deduction and inference and observation which I have heard you inculcate I have tried to build up a man". It was met with positive reviews in The Scotsman and The Herald and this success encouraged Ward Lock & Co to commission a sequel, The Sign of Four, which appeared in Lippincott's Magazine in February 1890, under agreement with the Ward Lock company. On 28th January 1889 his first child was born, Mary Louise, and three years later on 15th November 1892 they had a boy, Arthur Alleyne Kingsley, who became known only as Kingsley.

Now that he had a family to look after, he began to look more closely at the arrangement he had with his publishers and Conan Doyle soon began to feel that, as a new, inexperienced writer, he had been somewhat exploited by them, resolving to curtail his involvement with their business and instead beginning to write for the Strand Magazine from his home at 2 Wimpole Street. Meanwhile Conan Doyle was enjoying something of a sporting career, playing under the pseudonym A.C. Smith as goalkeeper for Portsmouth Association Football Club (though this club had no connection to present-day Portsmouth F.C, founded two years after Conan Doyle's amateur side disbanded in 1896). He was also a keen cricketer and played ten first-class matches between 1899 and 1907 for the Marylebone Cricket Club, making a highest score with the bat of 43 against London County. As an occasional bowler he only took one wicket in these ten matches, though it was W.G. Grace's stumps which he hit; a notable triumph of the right arm. His sporting interests extended to golf, for which he was elected captain of the Crowborough Beacon Golf Club in East Sussex for 1910. He once even visited Rudyard Kipling at his farm in America, bringing with him a set of golf clubs and giving his fellow famous writer an extended two-day lesson.

He went to Vienna to study ophthalmology in 1890 before returning to London and setting up a practice as an ophthalmologist, though he recorded in his autobiography that not a single patient ever crossed his doorway. This left him with more time for his writing, though by now he was beginning to feel somewhat exhausted by Holmes and wrote to his mother in 1891 "I think of slaying Holmes ... and winding him up for good and all. He takes my mind from better things." This was met with an entreaty from his mother of "you won't! You can't! You mustn't!" These "better things" were his historical novels such as The White Company (1891) and The Great Shadow (1892). Then, in defiance of his mother and the wishes of the general public, in December 1893 he wrote Holmes's apparent death in the clutches of a high-consequence brawl with arch-nemesis Moriarty above the Reichenbach Falls in Germany. Both of their deaths seemed certain, and it seemed the end of the Sherlock Holmes phenomenon. He now had time to focus on other work, most notably his pamphlet justifying the United

Kingdom's involvement with the Boer War, an involvement for which they were frequently and heavily criticised. The War in South Africa: Its Cause and Conduct was widely translated after its publication in 1902, and was based to a certain extent on the time he had spent as a volunteer doctor in the Langman Field Hospital at Bloemfontein between March and June 1900. It was this and his book The Great Boer War, written in 1900, which he considered the reasons for his knighthood in 1902 by King Edward VII, and he was subsequently appointed Deputy-Lieutenant of Surrey. In 1903 however, owing to the public demand of which he became increasingly aware after successive letters from fans pleading for the resurrection of their great hero, he seemingly brought Holmes back from the dead; in 'The Adventure of the Empty House', the first story for ten years, he reassures the reader that Holmes had merely arranged for his fall to appear fatal in order that his other enemies (particularly Colonel Sebastian Moran) might consider him dead also, whereas in reality he never falls at all. Fans were ecstatic and Conan Doyle continued to write Holmes stories.

His interest in politics piqued by the issues surrounding the Boer War, the interest he had in criminal justice which was so prominent in his crime fiction transferred to that of real-life and he became a fervent advocate of justice, investigating two closed cases of incorrect conviction. The first, in 1906, saw the shy half-British, half- Indian lawyer George Edalji exonerated for imprisonment for crimes of mutilation towards animals which he hadn't committed. Though the police were convinced of their prosecution, the crimes continued even after he was imprisoned and Conan Doyle, analytical and methodical as his invention, proceeded to privately investigate the case and the outcome, Edalji's acquittal, encouraged the establishment of the Court of Criminal Appeal in 1907. Meanwhile his wife Louisa had been suffering from tuberculosis and died on the 4th July, and Conan Doyle married Jean Elizabeth Leckie, the woman with whom he had fallen in love in 1897, the year after. The second case of injustice was some twenty years later, though pertaining to a crime committed in 1908 allegedly by one Oscar

Slater, a German Jew and gambling-den operator convicted of bludgeoning an 82 year old woman to death. Conan Doyle noticed inconsistencies in the evidence which, combined with his general sense of unease about the case, motivated him to pay for the majority of Slater's legal fees and eventually see him released in 1928.

He now had his first child with Jean, whom they named Denis Percy Stewart and was born on 17th March 1909, and then on 19th November 1910 they had Adrian Malcolm. Jean Lena Annette followed on 21st December 1912. Over the next few years there would be various deaths in his family. His first wife having already passed away, Kingsley was taken ill after complications of pneumonia following injury near the Somme in 1917. His two brothers-in-law also died, and after Kingsley's condition worsened and he passed away on 28th October owing to the complications of his convalescence and his brother Innes, now Brigadier-General died of the same, Conan Doyle sank into a deep depression, eventually finding solace in Christian spiritualism. Despite the veracity of his writing, he was not free from misunderstanding. Convinced of the authenticity of five (now known to be) hoaxed photographs of fairies by ELsie Wright in June 1917, he wrote a book The Coming of the Fairies in 1921 exploring them and other supernatural phenomena, followed up in 1926 by The History of Spiritualism, a broader look at the particulars of the movement. Encouraging the Spiritualists' National Union to modify their precepts, his turn to spiritualism was so strong that he wrote a Professor Challenger novel on the subject, entitled The Land of Mist, in 1926.

His friendship with Harry Houdini, another noted Spiritualist, led him to believe that Houdini was possessed of supernatural powers and that his feats were not tricks but proof of the supernatural. He expresses this view in The Edge of the Unknown (1930), and Houdini's inability to convince Conan Doyle of the illusory nature of his feats led to a bitter and very public falling-out. Conan Doyle has been posthumously implicated in the Piltdown Man hoax (and even accused of being its perpetrator by Richard Milner), a discovery of fossilised hominid remains which fooled the scientific world for over 40 years. Milner posits that Conan Doyle's motive was revenge on the scientific establishment for their debunking of Houdini, and that within The Lost World which was released the year the remains were found contains several hidden and encrypted clues indicating his involvement.

On 7th July 1930 Conan Doyle was discovered in the hall of Windlesham Manor, his house in Crowborough, East Sussex, clutching his chest. He died of a heart attack at the age of 71, and his last words, directed to his wife, were "you are wonderful". As a Spiritualist, his burial brought controversy as there was debate as to where he should properly be buried. Eventually he was interred on 11th July in Windlesham rose garden, though he was later removed and buried with his wife in Minstead churchyard in the New Forest, Hampshire. The epitaph on that gravestone reads

Steel true
Blade straight
Arthur Conan Doyle
Knight
Patriot, Physician and man of letters

www.ingramcontent.com/pod-product-compliance
Lightning Source LLC
Chambersburg PA
CBHW062207080426
42734CB00010B/1828

Open Pages

in South Asian Studies

Also available from SASA Books:

Beginning the Mahābhārata:
A Reader's Guide to the Frame Stories
  James W. Earl, University of Oregon

Yaśodā's Songs to her Playful Son, Kṛṣṇa
  Lynn Ate, Washington State University

The Multicultural Challenge:
A Visual-Cultural Guide to Coping in the Global Era
  Ingrid Aall, California State University, Long Beach

Decoding a Hindu Temple: Royalty and Religion in the Iconographic Program of the Virupaksha Temple, Pattadakal
  Cathleen Cummings, University of Alabama, Birmingham

Open Pages in South Asian Studies

Alexander Stolyarov, convenor
Joe Pellegrino, editor

THE RUSSIAN STATE
UNIVERSITY FOR THE HUMANITIES

South Asian Studies Association
Woodland Hills, California
www.sasaonline.net

Copyright © 2014 by Joe Pellegrino

Published by SASA Books
A Project of the South Asian Studies Association
Woodland Hills, California 91367
A public benefit, non-profit corporation,
EID 26-143783
www.sasaonline.net

Version Control:
1) 15 July 2014

All rights reserved. No part of this book may be reproduced in any form or by any electronic or mechanical means, including information storage and retrieval systems, without permission in writing from the publisher, except by a reviewer who may quote brief passages in critical articles and reviews. Contributions are the intellectual property of their individual authors.

ISBN 978-0-9834472-8-3 (paperback)
ISBN 978-0-9834472-9-0 (electronic, PDF)
LCCN: 2014942506

Cover painting courtesy of William and Judith Vanderbok.

CONTENTS

Preface
   William Vanderbok   vi

Introduction
   Alexander Stolyarov   ix

INDOLOGY PAGES

Some Problems in the Study of
Old Tamil Literature
   Alexander Dubianski   1

Aryan Prehistory and the
Indian Civilization
   Sergey Kullanda   15

The Prescriptive Function of Language in the
Nyāyamañjarī and in Speech Act Theory
   Elisa Fresci   27

Was there a Chinese Form of Atomism?
The *Vaiśeṣika* Atomistic Text in the
Chinese Philosophical Tradition
   Victoria Lysenko and Artem Kobzev   63

Open Pages in South Asian Studies

MODERN PAGES

The Western Tribal Region in South Asia:
The Limits of Our Knowledge
   Vyacheslav Y. Belokrenitsky   77

Modernity, Diversity, and the Public Sphere:
Religious Identities in 18th-20th Century India.
Some Ideas on Pre-Colonial Modernity:
The Case of the Indian Muslim Pietists
   Jamal Malik   111

The Past and Present of Theravada Buddhism
in Sri Lanka: Traditional Heritage v. the
Challenge of Modernity
   A.L. Safronova   137

Netaji Subhas Chandra Bose:
His Life and Fate
   Tatiana Shaumyan   155

FUTURE PAGES

How to Choose a Good
Indological Problem
   Dominik Wujastyk   173

Where Are We Going?
A South Asian Studies Trend Analysis
   William Vanderbok   195

Open Pages in South Asian Studies

PREFACE

WILLIAM VANDERBOK

The 2011 Open Pages in South Asian Studies conference celebrated the launching of Russia's first South Asian Studies program housed at the Russian State University for the Humanities, Moscow. Participants included scholars from Russia, Europe, the United States and India. This volume is dedicated to their budding friendship and continued collaboration.

Without the steady, guiding hand of Dr. Alexander Stolyarov, neither the RSUH program on South Asia nor the Open Pages conference would have been possible. Almost immediately collaboration between the Open Pages participants and the South Asian Studies Association took root. Conference participants Vyacheslav Y. Belokrenitsky, Jamal Malik, Alexandra L. Safronova, Alexander Stolyarov, and William Vanderbok have all subsequently published in SASA's journal, *Exemplar: The Journal of South Asian Studies.*

Finally, the Open Pages conference would have moved forward although the Russian-SASA collaboration would not have been possible but for the timely, critical travel support provided by the American Councils for International Education. Joe Pellegrino and I owe a great debt of gratitude to Dan E. Davidson, President of the American Councils, for his vision in anticipating what was possible.

Dr. William Vanderbok is the President of the South Asian Studies Association, USA.

Dr. Joe Pellegrino is a Associate Professor in the Department of Literature and Philosophy at Georgia Southern University, and editor of *Exemplar: The Journal of South Asian Studies,* a publication of the South Asian Studies Association.

Open Pages in South Asian Studies

INTRODUCTION

ALEXANDER STOLYAROV

Open Pages in South Asian Studies: I

While sitting at numerous conferences and workshops and listening to long presentations, I caught myself thinking of the most interesting things that every specialist wished to know:

- How do our close colleagues approach their work?
- What is their mode of working?
- How do they come to their results?
- What questions do they put to the subject of their study?
- What questions can they answer?
- What questions are currently unanswered?
- Why does this current state of affairs exist?

The latter point seemed to me the most important and interesting. Being keen specialists and knowing the subject of their study in depth, our colleagues could present a thorough vision of it: not only what is known, but also what is unknown. To my mind, in our work, to know the borders of the unknown is probably the most important thing that helps us define proper directions for further research.

First of all, this way of addressing our discipline helps to estimate the scale of the problems we are thinking over, link them with other problems, both solved and unsolved, and understand the main reasons that prevent this or that problem from being solved.

That is why and how the idea emerged to make a workshop about such unsolved problems in South Asian studies. It was the International Centre for South Asian Studies of the Russian State University for the Humanities that invited colleagues to discuss the problems of the unknown in their research work. The workshop was entitled "Open Pages in South Asian Studies." It was held at the Russian State University for the Humanities in Moscow on April 27-28, 2011.

The purpose of the workshop was to draw the attention of scholars not to achievements and results, as with our usual academic conferences, but to allow us to focus on problems and questions, to concentrate on details that still remain "blank" or "unrevealed" for this or that reason, whether objective or subjective, deliberately or accidentally. Workshop panelists were asked to explore such "open pages," and this volume presents a collection of articles based on papers delivered at the workshop.

The volume is evenly divided in terms of historical research. The first four papers of the book may be regarded as belonging to "classical Indological" studies, while the next four papers address so-called modern studies. The final two papers consider the discipline as a whole, looking at who we are and how we work. Collectively, the papers included in this book show that the most common reason for "pages" to remain "open" is just the lack of data, the lack of information.

In the "classical" papers here, the common denominator is the problem(s) of origin(s) (or the absence, the non-originating) of various cultural traditions. Thus Alexander Dubianski treats the problem of the origins of Old Tamil poetry. Sergey Kullanda tries to find linguistic data which would shed light on the origin of the *varṇa* system. Elisa Fresci considers the problems of the origin of Mīmāṃsā linguistics. Two historians of philosophy, Victoria Lysenko and Artemiy Kobzev, try to find explanations for the fact that atomistic theories were conspicuously absent in Chinese thought. The authors put forward the hypothesis that the origins of atomism and atomistic thinking are connected with the alphabetic (analytical) principle of writing in India (as in Greece), while in China, with its ideographic writing system, atomism could not be easily evolved and/or assimilated.

In modern studies the paucity of information is also one of the main problems. It is clearly demonstrated by all the papers of this section. Professor Vyacheslav Belokrenitsky assesses the situation in South Asia's Western Tribal Region. Professor Jamal Malik deals with phenomena of "messianism," "pietism," and "fundamentalism" in "Greater South Asia" from the 16th century until the end of the 20th century. Professor Alexandra Safronova writes about the past and present of Theravada Buddhism in Sri Lanka. Professor Tatyana Shaumyan treats the mystery of the death of legendary Subhas Chandra Bose.

In two papers some theoretical as well as practical questions of South Asian studies in general have been raised. These are, first, the paper of Dominik Wujastyk, who speculates on the prospects for future scholars to find unexplored problems and, second, the paper of Professor William Vanderbok, who analyzes the main trends of South Asian studies in the USA for the last sixty years as compared to European approaches.

Open Pages in South Asian Studies

The workshop has shown that there is no shortage of both "open pages" in South Asian studies and efforts to explore and "close" them. It is encouraging to observe that nobody tries to stop these efforts. So we may hope for future growth of our discipline.

The workshop participants believe that this book will be interesting not only for specialists and students but also for a wide circle of readers who want to know the history, culture and modern development of the South Asian nations.

Dr. Alexander Stolyarov is a Senior Scientist in the Department of Eastern History at the Institute of Oriental Studies of the Russian Academy of Sciences, Moscow. As Director of Russia's first South Asian Studies program, located at the Russian State University for the Humanities, he organizes the biannual Open Pages conferences in Moscow.

CHAPTER 1

ALEXANDER DUBIANSKI

Some Problems in the Study of Old Tamil Literature

When considering the contribution of Tamilnadu to Indian culture in general we note its many achievements: in the sphere of architecture and sculpture, in the arts of dance, music and many others. But perhaps the most remarkable among them is the corpus of literary works traditionally called "*cankam* poetry," rich in volume, aesthetical beauty, and artistic skill. This poetry is nowadays recognized as an indispensable part of the old Indian literary tradition, which is represented mostly in the Sanskrit and Prakrit languages.

The three main branches of this tradition (that is, Sanskrit, Prakrit and Tamil) have much in common, and one of the urgent tasks of research scholars is to understand and explain their interrelation, mutual influence, and development. An overall and coherent picture of the literary processes in ancient India is still to be drawn. Obviously, such a task cannot be solved without fundamental research in each branch of the tradition. From this point of view a research work on Tamil *cańkam* poetry seems especially important because, in my opinion, this poetry, in spite of the fact that it possesses features of a well-developed and refined art, preserves easily recognizable traces of the early stages of literary development, including elements of folklore. Such a situation makes it possible to follow the development of literary forms, conventions, and canonic images more closely. But one should not forget that studies of Tamil literature represent a comparatively new field of Indological research, and Tamil literature still contains many "open pages" for future scholars. In other words, there are many problems present, concerning the history of Tamil literature, its characteristic features, definitions, estimations etc., which give room for debates and controversies.

There is, for instance, an oft-recurring statement that the old Tamil literature was "rediscovered" at the end of the 19th and the beginning of the 20th centuries by some patriots of Tamil culture (like U.V. Swaminathaiyar, C.V. Damodaran Pillai). As H. Tieken has recently pointed out (*Blaming the Brahmins*, 235), this notion recurs in works by famous scholars like, for instance, A.K. Ramanujan, who gave to one of the chapters of the introduction to translations from *cańkam* poetry the heading, "A Tradition Lost and Found" (XI). This position was also shared by K. Zvelebil (*Companion*, 147). However, there are different opinions on the subject which take into consideration the fact that though some manuscripts (nobody knows how many) perished in the course of time, the old poetic tradition has certainly survived and, as Tieken correctly states "was never lost" (*Blaming the Brahmins*, 235). Putting aside historical, cultural, and even political reasons for privileging the concept of "rediscovery," I'd like to stress that this tradition had persisted throughout the long middle ages, revealing itself in the form of genres, images, conventions and literary terms.

At the same time we must admit that the so-called "rediscovery" first of all meant the creation of editions of texts which made them known to a large audience and made possible the beginning of their research. The pioneering work on ancient Tamils and their culture was written by V. Kanakasabhai and published in 1904. It was called *The Tamils Eighteen Hundred Years Ago*, and contained a lot of material—geographical, historical, and sociological—extracted mostly from the literary texts. This book was a starting point for a tradition of treating the *cańkam* poetry as a source of information, a tradition that still exists (mostly in Tamilnadu), though in a modified, more topical, so to speak, form. There are numerous works which present and treat one special object or phenomenon singled out of the poetry. They do not claim to be conceptual, but can be very useful because they collect and present specific facts in a concentrated and systematic way. As one example I offer the monograph by M. Varadarajan, "The Treatment of Nature in Sangam Literature," in which the author describes the objects of nature and gives quotations from the poems. Some authors narrow their field of research to a single-case study. The works by D. Nataraja are also significant in this respect: "*Gloriosa Superba* in Classical Tamil Poetry," and "*Kāman* in Tamil Classical poetry," among others.

For a scholar who studies ancient Tamil lyrics, works like Sundaramati's "The Theme of *Marutam* in *Cańkam* Literature" or Ceyeraman's "Neytal Songs," which give carefully collected and rubricated information concerning the themes of old love-poetry, are very good and useful, but they lack an analytical approach

Open Pages in South Asian Studies

from the point of view of the science of literature in the Western sense of the word.

It seems that only in the 1960s were efforts to analyze *cankam* poetry in terms of the literary theory undertaken. The first work to be mentioned in this connection is *Tamil Heroic Poetry*, by K. Kailasapathy, who tried to place Tamil poetry in the context of world literature, and interpreted it as belonging to the epic tradition (like *The Iliad* or *The Mahabharata*). He stated that Tamil songs belong to the same category of literature and possess its important features: formulas, typical motives, and cycles. It was a new word in Tamilology which produced an impression on scholars, but not all of them accepted it readily. For instance, I supported the idea that the origin of the tradition should be looked for in the situation of oral performance, but could not accept the thesis that Tamil heroic poetry is equal to the epic heroic poems just mentioned. I pointed out that the typical situation in which these poems were composed and sung, their aim and character (they are mostly praise-poems), the mode of performance and the figures of performers, differ considerably from those of the big poems. Tamil poems are not narrative, but mainly descriptive and in principle oriented to the task of praising a person or some events belonging, not to a faraway past, but to a moment more or less contemporary to the performer. In my understanding they formed a part of a certain ritual (a panegyric ritual, let us say) performed jointly by a ruler (a king or a chieftain) and a performer in order to sustain the life-giving power of the ruler on the one hand and the prosperity of the land and the people on the other (*Ritual and Mythological Sources*, 71). The ritual had formed not only the contents of the panegyrics but also influenced their stylistic, poetic features and artistic devices.

In this connection there arises a question: what is the role of rituals or ritual structures in forming the Tamil poetic tradition? As I tried to show, it is possible to consider the main situation of Tamil lyrical poetry (*akam*), namely, the separation of lovers, in ritual terms, namely as a rite of passage (*Ritual and Mythological Sources*, 138). That is to say, this situation is depicted in poetry as following a certain model of behavior which, when a woman is concerned, is known in Tamil culture as *noṉpu*, or *pāvai noṉpu* (*Ritual and Mythological Sources*, 126-129). This behavior in its turn presupposes the existence of a kind of a feminine energy which was qualified by the American scholar George Hart as *aṉaṅku* (the Tamil word that primarily denotes "suffering, affliction, distress, fear") and called by him, "sacred energy." According to Hart, this energy is immanent in many objects (including humans) and especially important when it is connected with figures of a Tamil king and a woman. Being ambivalent by nature (it is able to give both good and evil), it needs a sort of a control which can be achieved by ritual measures (*The Poems of Ancient Tamil*, 96; *The Relation between Tamil and Classical Sanskrit Literature*, 321).

Hart's theory had garnered some support (for example, Zvelebil's *Tamil Literature* and my own *Ritual and Mythological Sources*), but at the same time was strongly criticized. In his review of Hart's work, T. Burrow pointed out that in early Tamil literature there was no notion of such energetic potential and the word *aṉaṅku* signified spirits, demons, or gods. This critical attitude was strengthened by V.S. Rajam's "Ananku: A Notion Semantically Reduced to Signify Female Sacred Power," where she meticulously collected and analyzed all the contexts where the word was used. She reproached

Hart for presenting an oversimplified, reductionistic interpretation of the term (257). She showed that the "the term *aṉaṅku* does not lend itself to a single interpretation" (250) and that over time it "has undergone a semantic change, a change of a shriveling quality, narrowing from a multi-dimensional concept of a celestial female" (266).

The last statement cannot raise objections, coupled as it is with the recognition that Hart was at times perhaps carried away by his ideas, and had allowed some exaggerations. But it does not prevent us from acknowledging the importance of *aṉaṅku* as the concept of some inner, particularly female, energy. Contrary, though, to Hart's understanding of it as a supernatural power (very much like the Polynesian *mana* (22), I consider this energy as a natural phenomenon, presenting itself in the form of heat or fire (cf. the concept of *tapas*). There are some conspicuous passages in the poetry proving this idea: "thick pieces [of meat] fried (*aṉaṅkiya*) on fire" [from the anthology *akanāṉūṟu* 237, 9], "a fireplace with *aṉaṅku*" (*aṉaṅkaṭuppu)*" [from the poem *maturaikkāñci,* 29]. Another important feature of *aṉaṅku* is its fluctuant nature, an ability to change forms, to be collected or wasted. The best example in this respect will be the figure of Kaṇṇaki, the heroine of the poem *cilappatikāram,* who became a goddess by means of accumulating a huge potential of inner energy which she unleashed in an attempt to burn up the city of Madurai.

In my opinion, the concept of *aṉaṅku* as the inner feminine energy enables us to understand the meaning of images and conventions in Tamil love poetry. For example, specific features of the canonic portrait of the heroine (vegetative code) are aptly explained with the help of it (Dubianski, "Constructing Poetic Images," 90), as well as the whole situation of separation which, as stated earlier, can be viewed as a kind of the ritual of passage. Moreover, this concept offers an interpretation of the meaning and origin of the system of five *tiṇai*, the basic poetic construction of the Tamil love-poetry, which regularly correlates landscapes and love-situations.

The origin of this system was discussed by many scholars, resulting in several with different suppositions. Thani Nayagam suggested a socio-geographical interpretation of this system (88); Sivatamby looked upon it from a socio-economic point of view, stating, for example, that the situation of separation reflects the mode of economic activity of the population of pasture-lands (*passim* in "An Analysis of the Anthropological Significance of the Economic Activities"). There was also the idea of explaining the origin of the five-fold system of landscapes on the basis of five natural elements (*pañcabhuta*) (Zvelebil, *The Smile of Murugan*, 93-95), which looks very artificial. The last attempt was undertaken by Tieken, who suggested that the system of Tamil poetic conventions was inspired by the Sanskrit theory of music (*Kavya in South India*).

Without entering into a discussion of all the suggestions, and recognizing that they all have their convincing points, I shall put forward my hypotheses based on the idea that the feminine energy mentioned above is consubstantial with the energy of nature, its productive and life-giving power. So, the states of the energy of a woman, its aspects, so to say, in different situations (or stages of life) are understood as replicas of the state of nature in different moments of the calendar cycle, or vice-versa. That is why it is not a mere coincidence that the state of a woman suffering in separation and the state of nature during the summer heat are described in poetry by the word *vāṭu,* ("to wither, to dry up").

To make this point more comprehensive, let us turn to the poetic themes. The beginning of the young lovers' romance is connected with the theme-*tiṇai* called *kuṟiñci*. The situation it presupposes is traditionally called *puṇartal* ("a union or copulation"), which contains a paradox, because poets when composing *kuṟiñci* poems avoided descriptions of trysts and depicted scenes around them, that are, in fact, the situation of separation. According to my reading of the theme, its essence consists not in the union itself, but in the concept of union and the readiness of the heroes for it, which addresses their maturity or, to be more precise, their sexual ripeness. This idea is more pronounced with regard to the girl, and it is her inner energy, or *aṇaṅku,* which constitutes the focus of the given theme. This explains, by the way, the origin of its name.

Kuṟiñci (*Strobilanthes*) is a shrub with blue flowers, belonging to mountain areas. Strangely enough, it is mentioned in *kuṟiñci*-poetry only five times, each time in comparison with some other plants (e.g., *mango* or *vēṅkai*-tree). Thus, its presence in this poetic tradition is practically nonexistent. A natural question arises: what made the tradition choose this flower for the name of the *tiṇai*? I think that the explanation is twofold. First of all, it is obvious that the blue color in Tamil culture is associated generally with a woman (*Ritual and Mythological Sources,* 90). The second point seems more interesting. *Kuṟiñci* is known in Tamilnadu as a plant which blossoms only once in twelve years. The marriageable age of a girl in Tamil culture, the age of her "blossoming," is also considered to be twelve years. If we take into consideration the above-mentioned correspondence between the natural and the feminine, the profound symbolic meaning of the flower and the name of the theme will become clear.

The motive of the sexual maturity of the girl is expressed in *kuṟiñci* poetry in two ways. The first is the direct indication of physical changes in her (cf. *Kuṟuntokai* 337):

> The buds of her breasts have blossomed,
> the soft thick hair falls from her head,
> the compact rows of her white teeth are full
> since she has lost her deciduous teeth,
> and a few *cuṇaṅku*-spots have appeared on
>   her body.

But the most common way is through a general description of the mountain landscape given at the time when flowers are blossoming, fruits and honey are ripening, the millet is ready for harvesting, and streams and lakes are full of water. Individual details also can be full of meaning. For example, the *vēṅkai* tree (*Pterocarpus*) in *kuṟiñci*-poetry plays the role of the hero's (and the god *Murukaṉ*'s) alter ego, so when the simultaneous blossoming of *vēṅkai* and *mango* (signifying the female principle) is mentioned, there is no doubt that the idea of the union of the heroes (including the matrimonial union) is symbolically introduced. In this way the *kuṟiñci* mytho-poetic landscape, saturated with symbolic meaning, is construed.

This principle is discerned in other *tiṇai*-themes. The heroine of the *mullai* poems (*mullai* is a variety of jasmine) is shown as patiently waiting (*iruttal*) for her husband in the state of ritually controlling and accumulating her inner energy, which signifies her marital chastity (*kaṟpu*), and is symbolically represented in Tamil culture by the white color, the main feature of jasmine. The *pālai* poetry symbolically expresses the dangerous aspect of this process (a potentially disastrous character of the situation of separation). In the theme of *marutam* the heroine is also in a dangerous state, this time in connection with her impurity after the birth of a child. This latter circumstance defines the main idea of the theme, which can be seen as feminine energy in its productive state, connected with progeny and fertility. This idea is aptly expressed by the *marutam*-landscape, the fertile lands of rice and the sugar-cane fields, usually shown in the moments of harvest (*pālai* and *marutam* are trees characteristic of these two landscapes). The last theme, the *neytal* (the theme of the blue lily), is also connected with separation and its sorrows. For the most part it utilizes the situations of other *tiṇais* and uses for its natural background the seascape and images which symbolically express the ideas characteristic for those *tiṇais* (*Ritual and Mythological Sources*, 162-167).

It is worth stressing here that I am considering now only the main, pivotal points of the themes, not touching upon their different topical aspects (like the rivalry between the heroine and the courtesan in *marutam*, for instance, or the feelings of the hero). This very schematic presentation of the main canonical themes of Tamil love poetry aims to show its essential features which tie it with the sphere of myth and ritual (and certainly folklore—another problem of Tamil studies). I maintain that the concept of *aṇaṅku* in the sense of inner feminine energy is able to explain many traditional features of the old Tamil poetry and the formation of its poetic canon. As a final example I shall recall the rule of the famous treatise *Tolkāppiyam,* stating that the heroes of *akam* poetry do not have any other names than their *tiṇai*-names (*tolkāppiyam. poruḷatikāram,* 22). This is an obvious recognition of the fact that the poetry deals not with individuals but with generalized types, which represent models of a certain behavior in certain situations, that is, a ritual behavior. We know well that many rituals are connected with the relationship between the sexes and in the context of Tamil culture with the process of controlling *aṇaṅku*, the female inner energy. Tamil love poetry, no doubt, could not avoid it, and showed situations when this power expressed itself in specific ways, which conditioned the behavior of the heroes of the poetry, thus forming the topical structure of the poems. I also have no doubt that some poetic pieces were actively used during rituals in the form of ritual songs of various melodic types and, perhaps, modes of performance. But this thesis still belongs to one of the open pages of the study of Tamil poetry, and is to be closed by future investigations.

Works Cited

Beck, B.E.F. "Colour and Heat in South Indian Ritual." *Man* 4.4 (1969): 553-572.

Burrow, T. 1979 – T. Burrow. "Review of Hart G.L. *The Relation between Tamil and Classical Sanskrit Literature*. Wiesbaden 1976." *Indo-Iranian Journal* 21 (1979): 4.

Ceyarāman, Nārāyaṇacāmi. *Neytal Pāṭalkaḷ: Tiraṉāyvum Pāṭalkaḷum (Neydal Songs)*. Kumaraṉ Patippaka Veḷiyīṭu, Volume 5. Madurai: Kumaraṉ Patippakam, 1978.

Dubianski, Alexander M. "Constructing Poetic Images in Ancient Tamil Poetry (*Pattuppāttu Anthology*)." *Problems of Indian Philology*. Eds. Gurov, N.V. and S.G. Rudin. Moscow: Moscow: Moscow UP, 1974.

———. *Ritual and Mythological Sources of the Early Tamil Poetry*. Gonda Indological Studies, Volume VIII. Groningen, The Netherlands: Egbert Forsten, 2000.

Hart, George L. *The Poems of Ancient Tamil: Their Milieu and Their Sanskrit Counterparts*. Berkley: U of California P, 1975.

———. "The Relation between Tamil and Classical Sanskrit Literature." *A History of Indian Literature: Vol. X: Dravidian Literature*. Ed., Jan Gonda. Wiesbaden: Harrassowitz, 1974.

Kailācapati, Ka. *Tamil Heroic Poetry*. Oxford: Clarendon Press, 1968.

Kanakasabhai, V. T*he Tamils Eighteen Hundred Years Ago*. Madras: Higginsbotham, 1904.

Nadarajah, D. "The *Gloriosa Superba* in Classical Tamil Poetry." *Tamil Culture* 11 (1963): 280-90.

———. "*Kāmaṉ* in Tamil Classical Poetry." *Jurnal Pengajan India (Journal of Indian Studies. Kuala-Lumpur)* 1 (1983): 73-87.

Rajam, V.S. "*Aṇaṅku*: A Notion Semantically Reduced to Signify Female Sacred Power." *Journal of the American Oriental Society* 106.2 (1986): 257-272.

Ramanujan, Attipat K. *Poems of Love and War: From the Eight Anthologies and the Ten Long Poems of Classical Tamil*. NY: Columbia UP, 1985.

Sivathamby, Karthigesu. "An Analysis of the Anthropological Significance of the Economic Activities and the Conduct Code Ascribed to Mullai Tinai." *Proceedings of the First International Conference Seminar of Tamil Studies: Kuala Lumpur, Malaysia, April 1966*. Dept. of Indian Studies, University of Malaya, 1968.

Thani, Nayagam X. S. *Landscape and Poetry: A Study of Nature and Classical Tamil Poetry*. Bombay: Asia Publishing House, 1966.

Tieken, Herman J. H. *Kāvya in South India: Old Tamil Caṅkam Poetry*. Gonda Indological Studies Vol. X. Groningen: E. Forsten, 2001.

———. "Early Tamil Poetics between *Nāṭyaśāstra* and

Rāgamālā." *Bilingual Discourse and Cross-Cultural Fertilisation: Sanskrit and Tamil in Medieval India*. Whitney Cox and Vincenzo Vergiani, eds. Pondicherry, India: Inst. Francais de Pondichery, 2013. pp. 69-92.

———. "Blaming the Brahmins." *Studies in History* 26.2 (2010): 227-243.

Varadarajan, M. *The Treatment of Nature in Sangam Literature (Ancient Tamil Literature)*. Madras: The South India Saiva Siddhanta Works Publishing Society, 1957.

Zvelebil, Kamil. *The Smile of Murugan: On Tamil Literature of South India*. Leiden: Brill, 1973.

———. *Tamil Literature*. Leiden: Brill, 1975.

———. *Companion Studies to the History of Tamil Literature*. Leiden: Brill, 1992.

Dr. Alexander Dubianski is an Associate Professor in the Institute of Asian and African Studies at Moscow State University.

14

Open Pages in South Asian Studies

CHAPTER 2

SERGEY KULLANDA

Aryan Prehistory and the Indian Civilization

The origin of many phenomena of Indian culture can be properly understood only against the background of Aryan prehistory. Thus, the search for an Aryan homeland necessarily involves an analysis of interactions between the Aryans and Indo-Iranians and their neighbors, based on the linguistic data. In what follows below, I shall pass over thoroughly investigated contacts between the Aryans and Finno-Ugrians and focus on less conspicuous facts.

It appears from the analysis of Aryan traditions that Proto-Aryans were the bearers of the steppe archaeological cultures. The latter were characterized, *inter alia*, by the use of handmade pottery, in contrast to the wheel-thrown vessels of the proto-urban cultures of the Near East and South Central Asia. Old Indian ritual texts (for the relevant passages see Rau, 1972) testify that wheel-thrown pottery was considered ritually unclean:

It (the vessel, *sthālī́*) is made by an Aryan (*āryakṛtī́*) with [horizontal] parts going upwards (*ūrdhvákapālā*) for the unity with divinity (*sadevatvá*); it is united with the gods (*sádevā*). Yet the vessel (*pā́tra*) made by a potter (*kúlālakṛta*) wheel-thrown (*cakrávṛtta*) is Asuric (*asuryà*). (*āryakṛtī́ bhavaty ūrdhvákapālā sadevatvā́ ya sā hí sádevāsuryàṁ vā́ etát pā́tram· yát kúlālakṛtaṁ cakrávṛttaṁ – Maitrāyaṇī-saṁhitā* 1, 8, 3)

One [vessel] is wheel-thrown (*cakravṛtta*), the other is non-wheel-thrown (*acakravṛtta*); the wheel-thrown one is Asuric, the non-wheel-thrown is the divine vessel (*devapātra*). That is why a non-wheel-thrown vessel (*tapanī*) must be made for the Agnihotra. (*cakravṛttam anyad acakravṛttam anyad yac cakravṛttaṁ tad asuryaṁ yad acakravṛttaṁ tad devapātraṁ tasmād acakravṛttām agnihotratapanīṁ kurvīta – Kāṭhaka-saṁhitā* 6, 3)

The linguistic data imply, however, that the Indo-Iranians contacted with the bearers of Northeast Caucasian and Kartvelian languages. It seems likely that Indo-Iranian **uštra* "camel" (Old Indian *úṣṭra-*, Avestan *uštra-* "id") was borrowed from Pra-Nakh **ŭstuv/jŕe* "bull" – cf. Chechen *stu*, genitive case *steran*, Ingush *ust*, genitive case *istar-o*, Batsbi *psṭu*, genitive case *psṭañ*) (O.A. Mudrak, personal communication.) Northeast Caucasian **u̯aran/l-* "camel" (Avar and Lak *warani*, Dargwa *walri*, Lezghi *lawar* "id" – cf. Old Indian *vāraṇá* "wild, dangerous"), **wěršē* "young bull; male" (Avar *basi* "calf," Chechen and Batsbi *borš* "young bull," Chechen *börša* "male [of species]," Archi *boš-or* "husband; man" – cf. Old Indian *vṛ́ṣan-*,

Avestan *varəšna-* "man; male"), **mHädwV* "kind of beverage" (Lezghi *med*, Tabasaran *med*, "treacle, syrup," Andian *medi*, Godoberi *medi* "beer" – cf. Old Indian *mádhu-* "sweet intoxicating drink," Avestan *maδu-* "berry wine," Sogdian *mδw* "wine," etc.) were Indo-Iranian loanwords (Klimov 1971: 228; Starostin 1988: 113-114.) Georgian-Zan (a branch of Kartvelian) **rdo-* "time; timespan" (Georgian *dro*, Megrelian *rdo-*; cf. Old Indian *r̥tú-* "fixed time; period," Avestan *ratu-* "timespan"), Georgian-Zan **bandγ-* "to tie, plait" (Georgian *bandγ-* "to tie, to net, to spin webs;" Megrelian *bondγ-* "id"; cf. Old Indian *bandh-*, Avestan *band-* "to tie, bind"), etc. were borrowed from Indo-Iranian (Климов 1994: 176-177; 93-95).

The Indo-Iranians, Northeast Caucasians and Kartvelians could have interacted either in the Near East, before the Indo-Iranians moved to the steppes, or in the Caucasus if they followed the Caucasian way north.

To study the origin of the *varṇa* system, one also has to look into Indo-Iranian and even Indo-European prehistory. Besides the famous *Puruṣasūkta* story (RV X, 90, 11-12), Vedic texts provide very little information on the matter. They imply, however, that the *kshatriya* social class charged with warring and political power bears traces of the age class of young men. The relevant data, collected and analyzed by Stig Wikander (1938, *passim*), can be amplified. Thus, the Vedic Indra, a king and warrior par excellence, is depicted in the Rigveda as an unageing (*ajuryá*) youth (*yúvan*) and *márya*. One can, without stretching the point, trace all the above meanings to a protolanguage etymon marking membership in an age-sex group of young warriors. The latter were likely to be a nuisance in peacetime, hence the meaning "rascal." In time of war, however, they constituted the main military force and, after performing the required warlike deeds, were allowed to enter the next age-grade and marry. Let us see if Indra and the Maruts as described in the Rigveda can be regarded as such a group.

The Maruts in the *Rigveda* are youths (*yúvānas* and *máryās*) mentioned exclusively as a group (*śárdha, gaṇá* or *vrā́ta*) without any individual characteristics. They were born simultaneously (*sākáṁ jajñire* [I, 164, 4]; *sākáṁ jātā́ḥ* [V, 55, 3]), they are of the same nest (*sánīḷāḥ* [I, 165, 1; VII, 56, 1], neither senior nor junior and middle- (*té ajyeṣṭhā́ ákaniṣṭhāsa udbhídó 'madhyamā́so...* [V, 59, 6]). They are equipped with the full panoply of weapons, namely battle-axes, spears, bows, arrows, quivers, helmets as well as with horses and chariots (*vā́śīmanta ṛṣṭimánto maṇīṣíṇaḥ sudhánvāna íṣumanto niṣaṅgíṇaḥ / sváśvā stha suráthāḥ...svāyudhā́...*, i.e. "[ye are] battle-axe bearers, spearmen, wise, bearers of good bows, arrow-bearers, quiver-bearers; [ye] are possessing of good horses, good chariots... well-armed" [V, 57, 2]. They have gilt helmets on their heads (*śíprāḥ śīrṣásu vítatā hiraṇyáyīḥ* [V, 54, 11]) and mighty bows and (other) weapons in their chariots (*sthirā́ dhhánvāny ā́yudhā ráthesu vó...* [VIII, 20, 12]).

According to the *Rigveda*, the Maruts are *sāṁtapanā́* [VII, 59, 9], that is, as Renou (1962: 46) put it, born of the total burn, *nés de la brûlure-totale*. However, since the prefix *sam-* (here in the *vṛddhi* form with a long vowel, *sām-*) implies the action of several agents one is entitled to interpret the word *sāṁtapanā́* as "those who passed through a common ordeal by fire" being an integral part of initiation rites.

A very interesting mention of Indra as a merchant (*vaṇíj*) in the Atharvaveda (*índram ahám vaṇíjaṁ codayāmi*, "I incite Indra the merchant" – XV 15, 1) that at first sight seems to be contradictory to his image of the war chief is in fact quite in keeping with it. Archaic trade was closely related to warring – suffice it to remember the Vikings who were both warriors and traders. This ambiguity was reflected in Indo-European languages where words meaning "war booty" (Sanskrit *lotra*) and "gain, profit" (Latin *lucrum*) go back to the same protolanguage etymon. A classic case of this situation is the image of Wodan, the Germanic war god who was at the same time the protector of trade and in this capacity was identified with Mercury, the god of commerce in Roman mythology. As a result, the day of Mercury in Romance languages (French *mercredi*, etc.) became the day of Wodan (Dutch *woensdag*, English *Wednesday*).

I think that the above materials enable one to trace the Kshatriya *varṇa* to the age-class of young warriors. Unfortunately, we have no information on the relation of the other two primary *varṇas* to age-sex classification in Indian tradition – at least I have not succeeded in unearthing it – but in this case it is Iranian tradition that helps us. Thus, according to a Scythian legend or myth recorded by Herodotus, (IV, 5-7), the Scythian progenitor, Targitaos, had three sons: Lipoxaïs, Arpoxaïs, and the youngest (νεοώτατος) Colaxaïs. As the youngest brother succeeded in getting hold of sacred objects fallen from the sky, the elder brothers ceded the royal power to him. The story goes that "From Lipoxaïs originated those Scythians who are called the clan (γένος) of Auchatae; from Arpoxaïs, those called Katiari and Traspians; from the youngest the kings called Paralatae" (Herodotus IV, 6). Evidently the social position of the three brothers has nothing to do with their birth-order, or the second son would have become the ancestor of kings. Neither can it be a mere error of Herodotus, since in an independent Iranian tradition, that of the Middle Persian Bundahišn, it is the youngest son of Zardusht that becomes the ancestor of the warriors, resp. kings, while the eldest son is the ancestor of priests, and the second son – the ancestor of agriculturalists. Moreover, parts of a system cannot be separated arbitrarily. If one of the social classes was related to an age class, the other two probably had the same origin.

Both Dumézil in 1930 and Grantovskij in 1960 argued that Scythian clans (γένεα) had been social groups going back to age classes (Brandenstein 183-ff.) It was E.O. Berzin who took the logical next step and suggested that Indian *varṇas* had originally been age-classes of young warriors, mature men providing agricultural goods, and old men performing religious duties (Berzin 46). Unfortunately, the works by Brandenstein and Berzin contained, besides convincing arguments in favor of the role of age-sex stratification in the formation of the *varṇa* system, a number of far-fetched statements and outright errors,[1] hence they were greeted with skepticism. Berzin's paper, moreover, was published in a popular magazine, and was thus overlooked by scholarly community. It is therefore appropriate to reiterate and amplify their arguments.

It seems likely that the Kshatriyas were originally warlike youths, the Vaishyas were mature men—having ceased to be warriors *par excellence* and charged mainly with farming and animal husbandry—and the Brahmans belonged to the age-class of elders performing priestly functions. It is all the more probable since there are mentions of age-sex classification in Vedic literature. Thus, the word *váyas* "vigor, strength" means in certain contexts "a stage of life." One can cite such passages from the *Rigveda* as "passing through one life period (*váyas*) after another" (*váyo-vayo vicarántaḥ*)

[VIII, 55. 4], "[Soma] circulates through life stages" (pári... váyāṁsi... yāti) (IX, 9. 1) or "when thou [i.e. Agni] growest old establishing one life stage after another, / thou goest circle-wise changing thy outlook" (váyo-vayo jarase yád dádhānaḥ / pári tmánā víṣurūpo jigāsi) (V, 15. 4), etc.

It is likely that here Agni and Soma personify the movement of human beings through life periods; when an age-group reaches the limit of the socially active age it leaves the system of age-classes and is substituted by a new group assuming its name, that is, the circle-wise movement mentioned in the above-cited passages takes place. As to the age-grades in Vedic tradition, it is worth noting that in the *Śatapatha Brāhmaṇa* (XII, 9, 1, 8) one encounters the word váyas meaning approximately "the active life, vigorous age" and -vayasá "life period" in such compounds as pūrvavayasá-, madhyamavayasá-, and uttamavayasá-, meaning the first, middle, and last stage of life, respectively. Let us cite this very instructive passage: "There are three sacrificial cakes, for this life (váyas) of man (púruṣa) consists of three parts. It is his life that [adhvaryú] wins for him by [means of] those [cakes]. The early life (pūrvavayasá) [he wins] by that of Indra, the middle [part of] life (madhymavayasá) by that of Savitar, and the last [part of] life (uttamavayasá) by that of Varuṇa. Having won the life from Death in the sequence [of its periods and] deities [yajamāna] makes it immortal" (tráyaḥ puroḍā́śā́ bhavanti / tredhā́vihitáṁ vā́ idáṁ púruṣasya váyaḥ / váya évāsyá taíḥ spr̥noti / pūrvavayasámévaindréṇa / madhymavayasáṁ sāvitréṇa / uttamavayasáṁ vāruṇéṇa / yathārūpámevá yathādevatáṁ váyo mr̥tyóḥ spŕ̥tvāmŕ̥taṅ kurute.)

All these and many other facts can only be explained as the result of the evolution of an age-stratified soci-

Open Pages in South Asian Studies

ety, all the more so since linguistic analysis is indicative of the existence of age-sex stratification in Proto-Indo-European community. I dwelt at length on this issue in my paper ("Indo-European 'Kinship Terms' Revisted"), so here I will confine myself to broad outline of my arguments.

The analysis of Indo-European kinship terminology implies that Proto-Indo-European society was characterized by age-sex stratification. There are about twenty PIE etyma regarded, in accordance with the meaning of the majority of their reflexes, as kinship and relationship-by-marriage (affinal) terms. The reconstructed PIE kinship-terms system is therefore usually divided into two subsystems:

  a. consanguineous or blood-kinship terms and
  b. affiliation or relationship-by-alliance terms.

In doing so, however, one imposes on the society whose language one is trying to reconstruct one's own perception of kinship, notwithstanding conflicting evidence.

Thus, PIE *bhréh₂tēr is traditionally included into the blood-kinship terms subsystem with the meaning "(consanguineous) brother." It is, however, at the same time traditionally and appropriately considered a designation of any male member of the community/extended family belonging to the ego's generation, and rightly so.[2] Nevertheless, the obvious discrepancy is tacitly ignored.

It appears that early Indo-European social structure was based on age-sex stratification, with classificatory kinship playing only a secondary role.

The obvious socio-cultural implication of this conclusion is that age-sex stratification underlay the classificatory and individual kinship patterns and may therefore have been the first stage of social evolution that under certain circumstances could have evolved into the *varṇa* system. Yet while the remnants of age-sex classification had survived in a number of the recorded Indo-European traditions, it was among the Indo-Iranians that it evolved into the *varṇa/pištra* system). What circumstances, then, were favorable to the formation of such a system?

There is also the question of where and when it emerged. Given that (1) age-sex stratification is mostly viable among pastoralists, and, more specifically, among those pastoralists who are not exactly nomadic but not quite settled, so to speak, as the Maasai, Gikuyu, Oromo, and other peoples of East Africa (the classical area of age-sex stratification), (2) the Vedic Indians considered wheel-thrown (*cakravṛtta*) pottery unknown to the bearers of the steppe pastoralist cultures unfit for ritual purposes, and (3) the Indo-Iranians contacted with the Finno-Ugrians of the West Siberian forest zone, it seems likely that the Proto-Indo-Iranians were primarily cattle-breeders inhabiting the steppes of Western Siberia and South Urals.

Thus, the correlation of linguistic evidence and narrative sources gives us an insight into Indo-Iranian prehistory, and, hopefully, into the origin of Indo-Iranian social stratification.

Notes

1. Thus, Brandenstein held that the Scythian γένεα were related to the subsequent inhabitants of the North Pontic area, i.e., the bearers of the Tripolye archaeological culture, resp. the descendants of the elder brother, the bearers of the battle-axe culture, resp. the descendants of the middle brother, and the Scythians proper,

resp. the descendants of the youngest brother, which does not seem likely. Berzin, in his turn, argued that the Indo-Europeans had been mounted warriors while horseback riding was not widespread even in the Indo-Iranian epoch.

2. See Abaev 438-439; Trubachev 58-ff.; Benveniste vol. I: 213-214; Benveniste and Lallot 170-171; Szemerényi 23-24; and Gamkrelidze and Ivanov 764 (666 in their English version).

Works Cited

Abaev, V.I. *Istoriko-Etimologicheskii Slovar' Osetinskogo Iazyka*, vol. I-V. Moscow-Leningrad: Izdatel'stvo Akademii nauk SSSR [Nauka], 1958-1995.

Benveniste, Emile. *Le Vocabulaire Des Institutions Indo-Européenes*. Paris: Les Editions de Minuit, 1969.

Benveniste, Émile, and Jean Lallot. *Indo-European Language and Society*. Coral Gables, FL: U of Miami Press, 1973.

Berzin, E.O. "Sivka-Burka, Veshchaia Kaurka, ili Drevniaia Evropa v zerkale mifov i skazok." *Znanie–sila* 11 (1986).

Brandenstein, Wilhelm. *Griechische Sprachwissenschaft*. Berlin: W. de Gruyter, 1954.

Dumézil, Georges. *La Préhistoire Indo-Iranienne Des Castes*. Paris: P. Geuthner, 1930.

Gamkrelidze, T.V., and V.S. Ivanov. 1984 /1995. *Indoevropeiskii Iazyk i Indoevropeitsy. Rekonstruktsiia i Istoriko-Tipologicheskii Analiz Praiazyka i Protokul'tury*. Tbilisi: Izdatel'stvo Tbilisskogo Universiteta, 1984.

———. *Indo-European and the Indo-Europeans. A Reconstruction and Historical Analysis of a Proto-Language and a Proto-Culture*. Trans. Johanna Nichols. Ed. Werner Winter. NY: Berlin: Mouton de Gruyter, 1995.

Grantovskij, E.A. *Indoiranische Kastengliederung bei den*

Skythen. Moskau: Verlag für Orientalische Literatur, 1960.

Klimov, G.A. "Kavkazskie Ètimologii." *Ètimologiia 1968.* Moscow: Nauka, 1971. pp. 1-8.

———. "O Nekotorykh Slovarnykh Obshchnostiakh Kartvel'skikh i Nakhsko-Dagestanskikh Iazykov." *Ètimologiia 1970.* Moscow: Nauka, 1972. pp. 349-355.

———. *Drevneishie Indoevropeizmy Kartvel'skikh Iazykov.* Moscow: Nasledie, 1994.

Kullanda, Sergey. "Indo-European 'Kinship Terms' Revisited." *Current Anthropology* 43.1 (2002).

Rau, Wilhelm. *Töpferei und Tongeschirr im Vedischen Indien.* Wiesbaden: Franz Steiner Verlag GMBH, 1972.

Starostin, S.A. "Indoevropeisko-Severnokavkazskie Izoglossy." *Drevniĭ Vostok: Ètnokul'turnye Sviazi.* Eds. G.M. Bongard-Levin and V.G. Ardzinba. Moscow: Nauka, 1988. pp. 112-163.

Szemerényi, Oswald. *Studies in the Kinship Terminology of the Indo-European Languages. With Special Reference to Indian, Iranian, Greek, and Latin.* (Acta Iranica 16). Téhéran-Liège: Édition Bibliothèque Pahlavi. Leiden: Brill, 1977.

Trubachev, O.N. *Istoriia Slavianskikh Terminov Rodstva i Nekotorykh Drevneishikh Terminov Obshchestvennogo Stroia.* Moscow: Izdatel'stvo AN SSSR, 1959.

Wikander, Stig. *Der Arische Männerbund. Studien zur Indo-Iranischen Sprach- und Religionsgeschichte.* Lund: Håkan Ohlssons Buchdruckerei, 1938.

Dr. Sergey Kullanda is a Senior Scientist in the Department of Ancient Orient at the Institute of Oriental Studies of the Russian Academy of Sciences, Moscow.

26

Open Pages in South Asian Studies

CHAPTER 3

ELISA FRESCHI

The Prescriptive Function of Language in the *Nyāyamañjarī* and in Speech Act Theory[1]

The title of the workshop organized by Alexander Stolyarov and of the consequent volume invites me to consider the problem of "what to do first": the problem of priorities. Why do we need priorities? Because *ars longa, vita brevis*—"art is long and life is short"; we have to acquire many skills and our time is limited. Hence, no matter how much we would like to do it, we will not be able to read all the 20 millions of Sanskrit manuscripts waiting to be edited.

Priorities are needed not just for practical purposes (lack of time) or theoretical purposes (a desire to focus on more significant texts), but even for historical purposes. For instance, no one could start her study of the linguistics of the Prābhākara branch of the Mīmāṃsā school with Prabhākara's texts, which are hardly intelligible in themselves. Before reaching Prabhākara, one should rather focus on texts which might, by contrast, be able to spread light on the others. Hence, setting priorities is a fundamental task.

I will focus here on priorities in Classical Indian philosophy, especially in Classical Indian philosophy of language and linguistics.

Priorities in Classical Indian Linguistics

If we leave behind the treatises on Phonetics (the *Prātiśākhyas*), which are highly technical and focused on the specific topic of the accurate pronunciation of Vedic mantras, and Yāska's *Nirukta*, which deals with semantics and has greatly influenced many fields of Indian culture, but has not originated a distinct school,[2] we are left with two kinds of sources for classical Indian linguistics:

- *padaśāstra* ("Teaching about words": mainly Grammar)
- *vākyaśāstra* ("Teaching about sentences": mainly Mīmāṃsā)

The first group badly needs further studies to detect its complex approach and possibly to discern the distinct voices of its authors. Although much work has been done by Ashok Aklujkar, Saroja Bhate, George Cardona, Madhav Deshpande, Ram Nath Sharma, to name only a few, we are in fact still far from mastering the intricacies of Pāṇini's grammar and to be able to have a solid grasp on the entire tradition he founded.

An intermediate condition is the one of studies on the linguistics of Nyāya and Buddhist epistemology, on which some high quality work has been produced, although much remains to be investigated.[3] These two fields of study have in fact benefited from the quality and quantity of scholars focusing on Nyāya and on Buddhist epistemology.

Due to the paucity of scholars focusing on Mīmāṃsā,

by contrast, the study of the second group of texts has hardly been undertaken, and the intricacies of its system are yet to be discovered.[4] Hence, in the context of an "Open Pages" workshop, one cannot help but highlight the need for studying Indian sentence-linguistics. But is the need to study *vākyaśāstra* only linked to the historical reconstruction of Indian thought? Or are there further reasons at all to focus on sentence-linguistics?

The question is generally linked to the problem of the purpose of studying the Sanskrit heritage. One might suggest that all human products are worth preserving (as argued by Jan Houben in his *Appeal to Safeguard Ideo-Diversity*, in Squarcini 2002). But this brings one back to the initial problem, i.e., the necessity of setting priorities. Now, Sanskrit thought particularly excelled in the field of linguistic and philosophy of language. As for *padaśāstra*, Western linguistics has reached the high level of abstraction of Pāṇini's grammar only in very recent times (see Keidan 2011) and, one might add, only after having been fertilized by it (see Alfieri forthcoming). Sentence-linguistics is a field where Indian linguistics may ask thought-provoking questions, add insightful solutions, and display a complex and accurate system of linguistic analysis. Furthermore, the sentence-context is fundamental in order to deal with complex linguistic phenomena, such as deixis, textual linguistics, investigation on the minimal elements of signification, but its study has only recently been undertaken in the West.

In the following, I will especially focus on one of such phenomena, exhortation. In fact, in Western linguistics and epistemology, exhortation is usually considered just an exception to the informative use of language. Even where language is described as having various functions (see Copi and Cohen 1986, chapter 4.1.1–3), the exhortative function is hardly dealt with at all. By contrast, Mīmāṃsakas especially focus on exhortation, as will be explained below.

Having thus established that the study of *vākyaśāstra* is worthwhile, let me now turn to the question of how to go about doing it. To begin with, which sources can one count on?

Unfortunately, there are several problems with the sources for *vākyaśāstra* (problems which mostly apply to all other fields of Indian Philosophy):

- Sanskrit texts were meant mostly for insiders: In India, self-learning is generally condemned (cf. the *Mahābhārata* story about Ekalavya, who has learnt archery by secretly watching Droṇa's lessons).
- Classical texts (and even more so, post-Classical ones) mostly adjust presupposed definitions, rather than explaining them anew.
- We lack the background considered to be the most obvious one: ritual. In fact, in most cases Mīmāṃsā texts presuppose the knowledge of rituals and use ritual examples as explanatory tools. By contrast, we tend to be able to understand examples only once we have understood what they should exemplify.

Before discussing these problems through the analysis of the specific case of exhortation, I shall address the nature of "exhortation."

A Case Study: Exhortation

By "exhortation" I mean the linguistic phenomenon of inducing an effect in the listener/reader. A standard Indian example of exhortation is "the one who is desirous of cattle should sacrifice with the citrā-ritual" (*paśukāmaś citrayā yajeta*). A more common one is "Give me a glass of water." Exhortation is, hence, distinguished from description. The latter includes all statements regarding states of affairs, such as, "Having much cattle means being rich" or "Drinking water is healthy."

Exhortation in Mīmāṃsā

Exhortation is of chief importance for Mīmāṃsā authors, due to their focus on the *Brāhmaṇas*. These are the prescriptive part of the *Vedas*, i.e., the parts of the *Vedas* which contain all sorts of sacrificial injunctions. Since Mīmāṃsā authors developed their linguistics theories in accordance with their focus on the exegesis of the Brāhmaṇas, they regarded the exhortative function as the fundamental function of language. In the next stage, Mīmāṃsā authors extended their theories beyond the *Vedas* and—especially the Prābhākara branch of Mīmāṃsā—argued also that ordinary language is primarily prescriptive. As evidence they mention the process of language acquisition. This does not occur through the descriptive use of language. Children could listen to adults uttering descriptive sentences for an unnaturally long time before they would be able to single out the meaning of single words. By contrast, the experience of exhortative sentences such as "Fetch the cow!" and of the consequent action makes the child easily understand what is going on. Through repeated experience of similar sentences, in which new words are inserted or deleted (e.g., "Tie the cow!" or "Fetch the horse!"), they will learn the language.[5]

One might suggest that in order to study exhortation the tools of *padaśāstra* are enough. An exhortative sentence would be one where an optative, imperative, subjunctive or gerundive verbal ending is found. But this is not correct. Verbal endings are not enough to identify an exhortative sentence, since there are exhortations even in the case of indicative verbal endings and only a sentence-context allows one to detect them. Since their linguistic theories depend on exegetical concerns, Mīmāṃsakas were well aware of this phenomenon and developed theories which took into account the larger context. For instance, in the context of the prescriptions regarding the Darśapūrṇamāsa sacrifice, a statement such as "The sacrificial spoon is made of parṇa wood" means, in fact, "One should use a parṇa-spoon for the present sacrifice." Similarly "I am thirsty" may mean "Please, give me a glass of water," in an appropriate context.[6]

Exhortation and Speech Act theory

By contrast, linguistic studies developed in the West having in view the "scientific" usage of language, i.e., its referential usage.[7] In the 20th century, however, the Western approach to non-descriptive statements received important contributions. A notable example is Roman Jakobson (1896–1982), who deals with the referential function along with other five (expressive, conative, poetic, phatic and metalingual). Among them, the conative function highlights the exhortative aspect of language. Further, in the last decades, the approach to exhortation has been modified through J.L. Austin's Speech Act theory (whose fundamental book is *How to Do Things with Words*, published posthumously in 1962). This analyzes language from the point of view of its pragmatic effects and distinguishes a locutionary, illocutionary, and perlocutionary aspect in it. Noteworthy is also Austin's successor, Searle. Thus, through Jakobson, Austin, and his successor, J.R. Searle, 20th-century linguistics "discovered" non-referential usages of language.

Speech act theory distinguishes the following types of speech acts:

- A locutionary act comprises the act of uttering a sentence and its phatic and rhetic aspects.[8] Austin defines it as the act of using words "as belonging to a certain vocabulary [...] and as conforming to a certain grammar, [...] with a certain more or less definite sense and reference" (Austin 1975, pp. 92-3). The locutionary act is needed in order to distinguish between cases where the locutionary act is the same, but the illocutionary or perlocutionary ones differ. For instance, "I will do everything by myself" could be a constative speech-act, express a threat, a regret…
- Illocutionary speech acts are the core of the theory: they could be of various sorts (greeting, baptizing…) and their characteristic is the fact that they actually perform what they seem to be describing (e.g., a priest telling to a couple "I declare you husband and wife" is not describing a state of affairs which would have existed independently of the statement itself; it rather performs it).
- A perlocutionary act consists of the effect of the illocutionary one (persuading, scaring…).

In a short formulation, "Austin [...] distinguishes the act of saying something, what one does in saying it, and what one does by saying it" (Bach 2006, p. 150). For instance, the bar keeper says "The bar closes in five" (locutionary act). Illocution: urging (to go soon). Perlocution: ordering a last drink.

Within this theory, exhortations are a sub-set of illocutionary speech acts, namely "directive illocutionary speech acts."

Open Pages in South Asian Studies

To whom does the illocutionary force belong?

Answers from Speech Act theory and Classical Indian linguistics: It is apparent that the Speech Act theory focuses on the role of the speaker. Locutionary and illocutionary acts, in particular, depend on what the speaker does while speaking, while perlocutionary acts regard the effect of the speaker's statements on the listener. By contrast, Mīmāṃsā theories must avoid referring to any speaker, since the paradigmatic instance of language they aim at explaining, the *Veda*, is thought to exist independently of any author. If we leave the historical origin of the *Veda* out of the picture, its author is *now* epistemologically irrelevant, so that it is impossible to claim that the illocutionary power of the *Veda* depends on him/her. In fact —Mīmāṃsā authors claim— one recognizes the authority of the Veda independently of its author, and one does not respect the Veda because of the alleged author of a certain section, but rather because the Veda in itself enjoins an absolute authority. It can be incidentally noted that this was possibly the standard stance in regard to the Veda until theism became the regular option (see McCrea forthcoming).

Thus, although one could be tempted to say that exhortation as seen in Mīmāṃsā is an "illocutionary force," like the one present in commands, Mīmāṃsā authors do not attribute any role to the speaker. This seems to oppose the whole theory of speech acts, since this originates from the observation of the performative use of some verbs and exhortations are classified as directive illocutionary speech acts insofar as a speaker can utter sentences such as, "I order you that...." Furthermore, from the *vākyaśāstra* point of view, the distinction between illocutionary speech acts (intended by a speaker to produce a certain effect) and perlocutionary ones (producing effects on the hearer) is hardly possible. From a certain point of view, a prescription (*vidhi*) is a "perlocutionary force," since it is recognized through its effects on the listeners, rather than through the intention of its speaker. However, according to the Mīmāṃsā standpoint, an exhortation cannot be easily identified through its effects either, since its output is the *undertaking* of an activity and not the activity itself. Thus, its effects are hardly perceivable, if not by the listener himself.

In other words, Classical Indian *vākyaśāstra* focuses on the characteristics of the exhortative function of language itself. This view has the advantage of accounting for cases of exhortations with no speaker, such as the Veda.

I am not aware of any version of the Speech Act theory which does not take into account the role of the speaker. The role of perlocutionary speech acts seems to only regard the description of the *effects* of an act which must have in it an illocutionary force.

In *How to Do Things with Words*, the distinction between illocution and perlocution was chiefly aimed at distinguishing between the meaning intended and the one achieved. Perlocution was never thought of as the *only* aspect of a Speech Act. Searle (Searle 1969) plays down even more the role of perlocution, insofar as he understands it as just an additional element, since "the intention of achieving a perlocutionary effect is not essential to the illocutionary act" (Sbisà 2009, p. 235). Further, perlocution identifies only (external) effects, and seems, therefore, unsuitable to account for exhortations, which seem to be more than just their result on a listener. Also, these appear to have a standard way of functioning, unlike the variety of their perlocutionary effects:

> The performance of a perlocutionary act does not depend on the satisfaction of conventional conditions, but on the actual achievement of a certain goal or (since a perlocutionary act can also be performed unintentionally) on the speech act's having actually caused certain extralinguistic consequences (Austin 1962: 107).[9]

Can the Speech Act theory be modified in order to emphasize the role of the listener alone? Apart from the Veda, such an approach could be used to explain the case of laws, which have an "illocutionary" power that does not depend on their author.

If relying on the listener alone is not a viable solution, one is left only with language. But how can a *force* inhere in a non-sentient thing like language? We shall see later how this point is central for the Indian *vākyaśāstra*, which indeed focuses on the following question: What makes *language* able to convey a perlocutionary effect? Thus, whereas, as already hinted at, the definition of exhortation according to its speaker or listener depends on something outside it, Classical Indian *vākyaśāstra* focuses on some characteristics of language itself.

To sum up, once we have admitted that the role of the speaker might be reduced, we might ask:

> Is language in itself able to convey a perlocutionary effect or does it depend on its listeners in order to attain its purpose? (1)[10]

As far as similar questions are concerned, Classical Indian *vākyaśāstra* could fruitfully interact with Speech

Act theorists. By "interact" I mean that the process ought to be bi-directional, since both interlocutors can enhance their knowledge through the dialogue. Apart from contemporary *vākyaśāstra*-exponents, scholars of Indian linguistics working on *vākyaśāstra* are also included in this suggestion.[11] But, in order to interact, they should be able to understand each other, and this is not always smooth in the case of most Indian sources for exhortation.

Classical Indian Sources

The first and foremost source for the study of exhortation within the Indian *vākyaśāstra* should be Kumārila Bhaṭṭa (beginning of the second half of the first millennium CE), since he is the chief author of the Bhāṭṭa Mīmāṃsā.

Kumārila labels the exhortative force *śabdabhāvanā* "the [force] causing [an action] to be [and] consisting of language." Much about this force is obscure, starting with the controversial analysis of the compound, which can be analyzed as a *karmadhāraya* (i.e., an attributive compound, 'a force causing to be which is language') or as a tatpuruṣa (i.e. 'a force of language'). Whatever its etymology, the name *śabdabhāvanā* evokes a previous author, i.e., Śabara (the first commentator of the root-text of Mīmāṃsā, before the V c. CE). Śabara defines action as *bhāvanā*, i.e., 'causing [a result] to be'.

Kumārila's definition of the two bhāvanās sounds as follows:

> *abhidhābhāvanām āhur anyām eva liṅādayaḥ | arthātmā bhāvanā tv anyā sarvākhyāteṣu gamyate ||*

The verbal endings of optative, etc., express the designation *bhāvanā*. The bhāvanā consisting of a purpose is, by contrast, something else, and it is understood in the case of all verbal endings (TV ad 2.1.1, Abhyankar and Jośī 1971-1980).

Within the Bhāṭṭa Mīmāṃsā, all later definitions of the *śabdabhāvanā* follow along the same lines. Consider, for instance, Mahādeva Vedāntin's one:

[...] the productive force based on the word (*śabdabhāvanā*) is denoted by the suffix in the form of the optative, and is established by the experience 'The veda instigates me'(Mahādeva Vedāntin 2010, p. 368).[12]

Here, there is the interesting addition of the experience of being enjoined, but the definition is still far from being clear and understandable.

It can be even worse than that, since in most cases Kumārila's definition is presupposed and the authors just elaborate on it.[13]

Maṇḍana Miśra,[14] who dedicated a whole treatise on exhortation (the Vidhiviveka 'Discernment about prescriptions'), is highly insightful, but his terse style and the lack of reliable editions make the text often obscure. The following lines are the first ones of the Vidhiviveka (the first "it" must refer to the prescriptive force, the second one to the linguistic element and the third to the meaning):

It is in fact a sort of linguistic element, or an additional function of it, or a sort of meaning. And the linguistic element is also called like that because it designates it.[15]

The situation might improve, though, if one reads

later primers, such as Laugākṣi Bhāskara's *Arthasaṅgraha*:

The linguistic force is a particular activity of someone who causes to be an undertaking of an activity in a person. It is expressed by the optative component [of the verbal suffix]. For, one necessarily understands 'this induces me to act, since it entails an activity conducive to my undertaking of an activity' when one hears an optative ending.[16]

But those primers have an overall different agenda (practical and not theoretical), since they aim at presenting a clear overlook of the system and not at a critical investigation of its tenets, and are by and large not written for philosophical purposes. Thus, they cannot be a viable option for a cross-philosophical enterprise.

Jayanta Bhaṭṭa on Exhortation

This leads us back to the priority-question we started with: Which texts shall we start reading/studying, in order to understand Indian sentence-theories and re-think linguistic studies along them?

The present author's answer is to suggest Jayanta Bhaṭṭa's Nyāyamañjarī.[17]

Jayanta lived during the reign of the king Śaṅkaravarman (883-902, dates based on the *Rājataraṅgiṇī*, see Stein 1961, p. 98) in Kaśmīr. He was a Naiyāyika (i.e., an adherent of the Nyāya school) and the Nyāyamañjarī is his opus magnum. This is an encyclopedic work dealing with instruments of knowledge (*pramāṇas*) and objects to be known (*prameyas*). Four books out of twelve are dedicated to language (which is included in the first group).

How can Jayanta be an answer to the problems sketched above?

- Because of historical advantages: Jayanta is earlier than many insiders (see Kataoka 2008, pp. 210-209, which explains how Jayanta offers in many cases the first extant interpretation of Kumārila) and definitely much earlier than all primers (which have been written only after the XV c.).
- Because he is himself a mediator (not an insider): Jayanta is indeed a Naiyāyika who knows a lot about Mīmāṃsā, but writes for a Naiyāyika public: Hence, he needs to explain the theories he deals with.
- Because he is a philosopher: Unlike the authors of primers, who are mainly concerned with giving an overall view of the whole system, Jayanta pauses on each topic and discusses it thoroughly.
- Because he writes in order to understand: As it is immediately evident out of the very bulkiness of the part of NM 5 dedicated to *śabdabhāvanā*, Jayanta carefully examines each definition rather than presupposing them.
- Because he is reliable in depicting his opponents' views: He is fair against opponents and his philosophical attitude does not make him interpret freely his predecessors' opinions, as it is often the case with other commentators who are either biased against a certain view, or more philosophically creative, such as Prajñākaragupta or Someśvara Bhaṭṭa. Such commentators end up being less reliable because they integrate what is not found in the original theories, develop them further, emend them, etc.

Jayanta on *śabdabhāvanā*

The discussion on *śabdabhāvanā* is found in NM 5, after (a) a discussion on what is the meaning of linguistic elements (śabda), and (b) a discussion on the nature of action (bhāvanā). Thus, Jayanta arrives at *śabdabhāvanā* because of the strength of the arguments he is dealing with. By contrast, in other texts, this and similar topics are dealt with in accordance with their place in the text they comment upon or in accordance with ritual purposes (e.g., the MNP and the AS do not deal with the restrictive prescription *niyamavidhi* while discussing the nature of exhortation, but rather while discussing the role of mantras within the Vedic ritual[18]). In other words, Jayanta is led by theoretical concerns.

Jayanta's definition of *śabdabhāvanā* runs as follows:

> The linguistic force is that function pertaining to language which causes people to undertake actions and in which the undertaking of the activity reaches the status of something to be done.[19]

The chief elements of this definitions are that the *śabdabhāvanā* is a function (*vyāpara*), related to language (*śabdagata*) and inherently prescriptive (*sādhyatāṃ pratipadyate*).

Jayanta on "To whom does the illocutionary force belong?"

This leads us back to the question mentioned above ((1), p.6), namely, "to whom does the illocutionary force belong?" In other words, "is language by itself able to convey a perlocutionary effect or does it depend on its listeners in order to do it?" In Jayanta's terminology, the first question can be specified as "How can the burden of expressing the illocutionary force rest on a function?"

Jayanta addresses the problem insofar as he investigates on the relation between exhortation and prescriptive verbal endings. Do prescriptive verbal endings directly induce one to act, or is it their functioning (*vyāpāra*), which induces one to act? The alternative reproduces the gist of question (1).

If exhortative verbal endings would in themselves express the exhortation, then everyone —just by hearing them— would undertake an activity. Even young children or strangers, who do not understand Sanskrit, would be induced to act by the force of exhortative endings, if this were intrinsic in them and did not depend on their function. Moreover, the relation between the exhortative endings and exhortation itself would be twofold, insofar as exhortation would be their product, i.e., it would not exist before them, but also their meaning. And how could a semanteme mean something which it itself produces just by the fact of being uttered? [20]

If, by contrast, one maintains that the exhortation is conveyed by a function of the exhortative endings, then the theory amounts to the following scheme:

exhortative endings

↓

exhortative endings' function, i.e., conveying a meaning

↓

comprehension of this meaning by the listener

↓

effect on the listener: exhortation